# Elizabeth Bowen's Psychoanalytic Fiction

**Midcentury Modern Writers**
Edited by Professor Maud Ellmann, The University of Chicago

This series contributes to the on-going expansion of Modernist Studies by redirecting attention to midcentury writing (c. 1928–1960). Some of the finest writing of this period resists the taxonomies of academic criticism, especially the so-called 'great divide' between high-brow and popular literature. This series aims to enrich the canon of modernist studies by restoring unjustly neglected writers, groups of writers and forms of writing to the prominence that they deserve.

**Published titles**
*Ivy Compton-Burnett*
Barbara Hardy

*London Writing of the 1930s*
Anna Cottrell

*Elizabeth Bowen's Psychoanalytic Fiction*
Victoria Coulson

Please find the series website at: www.edinburghuniversitypress.com/series/MCMW

# Elizabeth Bowen's Psychoanalytic Fiction

Victoria Coulson

EDINBURGH
University Press

Edinburgh University Press is one of the leading university presses in the UK. We publish academic books and journals in our selected subject areas across the humanities and social sciences, combining cutting-edge scholarship with high editorial and production values to produce academic works of lasting importance. For more information visit our website: edinburghuniversitypress.com

© Victoria Coulson, 2020, 2022

Edinburgh University Press Ltd
The Tun – Holyrood Road
12(2f) Jackson's Entry
Edinburgh EH8 8PJ

First published in hardback by Edinburgh University Press 2020

Typeset in 10.5/13 Adobe Sabon by
IDSUK (DataConnection) Ltd, and
printed and bound by CPI Group (UK) Ltd,
Croydon, CR0 4YY

A CIP record for this book is available from the British Library

ISBN 978 1 4744 8049 9 (hardback)
ISBN 978 1 4744 8050 5 (paperback)
ISBN 978 1 4744 8051 2 (webready PDF)
ISBN 978 1 4744 8052 9 (epub)

The right of Victoria Coulson to be identified as the author of this work has been asserted in accordance with the Copyright, Designs and Patents Act 1988, and the Copyright and Related Rights Regulations 2003 (SI No. 2498).

# Contents

Acknowledgements vii
Series Editor's Preface ix

Introduction 1
1. Development 21
2. Sexuality 105
3. Reproduction; or, Legacy 173

Bibliography 213
Index 219

# Acknowledgements

For encouraging me to write this book, and for her warm support and expert (as well as tactful) critique at every stage of its creation, I owe a great debt of gratitude to Maud Ellmann.

I gratefully acknowledge the financial support of my department, in the form of the Leavis Fund, with respect to the book's index.

And with all my heart I thank my dear friend Jason Edwards. He will not need to read this book, as he has already entered enthusiastically into its every twist and turn over the course of uncountable conversations by his fireside, and knows its features and figures as well as I do.

# Series Editor's Preface

Midcentury Modern Writers opens new vistas in modernist studies by restoring undervalued writers, genres, and literary movements to the twentieth-century literary canon. The reasons for this critical neglect are manifold, but they include a tenacious bias in favour of male writers associated with the European metropolis, especially London and Paris. Even Virginia Woolf was begrudged a place in the pantheon of 'High Modernism' until the resurgence of feminism in the 1970s. Meanwhile, other distinguished women writers of the midcentury, along with their male contemporaries, have receded from view, overshadowed by towering figures like Joyce and Eliot.

The purpose of this series is not to topple these figures but to enrich our sense of the contestation between forms and genres in the midcentury period, roughly from 1928 (when British women were finally granted the vote on equal terms with men) to the 1960s. The traditional modernist canon, comprising a small band of experimental pioneers, obscures not only the creative wealth and variety of these five decades but even those features that distinguish modernists from their literary rivals. A fresh view of the period, undistorted by the fetishisation of modernism, reveals that the mainstream is often difficult to distinguish from its tributaries; tradition and experiment overlap in ways that disrupt conventional critical taxonomies and hierarchies. Likewise, highbrow and popular literary forms galvanise each other, despite the so-called 'great divide' that critics have imposed between them.

Midcentury Modern Writers include both single-author studies and wide-ranging thematic and generic surveys of the period. The authors of these original studies have been selected from established and emergent voices in Anglophone literary studies on the basis of their expertise, inventiveness, and clarity, in the expectation that this series will open up new avenues of investigation for students and their teachers, as well as for specialists in the field. Ultimately, this series strives to change the way we read, teach, and study modern writing in English.

General Editor
Maud Ellmann

# Introduction

In 1949 *The Saturday Book* posed a set of questions to nine distinguished men and women, one of whom was the Anglo-Irish writer Elizabeth Bowen (1899–1973). To the inquiry '*Is there any other profession you might have been good at?*' Bowen replied: 'I should like to have been an architect. Or (if I had been a man) a barrister.'[1] Her response suggests some important aspects of her thought – above all, her passionate investment in the social and psychological institution of law. Perhaps more obviously than is the case with other creative practices, architecture submits itself to the real limitations of matter that we think of as 'laws of nature' as the basis on which to promote individual and social wellbeing. A building may be designed to look as if it defies material possibility, but it of course can never do so in practice, and the appearance of such a supernatural feat – when that is what is aimed for – can only be achieved by way of a skilful acceptance of the physical limitations whose abrogation is conjured up by such a construction. In a very similar way, if to less concrete effect, the barrister seeks his creative triumph within the limits of the laws of the land, at once a set of constraints upon his arguments and the very condition of their possibility. In a 1941 radio talk entitled 'Do Conventions Matter?' Bowen had insisted on the constructive function of limits, or rules, in cultural development: that, in her words, 'conventions are aids rather than hindrances to social life'. '[I]f society', she argues,

> or any section of society, because it was out of patience with the restricting influence of its conventions, were to try and make a new life possible, by sweeping away the conventions it knew, it

would have to be content with stepping down from the level of culture it had been accustomed to to a primitive state of life.²

Bowen's response points also to an acceptance of highly differentiated gender roles. In her replies to a series of questions posed her in September 1946 for an article on 'The Cost of Letters' in *Horizon* she had similarly characterised the barrister's job as a profession for men. Asked what she considered the most suitable second occupation for a writer, she replied:

> I should say in a man's case a suitable second occupation would be either medicine, architecture or law. Very few women would have time to carry on two professions simultaneously as their personal life and domestic responsibilities take up a good deal of time in themselves.³

While we should bear in mind that Bowen is speaking here specifically about the situation of a writer – of either sex – seeking to supplement his or her income by means of an additional, better-paid job, it is worth noting nonetheless that her remarks tend to endorse a conservative view of the different social functions, or symbolic responsibilities, proper to women and to men. Elizabeth's father, Henry, was a lawyer, a profession that he adopted in defiance of his own father's wish that he devote himself full time to the management of the family's estate in the south of Ireland. Yet Henry Bowen's evident commitment to the practice of law was not matched by any great success in his professional life. His career was badly disrupted by a long period of mental illness in middle age; as he recovered he began to work on a legal magnum opus. 'Sixteen years of my father's concentration and energy went into his book on Statutory Land Purchase', Bowen writes in her family biography *Bowen's Court*: 'His life grew to centre very much round it.'⁴ But the authority of the tome was evacuated by the end of Anglo-Irish rule in 1921 and the establishment of the Irish Republic and its new constitution.

So, before [Henry Bowen's] long book, carried out on the scale of a standard work of reference, had so much as gone to the publishers, it had become, in the phrase he preferred to use, 'a work of historic interest only.' It could no longer have a functional part in law. (BC 444)

If Elizabeth Bowen looked to her father to demonstrate competence in the operation of law – a role that had been ruled out as unsuitable for women, or at least for women writers, such as herself – she can hardly have been satisfied by Henry's performance of this crucial symbolic function.

The Elizabeth Bowen that I present in this book is a figure rich in such seeming paradoxes of politics and power. The author – across her writing life – of ten novels and around one hundred short stories, Bowen was the only child of an Anglo-Irish landowner, and upon his death she inherited the family estate in County Cork complete with a neoclassical Big House, 'Bowen's Court.' In her fiction, Bowen explores contemporary social milieus in which masculine and feminine subject positions are characterised by markedly different relations to socio-symbolic power. We might therefore, perhaps, imagine that the writer's self-experience as a woman would consort uncomfortably with her identity as a representative of the historical ruling class in Ireland. Certainly, Bowen's inherited position endowed her from birth with extraordinary social, financial and political power in contradistinction to the Irish tenantry from whom her family exacted rents in return for the right to live and work on the land. In *Bowen's Court*, Bowen describes the Cromwellian appropriation of Ireland in the seventeenth century as an 'inherent wrong', and chronicles in mordant detail the multiple personal mistakes, weaknesses and failings of her settler-colonial ancestors down to the generation of her own parents. But she never sought to repudiate her inherited privilege, and her eventual selling-off of the Big House was necessitated, as she saw it, by financial exigency, not by any desire to divest herself symbolically of the legacy of her class. Certainly, too, Bowen's concern, in her writing, with the question of gender might seem apt to undergird a feminist critique of patriarchal social organisation. Her texts never waver in their insistence on the family, class and cultural determinants of gender identity, or on the inequality of access to symbolic law by which masculinity and femininity are mutually differentiated and defined in the mid-twentieth century societies of Britain and Ireland in which Bowen's characters have their fictional being. Irreducibly political, the inequitable formations of gender explored in Bowen's writing might thus appear to open the way for a progressive critique of social inequality *tout court*, and to reflect with particular salience, we might think, upon the 'inherent wrong' of settler-colonial rule in Ireland. For by her own lights, Bowen's experience as a woman under the mandate of a patriarchal culture equipped her with a personal understanding of what it means to belong to a class whose exclusion from the active operation of law is the indispensable structural correlative of another group's pre-eminence.

In fact, Bowen's belief in the institution of law – her certainty about the importance of the task to which it must address itself, and her confidence in its capacity to function as the task requires – underlies both her unapologetic self-acceptance as a beneficiary and a present-day embodiment of the Anglo-Irish landowning class and her sanguine endorsement of the very socio-sexual order that she herself identifies with the differential construction of masculine and feminine gender identities in terms of their relations to a certain kind of power. For what takes precedence for Bowen over any democratic aspiration to social or sexual equality is a traditional conservative conception of the paramount importance of order as against anarchy and absolutism both: the rule of law as against either its absence, or its absorption into a totalitarian state. From such a perspective, law is not understood primarily as a basis for the equitable distribution or protection of rights, nor as a system for arbitrating conflicts between individuals, or between individuals and the state, but rather as the definitive symbolic mandate by which a culture regulates its subjects' relation to reality. In Bowen's eyes, reality is sometimes very hard to bear, which is why the effective operation of symbolic law is crucial for the wellbeing of individuals and societies alike. Thus, while perfectly willing to pronounce against the specific historical injustice of the land-grab perpetrated upon the indigenous people of Ireland, Bowen's imaginative energies are much more seriously engaged by what is almost the opposite problem, a 'problem' that only appears as such from an almost opposite point of view: the misjudgements and incompetence – as Bowen sees it – with which many of her Anglo-Irish forefathers exercised their class- and gender-based entitlement to rule over the estate lands whose origins as family property lie in acts of colonial rapine.

Such an account presents quite a contrast to the reading set out in what could be described as the inaugural text of modern literary criticism on the work of Elizabeth Bowen: *Elizabeth Bowen and the Dissolution of the Novel* by Andrew Bennett and Nicholas Royle (1995). A high-style exercise in poststructuralist critique, the book made a claim for Bowen's exceptional interest on the basis of her intellectual radicalism; her work, these critics argued, systematically undermined the epistemological and ontological verities of classic realism and the conservative social order promoted by such a form. 'From *The Hotel* (1927) to *Eva Trout* (1968)', write Bennett and Royle,

> Bowen's writing is concerned with dissolution – with dispersion, melting, break-up and death. [. . .] Ranging between the tragic and the comic, between the poignant and the scrupulously prosaic, Bowen's novels present dissolutions at the level of personal identity, patriarchy, social conventions and language itself – up to and including the language of fiction and criticism.[5]

This account reinvigorated scholarship on Bowen to wonderfully creative effect – in 2003, for example, Maud Ellmann identified Bennett and Royle's book as the most important influence on her own *Elizabeth Bowen: The Shadow Across the Page* – and it continues to make an impact today. Jessica Gildersleeve's *Elizabeth Bowen and the Writing of Trauma* (2014), the most recent monograph on Bowen to appear before the present study, engages with Bennett and Royle's ideas throughout.

It has to be admitted, however, that the galvanising theoretical ambition of the book by Bennett and Royle was not consistently matched by the quality of its textual analysis. Ellmann's monograph of 2003 and Neil Corcoran's of 2004 (*Elizabeth*

*Bowen: The Enforced Return*) each offered expert sustained attention to Bowen's writing in ways that enabled these critics to found their claims for the importance of Bowen's fiction in the literary specificities of her work. For both scholars – as also for Bennett and Royle – that special value or significance was intrinsically related to the peculiarly challenging, and challengingly peculiar, nature of Bowen's writing. 'As an anatomist of consciousness', Ellmann writes, in a formulation that remains authoritative for any consideration of Bowen's writing today,

> [Bowen] rivals Henry James; as an observer of social mores she rivals E. M. Forster; as a journalist of the sensations she rivals Joyce; as a lyricist of obsession she rivals Patrick Hamilton. Her narratives are as compelling as Graham Greene's, her satires as sharp as Evelyn Waugh's, her sentences as multivalent as Virginia Woolf's. Yet Bowen is stranger than her rivals: ethically, psychologically, stylistically, her fiction constantly takes our categories by surprise.[6]

Corcoran characterises Bowen's idiosyncratic prose style to comparable effect (and, similarly, with a precision that has yet to be bettered):

> Stylistically, [Bowen's] writing is controversially eventful: it has been accused, even by some of her admirers, of mannerism, and it is certainly often deeply unconventional in its syntactical and grammatical structures; in some forms of negative construction, repetition, inversion, and ellipsis; in a reflexive turning back in upon itself rather than a committed motion forward; in its unyielding refusal of the obvious in spirited but sometimes very demanding favour of what she calls 'the affray of words, the vibrating force of their unforeseenness', which sounds as though she regards writing, or at least certain types of writing, as almost a kind of jazz improvisation.[7]

Responsive to the defamiliarising thrust of Bennett and Royle's analysis, the emphasis in Ellmann's work and in Corcoran's on the 'arresting oddness' or 'profoundly disconcerting' quality of Bowen's writing proved so influential on subsequent scholarship as to constitute a virtual rubric for new criticism and a theme for meta-analysis.[8] In her editor's introduction to *Elizabeth Bowen: New Critical Perspectives* (2009), Susan Osborn describes the essays in the book as 'examin[ing] [. . .] some of the stranger pressures and unfamiliar tensions' in Bowen's writing, 'tensions that make her work uncommonly difficult to conceptualise, describe, and evaluate', while the 2009 essay collection *Elizabeth Bowen*, edited by Eibhear Walshe, includes an essay by Julie Anne Stevens devoted to 'explor[ing] critical reactions to Bowen's strangeness'.[9]

In the modern history of critical responses to Bowen's work, the 'unnerv[ing]' quality of Bowen's writing – as Corcoran describes it – has often been linked to elements of formal experimentation in her writing.[10] Bowen 'is a writer deeply impressed by the ambitions of High Modernism', Corcoran argues, 'even if, until the final two novels, she never entirely loses touch with classic realism and its customary methods'.[11] On numerous occasions such a focus on the modernist aspects of Bowen's style has extended as if seamlessly to the identification of a more thoroughgoing negativity in Bowen's plots and projection of characters as well. After highlighting the 'reflexivity and material intrusiveness' of Bowen's prose, Ellmann, for example, goes on to write of '[the] many different kinds of nothingness in Bowen's work, ranging from the ruins of the Irish countryside to the silence of the inarticulate imagination'.[12] In a notably ambitious essay of 2007, Sinéad Mooney argued that Bowen's work could be usefully compared to Beckett's, in light of the 'dramatizations of impasse, paralysis and lack of presence, deliberate narrative unpicking, [and] actions repeatedly arrested or aborted' that characterise her texts.[13] 'Bowen is, like Beckett, a specialist in inertia, a sculptor of the void', Mooney writes. 'Both operate a perverse endorsement of negative states and demonstrate a strong sense of underlying identification with stillness, paralysis, and states of abeyance.'[14] ('Abeyances', we might note, is the title of Bennett and Royle's first chapter.) 'The novel', Osborn writes of *The Last September*, 'is strangely unburdened of content.'[15] Claire Seiler questions whether *The Heat of the Day* 'is really about anything'.[16]

Yet both Ellmann and Corcoran had insisted also that Bowen's fiction 'has an ethical, not merely an aesthetic, message to convey'.[17] In Ellmann's account, the ineluctable return of nothingness in Bowen's writing is counterpointed, if not contested, by the intimation of moral law. 'Responsibility for the other is the law of our existence', Ellmann writes of the ethical burden of *The Death of the Heart*; 'whether we embrace this law or not, our lives are shaped by its imperative'.[18] A particularly significant stress in her book falls on the near-global predicament of bereavement and the work of personal and cultural mourning in the aftermath of the First World War. For his part, 'I think', Corcoran writes,

> that there is an apprehensible and sometimes peculiar or disconcerting ethics in [Bowen's] work, and that it is to our advantage to discover it, and that, although she is drawn to fracture and disintegration, this is more inflected with affirmation [...] than some recent criticism has made it seem.[19]

Like Ellmann, Corcoran too investigates Bowen's understanding of the necessity of mourning as the basis for a creative conception of the future.

The explicit reorientation towards ethics in twenty-first century literary criticism is writ large in the two most recent monographs on Bowen to appear – although in both books a continuing emphasis on the unorthodox or unsettling quality of Bowen's writing persists alongside a foregrounded concern with the moral dimension of the fiction. Thus Nicola Darwood, in her *A World of Lost Innocence: The Fiction of Elizabeth Bowen* (2012), tempers the sturdy traditionalism of her topic with a stress on Bowen's denial or failure of closure, by which means Bowen's fiction 'resists the notion that she is enforcing any moral judgement [...] on her readers',[20] while Gildersleeve unites directly the well-attested idiosyncrasies of Bowen's style with what she identifies as the dominant thematic concern of her texts. 'This book attempts to do justice to the strangeness of Bowen's writing', Gildersleeve explains, in its concern with the ways in which writing survives, integrates (or fails to integrate), and represents trauma. I argue that Bowen's writing is always and everywhere the narrative of trauma, and show that throughout her life she experimented with the methodology of trauma writing.[21]

In its own way as representative of the ethical turn in literary theory, and of a prominent contemporary interest in trauma, as was Bennett and Royle's work of an earlier deconstructive moment in criticism, Gildersleeve's book similarly identifies in Bowen's writing an exemplary philosophical trajectory, although to almost opposite effect. Whereas Bennett and Royle discovered in Bowen's writing a demonstration of the negativity of being and of writing alike – 'Living, in the work of Bowen, is dissolving [. . .] Bowen's novels figure a dissolution of the novel as such'[22] – Gildersleeve sets out to 'explore [Bowen's work] as a lifelong project of ethical representation and of understanding the narrative responsibilities of the survivor', 'suggest[ing] that her work is most importantly seen as an example of the inextricability of twentieth-century literature, suffering, and bearing witness'.[23] Thus Bowen's writing, still celebrated for its strangeness, has been fully reconceived in recent years not only in terms of a symptomatic relation to world-historical trauma but also as a project with aspirations to figure a kind of justice and to gesture towards the possibility of personal and cultural recovery or renewal. In a striking essay of 2017, which seeks to restore to Bowen scholarship a sensitivity to the specifically Christian valences of the writer's work, Annette Oxindine has redescribed the notorious uneasiness elicited by *The Heat of the Day*, in particular, as a function of its focus on re-birth, or what Oxindine terms its 'complexly rendered regenerations'.[24] '[I]t is the profusion and excess of life', Oxindine argues, 'rather than its attendant dearth and nullity that is most unsettling. Potentially more unnerving than the novel's profound absences are its unorthodox fecundities.'[25]

This is not to say that Oxindine signals much confidence in the likely response of her readers to such a biblically attuned account of 'the various ways in which *The Heat of the Day*'s proliferating uncertainties and unstable subjectivities [...] work against nullity'.[26] 'Over four decades ago', Oxindine acknowledges, nervously, '[Harriet] Blodgett concluded that characterizing Bowen's novels as "essentially Christian" was "not a completely new idea in Bowen criticism, although [...] scarcely a popular one" (Blodgett 1975: 9–10). And while it is not my intention', Oxindine continues, 'to claim that *The Heat of the Day* is "essentially" a Christian novel [...] I do think if we continue to mention only in passing or to sidestep altogether Bowen's well-documented spiritual faith, we also sidestep promising critical terrain.'[27] It is not my intention, either, to present Bowen's texts as 'essentially Christian'; but as I have signalled already, Bowen's fiction will emerge from my analysis as the work of a rigorous conservative thinker with a profound belief in symbolic law. Apt as such a disposition might be for expression in theological terms, it is in the conceptual and figurative fields of politics and – above all – psychology that Bowen's thought finds its most detailed, sustained and complex articulation in her writing, and it is upon these particular thematic dimensions or aspects of her texts that I concentrate in this book.

Along with the conservative cast of Bowen's thinking I want also at this introductory moment to draw attention to its qualities of conceptual originality, intra-textual coherence and career-long consistency. In fact it is a significant part of my project in this book to show that there is operative in Bowen's writing a sophisticated implicit account or understanding of psychological development, of sexuality, and of the structure and function of gender identities that is as fully discernible in her first novel *The Hotel* (1927) as it is throughout the whole chronological span of her work. It will immediately be apparent that in thus highlighting the local clarity and inter-textual integrity of Bowen's thinking my analysis offers a different emphasis from that of critical accounts that stress the overweening strangeness or negativity of her work. As I hope my readings will show, Bowen's writing is complex but crystalline; her work makes up a powerful body of thought that is no less elegant, distinctive, or arresting, for being thoroughly comprehensible. By the same token, my characterisation of Bowen, the novelist, as a kind of virtual or de facto 'theorist' of psychic life pulls against some of the most persuasive modern interpretations of her work. Both Ellmann and Corcoran highlight in their Introductions the importance to their thinking of Bowen's essay 'Out of a Book', in which Bowen identifies a certain compulsion in the structure or function of art. Ellmann quotes the essay in the first pages of her book – '"The apparent choices of art are nothing but addictions, pre-dispositions," Elizabeth Bowen wrote in 1946. "The aesthetic is nothing but a return to images that will allow nothing to take their place; the aesthetic is nothing but an attempt to disguise and glorify the enforced return"' – and subsequently deploys the term 'addictions' with reference to the characteristic tropes and preoccupations of Bowen's texts.[28] Corcoran picks up from the same passage Bowen's phrase 'the enforced return' for the title of his book; characterises 'Bowen's writing [as] manifest[ing] the entrapment of obsessive return, the inability to shake off a distressing, or distressed, past in a way which virtually demands to be read under the rubric of a Freudian return of the repressed'; and points to the prevalence in Bowen's work of 'images which are [. . .] close to being obsessions'.[29] Shafquat Towheed writes similarly of Bowen's 'repeated, insistent and enforced returns in her fiction to the place of an earlier event', a behaviour that he says 'verges on the obsessive'.[30] And as we have seen, Gildersleeve's book associates the whole of Bowen's oeuvre with the symptoms of trauma, as well as with an ethical project of witnessing.

I share with these critics a sense of the profound suitability of psychoanalytically inspired practices of reading and interpretation for investigating Bowen's work. At the same time I wish to emphasise, in contrast to such readings, a significant degree of creative and conceptual intentionality, as it were, in Bowen's literary explorations of psychic life. My identification in Bowen's writing of some non-professional discursive competence in the area of psychoanalytic thought, broadly defined, builds on Elizabeth Cullingford's characterisation of the impact on Bowen of the intellectual and social milieu in which she moved in early adulthood. In the context of a discussion of the meaning of 'onliness' – the experience of having no siblings – in Bowen's work, Cullingford writes:

> Bowen represents onliness as inseparable from the questions about gender identity and sexual orientation that were raised in the late-nineteenth century by the sexologists Karl Ulrichs, Richard von Krafft-Ebing, and Havelock Ellis, and answered in a different key by Freud. She absorbed these modern discourses of sexuality in postwar London, where she moved in 1919: her friends Rose Macaulay and Naomi Royde-Smith, later among the most steadfast defenders of Radclyffe Hall's lesbian novel *The Well of Loneliness*, gave regular Thursday parties at which Bowen encountered advanced ideas about sexuality. In 1924, Virginia and Leonard Woolf's Hogarth Press began issuing Freud's *Collected Papers*, and although we have no hard evidence that Bowen read them, the concepts and vocabulary of both sexology and psychoanalysis ('hyperaesthesia,' 'tabu,' 'repression,' 'complex,' 'fetishism,' and 'Oedipus-trap') permeate her work.[31]

We may see in Bowen's short story of 1934, 'The Cat Jumps,' suggestive support for Cullingford's account of Bowen's social context in the post-war years, and of the evidence of its intellectual significance in the development of Bowen's thought in young adulthood. The story offers an exquisitely amusing insider take-down of a slightly later iteration of the advanced Freudian milieu that Cullingford describes. Harold and Jocelyn Wright, the couple at the centre of 'The Cat Jumps',

> had light, bright, shadowless, thoroughly disinfected minds. They believed that they disbelieved in most things but were unprejudiced; they enjoyed frank discussions. They dreaded nothing but inhibitions; they had no inhibitions. They were pious agnostics, earnest for social reform; they explained everything to their children, and were annoyed to find their children could not sleep at nights because they thought there was a complex under the bed. They knew all crime to be pathological, and read their murders only in scientific books.[32]

Introduction    13

What these scientific books consist of is spelled out in a scene set in the couple's new country residence, to which they have invited their equally educated, upper-middle-class friends for a house-warming weekend: 'The library stools, rugs and divans were strewn with Krafft-Ebing, Freud, Forel, Weiniger and the heterosexual volume of Havelock Ellis. (Harold had thought it right to install his reference library; his friends hated to discuss without basis.)'[33] Arguably the single funniest fiction in Bowen's oeuvre – for the pure joy of it, I note that another activity engaged in by the house-warming guests is 'a pleasant discussion, in a punt, on marriage under the Soviet' – the story advances a sophisticated psychoanalytic critique of the protagonists' fundamental misconception of psychoanalysis.[34] For the satire of 'The Cat Jumps' is directed not at the ideas represented by the volumes stocking the Wrights' library but at the spectacle of their complacent uptake by a social group motivated primarily by a tribal desire to instantiate its intellectual superiority.

Cullingford's characterisation of Bowen's work as 'permeate[d]' by the concepts and vocabulary of sexology and psychoanalysis may be fortified by a wealth of local evidence.[35] This includes the letters that Bowen wrote to her lover Charles Ritchie, in which she displays a zestful non-specialist familiarity with psychoanalytic terminology and thought. If we confine ourselves, for example, to the year 1945, we find Bowen describing the results of the General Election as 'a terrific psychic shock', wondering about 'the psychic drive behind the brain (that makes one's work part of oneself)', and contrasting the way in which 'war brutalised physical life' with the effect of the post-war period, which 'seems to dissipate, in a way that is almost brutalising, psychic life'.[36] On 14 August she notes her 'cigarette-less neurosis', writes, on 24 August, that 'attacks on weeds in the walled garden and groves of nettles about the grounds are an excellent outlet for [her] aggressive instinct', asks on 22 October: 'Do you think I have got a vampire complex?' and confesses, on 18 November: 'I'm developing a positive narcissism [. . .] and am always rushing to look at myself in the glass.'[37] Or we might consider Bowen's judicious use of psychoanalytic terms in talks such as 'The Idea of the

Home' (1953), in which she asks, rhetorically, 'Is there not a suggestion that the home is simply a consolidation of the ego?',[38] or 'The Cult of Nostalgia' (1951), in which she muses on the activity of the novelist. 'One of the dangerous powers of the writer', Bowen suggests,

> is that he feeds, or plays up to, fantasies he knows to exist. He knows of their existence for the good reason that they are probably active in himself. In contacting the same fantasies in his readers he does something to break down his isolation.[39]

This latter example illustrates also how Bowen at times characterises at least some varieties of writing in terms of a simple Freudian wish-fulfilment. '[R]eally I think there's something pathological about the best-seller', she remarks in 1942. 'The book happens to be based on some craving or daydream and it happens to chime in with a similar mood or ways of feeling among the public.'[40] Even in good art – as in life itself – the unconscious plays a major part, if also an obscure one. '[G]ood dialogue [. . .] is very difficult to write', Bowen says in 'The Living Image – 1' (1941), 'because you are trying to get the unconscious emotional content of your character into the words.'[41] Similarly, Bowen describes her own 'Notes on Writing a Novel' as 'an attempt to externalise or to pin down, or to bring up on to the plane of consciousness what is, in the main, an unconscious process'.[42]

We know a little, from Charles Ritchie's diary, of Bowen's experience of psychoanalysis as a patient: on 3 December 1941 Ritchie noted that Bowen 'is going to a psychoanalyst to be cured of her stammer which is so much part of her'.[43] Seven weeks later, Ritchie describes 'A rather sad and painful evening with E. She suddenly said in that cool voice of hers, "One interesting thing my psychoanalyst got out of me, that I have a hidden wish that all my acquaintances should die, should be eliminated or at least disappear to South America."'[44] Characters strongly suggestive of the figure of the psychoanalyst appear throughout Bowen's fictions, and range from targets of merciless satire to enigmatic visions of compassion and care. In the former category we should mention *To the North*'s Lady Waters, who attends lectures on Adler and Havelock Ellis; driven by 'a cosmic and ravenous curiosity', she fancies herself quite the lay analyst.[45] 'One may do so much, with a little judgement, by bringing theory to bear on life', Lady Waters remarks, self-preeningly. 'Knowing that I am always willing to listen, friends bring me their difficulties; I am often surprised to find how a little talk, with a touch of some knowledge and penetration, may set things right.'[46] Mrs Bettersley, the analyst-figure in 'The Apple Tree' (1934), is similarly orthodox in her methodology: correctly discerning in her hostess the symptoms of unresolved trauma, Mrs Bettersley corners her in her bedroom and demands details of the terrible event.

> 'We've got three-quarters of an hour alone,' she said. 'You've got to tell me. Make it come into words. When it's once out it won't hurt any more – like a tooth, you know. Talk about it like anything. [. . .] You never have, have you? You never do?'[47]

A much more nuanced figure than Lady Waters, Mrs Bettersley – although similarly motivated by 'wolfish [. . .] curiosity' and intellectual vanity – is acutely perspicacious and highly effective in making her 'patients' better.[48] She completely cures the traumatised hostess and she is said never to have failed in her informal therapeutic practice. In tonal contrast to both of these rich, self-satisfied 'analysts', we might think of the nameless young woman encountered on a park bench in 'Tears, Idle Tears' (1934), whose recognition and understanding enable the child protagonist to survive an experience of emotional agony. Working-class, unemployed, this striking figure of disinterested empathy is motivated by her perception of 'wounds, in the world's surface, through which its inner, terrible unassuageable, necessary sorrow constantly bled away and as constantly welled up'.[49]

In the following chapters I seek to do justice to the clarity, elegance and originality of Bowen's thinking about development, sexuality and gender, highlighting in particular her principled conservative emphasis on the importance of symbolic law. The book is composed of six sections of equal length, organised into three interrelated chapters. The three sections of Chapter 1, 'Development,' concern Bowen's understanding of psychological maturation in the matrix of the family. In the first section I concentrate on *The Hotel* (1927) and *The House in Paris* (1935). I look at Bowen's view of early infancy, exploring her implicit account of the different roles to be undertaken by parents in the child's psychic life and development. It is the responsibility of the primary caregiver – 'Mother' – to introduce separation into the baby's experience. Separation may take the form of weaning, for example, or putting the child to sleep alone at night. The reason that Mother must do this is that it represents and acknowledges the real existence of limits in the world, up to and including the fact of mortality itself. Separation is therefore a terrible shock to the child, who may as a result begin to perceive his or her beloved mother as a figure of Death. And this is why, in Bowen's view, the role of the secondary parent, 'Father,' is so crucial to the process of development. Father's job is to take on responsibility for the separation that Mother has imposed, thereby at once confirming its necessity and making it a great deal more tolerable. By shouldering the blame, as it were, for mortality, Father symbolically revitalises Mother in the child's eyes, restoring the child's love for her, and for life itself, on the basis of a new respect for reality.

In the second section of Chapter 1 I focus on the very substantial story 'Ivy Gripped the Steps' (1945) to explore the two factors that Bowen consistently identifies as posing a serious threat to the developmental process. On the one hand, Mother may be unwilling to separate herself from her child, or may try to undo what separation she has managed to achieve; on the other hand, Father may be too weak to confirm the necessity of separation, and may thus be unable to bolster Mother's efforts in this direction, let alone redeem her in the eyes of her child if she succeeds.

In the third section of the chapter, I show how Bowen's analysis of developmental failure underlies the structural and thematic complexity of her major political novel of the Second World War, *The Heat of the Day* (1948). My discussion focuses here with increasing intensity on a big question raised by the

Introduction    17

book as a whole: the question, that is, of how Bowen explores the psychodrama of individual development in relation to contemporary world-historical events. Here, I argue that Bowen uses the war between Germany and England as a symbolic representation of the conflict that breaks out between mothers and children in the wake of separation.

In Chapter 2, 'Sexuality,' I extend my discussion of Bowen's symbolic correlation of political and psychic life to the image of the Big House, the prestigious country residence of Anglo-Irish landowning families. In the first section, I focus on *The Last September* (1929), and show that Bowen conceives of the Big House as a prototypical object of desire. In this novel, I argue, Bowen analyses the Irish War of Independence as a deadly struggle between sexual rivals. My discussion builds also on my work in Chapter 1 of setting out Bowen's understanding of development, because I argue here that Bowen views sexuality as an index of the subject's developmental state. A subject's style of desire, and the object that it takes, provide detailed information about that character's experiences of separation at Mother's hands and the success of its subsequent redemption by paternal law. Thus in Bowen's view, as I show in the second section of the chapter, forms of sexuality that express or evoke immature states of development offer rich imaginative access to the earliest stages of life. In light of Bowen's emphasis on the regulatory importance of symbolic law, it is not surprising, I think, that we may observe in her work a competing fascination with some very primitive states of being.

Bowen's account of mature sexuality, as it emerges from Chapter 2, is confident as to function and egalitarian as to sex. Both masculine and feminine subject positions secure access to the object of desire, and for neither male nor female children is the assumption of gender either prescribed or proscribed by biological sex. In Chapter 3, 'Reproduction; or, Legacy,' I show how under a specific combination of personal and historical pressures Bowen's sanguine analysis of mature sexuality is overborne by a constellation of anxieties about the reproductive capability of her own family and of the Anglo-Irish as a class. In this final, single-section chapter of the book, I explore

Bowen's figuration of reproductive dysfunction in *The Heat of the Day* (1948), *A World of Love* (1955) and *Eva Trout* (1969). Here again I look at the contemporary political expression of Bowen's thought, for in these mid-century fictions too Bowen's imagination takes shape from the historical context of its time, referencing in particular the decline of British global power and the consolidation of a new American world order in the years after the Second World War. My work in this concluding chapter of the book thus highlights the particular psychological and political risk to which Bowen's conservative sensibility is vulnerable: the risk, that is, of an increasingly authoritarian conception of order. Confronted by the prospect of symbolic extinction, Bowen's ethical investment in the psychosocial institution of law morphs into a neo-imperial imagination of dominance and submission.

## Notes

1. Bowen, 'Confessions', p. 232. The article was originally published in *The Saturday Book: Being the Ninth Annual Issue of this Celebrated Repository of Curiosities and Looking-Glass of Past and Present*, ed. Leonard Russell, London: Hutchinson, 1949, pp. 108–9.
2. Bowen, 'Do Conventions Matter?', p. 301.
3. Bowen, 'The Cost of Letters', p. 233.
4. Bowen, *Bowen's Court*, p. 443; hereafter cited as BC.
5. Bennett and Royle, *Elizabeth Bowen and the Dissolution of the Novel*, p. xix.
6. Ellmann, *Elizabeth Bowen: The Shadow Across the Page*, p. xi.
7. Corcoran, *Elizabeth Bowen: The Enforced Return*, p. 3.
8. Ellmann, *Elizabeth Bowen: The Shadow Across the Page*, p. x.
9. Osborn, 'Introduction', in Osborn (ed.), *Elizabeth Bowen: New Critical Perspectives*, p. 7. Stevens, 'Bowen: The Critical Response', p. 179.
10. Corcoran, *Elizabeth Bowen: The Enforced Return*, p. 3.
11. Corcoran, *Elizabeth Bowen: The Enforced Return*, p. 4.
12. Ellmann, *Elizabeth Bowen: The Shadow Across the Page*, pp. x, 8.

13. Mooney, 'Unstable Compounds: Bowen's Beckettian Affinities', p. 13.
14. Mooney, 'Unstable Compounds: Bowen's Beckettian Affinities', p. 15.
15. Osborn, '"How to measure this unaccountable darkness between the trees"', p. 36.
16. Seiler, 'At Midcentury: Elizabeth Bowen's *The Heat of the Day*', p. 127.
17. Ellmann, *Elizabeth Bowen: The Shadow Across the Page*, p. 20.
18. Ellmann, *Elizabeth Bowen: The Shadow Across the Page*, p. 20.
19. Corcoran, *Elizabeth Bowen: The Enforced Return*, p. 13.
20. Darwood, *A World of Lost Innocence*, p. 1.
21. Gildersleeve, *Elizabeth Bowen and the Writing of Trauma*, p. 2.
22. Gildersleeve, *Elizabeth Bowen and the Writing of Trauma*, p. xix.
23. Gildersleeve, *Elizabeth Bowen and the Writing of Trauma*, p. 2.
24. Oxindine, 'Resisting Dissolution', p. 200.
25. Oxindine, 'Resisting Dissolution', p. 214.
26. Oxindine, 'Resisting Dissolution', p. 200.
27. Oxindine, 'Resisting Dissolution', p. 205.
28. Ellmann, *Elizabeth Bowen: The Shadow Across the Page*, p. 2.
29. Corcoran, *Elizabeth Bowen: The Enforced Return*, pp. 9, 11.
30. Towheed, 'Territory, Space, Modernity', p. 113.
31. Cullingford, '"Something else"', p. 280.
32. Bowen, 'The Cat Jumps', p. 362.
33. Bowen, 'The Cat Jumps', p. 366.
34. Bowen, 'The Cat Jumps', p. 364.
35. Cullingford, '"Something else"', p. 280.
36. Bowen and Ritchie, *Love's Civil War*, 29 July 1945, p. 53; 17 September 1945, p. 63; 17 September 1945, p. 64.
37. Bowen and Ritchie, *Love's Civil War*, 14 August 1945, p. 68; 24 August 1945, p. 55; 22 October 1945, p. 71; 18 November 1945, p. 75.
38. Bowen, 'The Idea of the Home', p. 171.
39. Bowen, 'The Cult of Nostalgia', p. 97.
40. Bowen, 'The Living Image – 2', p. 258.

41. Bowen, 'The Living Image – 1', p. 246.
42. Bowen, 'A Conversation between Elizabeth Bowen and Jocelyn Brooke', p. 275.
43. Bowen and Ritchie, *Love's Civil War*, 3 December 1941, p. 26.
44. Bowen and Ritchie, *Love's Civil War*, 26 January 1941, p. 28.
45. Bowen, *To the North*, pp. 52, 93, 88.
46. Bowen, *To the North*, p. 171.
47. Bowen, 'The Apple Tree', p. 467.
48. Bowen, 'The Apple Tree', pp. 465, 470.
49. Bowen, 'Tears, Idle Tears', p. 486.

# Chapter 1
# Development

Elizabeth Bowen spent her first seven winters in Dublin, at 15 Herbert Place, the primary residence of her father, who occupied himself for the greater part of the year in working as a barrister in the city. In *Seven Winters*, a memoir of her early childhood, Bowen notes that her nursery was at the front of the house: 'under its windows lay the road, the canal and a row of trees':[1]

> My nursery reached across the breadth of the house; being high up it had low windows, and bars had been fixed across these to keep me from falling out. On the blue-grey walls hung pictures, and two of these pictures I do remember sharply – they were openings into a second, more threatening reality. The first must, I think, have been chosen for its heroic subject when my mother still expected me to be Robert:[2] it was Casabianca standing against the flames. The boy stood in ecstasy on the burning deck. In the other, a baby in a wooden cradle floated smilingly on an immense flood, stretching out its two hands to a guardian cat that sat upright on the quilt at the cradle's foot. All round, from the lonely expanse of water rose only the tips of gables, chimneys and trees. The composure of the cat and the baby had been meant, I suppose, to rule all disaster out of the scene. But for me there was constant anxiety – what would become of the cradle in a world in which everyone else was drowned? (SW 471–2)

I think we may see in these striking nursery pictures the illustration of some important aspects of Bowen's thinking about psychological development. The uncanny image of the waterborne baby suggests that even the most ordinary separations from Mother are, for an infant, as terrifying as they are uncontestable. In particular, the picture reflects upon the baby's routine desertion at bedtime, when Mother's arms are withdrawn in favour of the bleakly functional cradle and the daytime view from the nursery windows of 'gables, chimneys and trees' is almost completely drowned out by the dark, the 'lonely expanse of water' a representation of the featureless wasteland of the night. No amount of tucking-in of the quilt or fobbing off with animal familiars, whether stuffed or unresponsively alive, can mitigate the desolation of this nightly rejection, or disguise from the infant what the infant will perceive as the neglectfulness or cruelty of the mother who insists on such a separation. The 'composure' of the scene has a coerced quality and the baby's smile, like the stretching-out of its hands, seems a gesture of supplication towards the departing mother, a final, futile plea not to be left alone. But Mother is a ruthless God, her nocturnal abandonment of her child in the Ark-like cradle recalling the infanticidal destructiveness of a deity who chose to put to death almost all of his own creation by sending upon them an immense flood. Dependence upon such a power seems likely to provoke intense ambivalence. I love Mother, such an infant may be imagined to feel, and yet she is close to annihilating me. I love Mother, and yet I find myself fearing and hating her, too.

The other picture also addresses itself to the agony of separation, in order to re-stage the scene as a problem to which a solution could be imagined – imagined, that is, in the form of Father. An admiral's son, the thirteen-year-old Casabianca perished with his father's ship, the *Orient*, at the Battle of the Nile because his father, fatally wounded, was unable to come to his son's aid or to release him from his honourable stand upon the burning deck. Thus although the picture shows us a hyperbolic instance of paternal inadequacy, it does thereby project as a kind of imaginary counterfactual the terms on which the relationship of mother and child might be reconfigured by the intervention of an external authority or law. For, in light of the conventionally feminine gendering of boats, and recalling also, in the case of the waterborne baby, the association of the floating cradle with the longed-for presence of Mother, I think we may recognise in the picture of the boy sticking fast to the beleaguered *Orient* an image of a baby clinging to the mother ship in defiance of separation, and understand the violence of the naval battle as a reflection of the infant's rage and fear in relation to the maternal vessel upon which he depends. In Felicia Hemans's poetic celebration of Casabianca's last stand, 'The flames roll'd on – he would not go / Without his father's word'. His father, 'faint in death below', cannot respond, but a crucial point, I think, for Bowen, as she counterposes this picture to the picture of the baby in the floating cradle, is that the scene of imperial heroism introduces a new position, a third person, Father, in this instance a great naval commander, whose responsibility it is to confirm the necessity of separation by refiguring it as a paternal mandate that neither mother nor child has any choice but to obey. In the historical event, of course, Casabianca waited in vain for the authoritative word that would order him to safety: 'He call'd aloud: – "Say, Father, say / If yet my task is done?" / He knew not that the chieftain lay / Unconscious of his son.' But, by highlighting this famous failure of paternal intervention, the picture indicates the nature of the remedy by which the trauma of separation from Mother could be redeemed by its re-presentation as a consequence of Father's command. The *Orient*, after all, is father's ship, and Casabianca has neither the power to protect her nor, properly, the responsibility for doing so.

This chapter is composed of three sections. In the first section, I will demonstrate that Bowen's writing implies a particular conception, on Bowen's part, of psychological development, and I will show that the primary plots of Bowen's first novel *The Hotel* (1927) and of her novel of the mid-thirties *The House in Paris* (1935) can be understood as fictional articulations of exactly this developmental drama. Implicit in Bowen's work, it appears to me, is the supposition that a baby's earliest life is experienced within an intimate, interdependent two-person system of mother and child. To refer to this two-person system

I shall use the phrase 'maternal dyad': the term has been deployed across a wide range of psychoanalytic and child-development discourses and may offer us here a sympathetic shorthand for the early-life experience that Bowen's writing repeatedly invokes. In Bowen's understanding, the maternal dyad comprehends both the paradise of an original state of perfect harmony, and the dystopia by which it is succeeded when the child first begins to experience separation at the hands of his or her mother.

I shall characterise the experience of separation – as Bowen's writing imagines it – as a 'trauma', my purpose being to indicate that in Bowen's view its impact on the child is that of a metaphorical assault, the emotional equivalent of a severing of – in particular – an intimate connection to Mother. Thus my employment of the term differs in a crucial way from Jessica Gildersleeve's in her *Elizabeth Bowen and the Writing of Trauma: The Ethics of Survival* (2014). Gildersleeve works with the specific conceptualisation of trauma developed in recent years by Cathy Caruth and others, a conceptualisation that tends to assume or imply the abnormal or anomalous nature of the traumatic event and that stresses the consequent impossibility, or at least extreme difficulty, of its conscious representation: 'trauma is a kind of psychological wounding caused by an event so extreme that it cannot be immediately assimilated, and is thus, paradoxically, only first experienced in its repetition, and as a function of its forgetting'.[3] I want to highlight in Bowen's thought, by contrast, the twin ideas that separation – for example, bedtime, or weaning – is normal, and necessary for development, and that, nonetheless, it causes the infant terrible pain, incomprehension and despair. That it is an excruciating experience – and one, certainly, that many of Bowen's characters seek more or less unconsciously to disavow or disallow by various forms of denial – indicates not that something has gone wrong for the child but that, on the contrary, something has gone right: Mother has instituted separation.

In Bowen's view, separation does not by itself restructure the dyadic relationship between mother and child, which remains, after separation, a two-person system. What changes dramatically, however, is the child's perception of each party to the relationship, for after separation Mother may seem to pose an existential threat to her infant and her infant, in turn, may experience acute ambivalence or straightforward hostility in relation to Mother. In Bowen's view what is needed to redeem this desperate state is the arrival of Father, whose responsibility it is to refigure the maternal No as paternal law, reconfiguring the two-person trauma of separation as a three-person crisis. Father's job is to lay a special claim to Mother for himself, an act that is at once – in relation to the child in question – prohibitive and powerfully enabling. By re-presenting Mother's withholding of herself in terms of a paternal sanction against certain kinds or degrees of intimacy in the relationship between mother and child, Father exculpates Mother from the child's charges of negligence, cruelty or deprivation and restores her to her child as a loved, loving and lovable object; at the same time, the child, too, is released from a state of fear and reactive aggression and restored to himself or herself as a loved, loving and lovable subject. In the first section of this chapter, I show that the central plots of both *The Hotel* and *The House in Paris* culminate in demonstrations of exactly such a developmental happy ending.

It is important to recognise, however, that notwithstanding these exemplary and indeed exhilarating fictions there appears with great frequency in Bowen's writing a story concerning the derailment of such a developmental trajectory: what we might think of as a 'signature story' detailing a specific combination of factors that can significantly compromise the process of development that Bowen regards as necessary for her characters' wellbeing. The picture of Casabianca on the burning deck of the *Orient* has shown us already how the confirmation of separation as the mandate of paternal law may be imperilled by Father's incapacitation. I think we may observe in the other nursery picture, as well, the shadow of some interference in the developmental stage there illustrated, because the image of the baby's ordinary separations from its mother – separations that the child cannot help but experience as a terrible abandonment – is complicated not only by God's declared intention that Noah should survive the flood but also by the picture's evocation of the infant Moses in his waterproof basket, consigned by his mother to the river in an attempt to save his life, Pharaoh having decreed death to all male babies of the Israelites. Indeed Moses's mother's action is less an abandonment than a strategic *staging* of an abandonment, a ploy by which the fatal separation of the infant from his mother could be indefinitely postponed: after floating the cradle on the water Moses's mother left her daughter to keep watch by the river, so that when the infant was discovered by Pharaoh's daughter, Moses's sister was on hand to offer her mother's services as a suitable nurse for the baby. The suitability of Moses's mother derives in particular from her ability to breastfeed the infant, a crucial capacity that is not to be found in Pharaoh's childless daughter or her attendants. We might, then, review with some scepticism the ostensible claim of the picture to offer an image of separation, for the result of Moses's 'abandonment' by his mother was the prolongation of the nursing dyad. The picture thus lodges within its presentation of separation the hint of an intransigent maternal resistance to weaning, an insistence on the uninterrupted harmony of the breastfeeding mother and child. Together, the pictures may thus stand as emblems of the twin commitment, in Bowen's writing, to a conception of a developmental trajectory that conduces to maturation and wellbeing, and to the tireless exploration of a particular sequence of conditions which might cause this trajectory to falter or fail.

In the second section of the chapter I explore three of Bowen's short stories: the enormously interesting, complex and substantial 'Ivy Gripped the Steps' (1945) – a virtual novella – and the compelling early stories 'Coming Home' (1923) and 'The Visitor' (1926). My focus will be on Bowen's 'signature story' about how a necessary process of development can be compromised, short-circuited or simply arrested by a specific combination of factors: that is to say, a mother who is extremely reluctant to effect separation between her child and herself, or who may be stricken with remorse at having done so, and may attempt, in earnest or as a pretence, to undo the separation that has been achieved; and a father whose authority is sufficiently debilitated so as to render him incapable of confirming the maternal No and refiguring it as a paternal prohibition, transforming the dyadic relation between mother and child into a three-position structure. I will show that Bowen repeatedly concludes the story of such a developmental derailment with the death of her protagonist's mother, a death whose particular impact on the child gives the measure of the extent of that developmental compromise or failure. Throughout this section of the chapter I pay close attention to Bowen's autobiographical writing, for her accounts of her childhood experience identify in Florence and Henry Bowen the parental archetypes of her signature account of the perils that threaten development. Florence died in 1912, a couple of months after Elizabeth's thirteenth birthday: the meaning and effect of her death in her daughter's life are subjected, by Elizabeth Bowen, to intense analysis in the fictional as well as the autobiographical texts that I discuss here.

In the third section of the chapter, I concentrate on Bowen's novel *The Heat of the Day*, and seek to show how an understanding of Bowen's signature story of developmental failure can illuminate the extraordinary structural and thematic complexity of her 1948 masterpiece. Much of my discussion concerns the big question of how, in Bowen's writing, the psychodrama of individual development is explored in relation to current affairs; it is a topic that will have been raised already by 'Ivy Gripped the Steps', a story whose account of the relationship between the First World War and the Second World War is integral to the symbolic work of the text as a whole. Nowhere, however, in Bowen's *oeuvre*, than in her wartime novel of espionage, intrigue and romance do we find a more substantial or sustained example of how the narrative structure and characteristic tropes of contemporary geopolitical reality may be pressed into service as elaborate world-historical correlatives to the psychological turmoil and developmental travails that constitute the primary subject of Bowen's interest and attention.

## Section One: Happy Endings

Bowen's first novel *The Hotel* (1927) examines the making and breaking of relationships among the English guests of a Riviera hotel over the course of a couple of weeks in the summer season. All the principle characters are adults, but, as we will see, the plot conceives of several of these figures as representing childlike states of being. *The House in Paris* (1935) has a more elaborate structure. Composed of three parts – 'The Present', 'The Past', 'The Present' – the novel's central recessed section offers a look back into the prehistory of the contemporary plot, which deals primarily with the re-uniting of an eight-year-old child, Leopold, with his birth mother, who had given him up for fostering and then adoption. Both novels showcase the state of the weaned dyad: they focus, that is to say, on the predicament of the child who has experienced separation at the hands of its mother, without that painful experience having yet been affirmed and refigured by paternal intervention. In Bowen's work, the most distinctive sign of this predicament is a yearning for intimacy with the mother who is felt to have been lost, without any marked sense of lack in relation to the equally missing father. Sydney Warren, heroine of *The Hotel*, a 'probable twenty-two', seems to have no closer relation than her cousin Tessa, with whom she is holidaying abroad, and it is stated explicitly, by another of the hotel's English guests, that Sydney 'ha[s]n't got a father at all'.[4] But Sydney's passionate attachment to Mrs Kerr, an attractive middle-aged widow, speaks powerfully of a desire for maternal attention without indicating any feeling of need in relation to her absent father.

The two child characters in *The House in Paris* have both been deprived of both parents, but in each case it is the mother that is grieved for. The eleven-year-old Henrietta's mother has died; her father, 'left helpless' by his wife's death, has given up his daughter to her maternal grandmother, a paternal abdication that does not seem to trouble Henrietta, who seems to mourn only her lost mother.[5] Nine-year-old Leopold can have no conscious memory of *his* mother, Karen, who gave him up, in his earliest babyhood, to the care of a foster mother, and subsequently to an adoptive family, but it is the original maternal relationship that Leopold longs to recover, seemingly giving little thought to the figure of his father, who died before he was born. In Bowen's work, it is a hallmark of the weaned dyad that although both parents appear to be missing, only the mother is mourned.

The primary plot of *The Hotel* concerns Sydney Warren's attempts to recreate, in young adulthood, the bliss of her dyadic relation to her mother prior to the trauma of separation, a project that motivates virtually all of her actions until almost the end of the book: as, for example, at the start of Chapter 9, 'My Little Boy'.

> From end to end of the town the principal long street ran like a funnel; as Sydney came out of the flower-shop, her side of the street was slate-grey in the shadow of early afternoon. It was characteristic of her as an intelligent young English lady that she should have come to buy carnations during the hour of the siesta, cutting for her a caprice of her own direct across the custom of the land. The carnations, among which, walking slowly, she now was burying her face, were scentless, but gave one an acute pleasure by the chilly contact of their petals. She had an armful of two colours – sulphur with a ragged edge of pink and ashy mauve with crimson at the centre, crimson-veined. [. . .] On account of their low cost, their strangeness to the Northern eye and the vehemence of their colouring, they have become the vehicle of much emotion. One cannot, however casually, present these native carnations to a friend and remain unaffected, while the pleasure with which carnations are received is intensified by some vague agitation.
> Sydney's day had been so far as perfect as a bubble; she felt careless of it, as though the bubble could not burst. (H 65)

The first thing that I want to highlight is the powerful yet indistinct eroticism that suffuses the passage, at once stimulating and evading specification: here is 'much emotion', an uncertain combination of 'acute pleasure' and 'vague agitation', an effect linked to the coincidence of intensity and indeterminateness that characterises the elusive representational work of the uncanny flowers.[6] This emphatic yet enigmatic effect may be understood, I think, in terms of the pre-linguistic origins of the experiential field in question, as well as in relation to the social and psychological need to obscure the essentially infantile nature of that experiential field, for it seems to me that an important experience called up by Sydney's interactions with the carnations is the dyadic activity of breastfeeding. Consider, for example, the tactile enjoyment that she experiences in the chilly touch of the petals, not against her hands but on her face. I would emphasise also the sense of fullness, of bountifulness, in the 'armful of two colours', an image of a floral cornucopia that suggests both a whole-body embrace and a large volume of relatively simple visual data, or of visual data that in a baby's perception has been simplified for ease of understanding. The vividly perceived colours – 'sulphur with a ragged edge of pink and ashy mauve with crimson at the centre, crimson-veined' – are strikingly corporeal: the yellows, purples, reds and greys of those tender-skinned, private parts of the so-called 'white' body whose coloration is unlikely to have been subdued by callusing, or tanned by exposure to the sun. The crimson veining is particularly evocative of the breasts, as are the 'ragged edge' of pink and the crimson centre on ashy mauve, both of which suggest the visual function of the areolae as a centralising focus for the baby's look, as well as the textural cues sought by the hungry baby's mouth. Carnations have a quite straightforward circular form, and the varieties that Sydney has chosen are patterned to accentuate their shape. '[S]ulphur with a ragged edge of pink' implies a centrifugal look, a moving outwards of the baby's eye from the centre of the mother's breast towards its circumference; 'ashy mauve with crimson at the centre' suggests a centripetal look, a moving back from the edge of the breast to the middle. Together, the two variants suggest a back and forth roving of the eye between centre and circumference, an ocular caressing of close-up objects that monopolise the viewer's interest, love and attention. Sydney's 'senses were absorbed by the carnations, and she could be conscious of the street only as a sharp distinction between sun and shadow' (H 65).

It is axiomatic, however, in the world of Bowen's fiction, that such attempts to restore the paradise of the nursing dyad are doomed to failure, for if Mother has burst that bubble once you may be sure that she will do it again. Sydney's presentation of the carnations to Mrs Kerr is followed almost immediately by Mrs Kerr's opening of a letter from her twenty-year-old son Ronald to discover that he is planning to join her at the hotel for a brief holiday: 'My little boy', as she puts it, 'is coming here.' 'Coming here?' Sydney echoes. 'Yes, here', Mrs Kerr confirms: 'Coming to the Hotel.' It is the first of two moments at which we see Sydney's life, and indeed the entire novel, pivot in its course, a moment of shock for Bowen's protagonist so profound as to be not only inexpressible but impossible to experience consciously: 'Sydney, sitting quite still, remained blank for a moment and did not say anything' (H 70). She does, quite swiftly, manage to move and speak again, and within a page, or a couple of minutes, 'had [. . .] made up her mind that their future must not be devastated by the descent upon them of Ronald' (H 71) – but this only confirms the scale of the catastrophe that is now in train. For Maud Ellmann the significance of Ronald's arrival can be understood in the context of Bowen's interest in the Oedipal triangle 'in which the primal dyad of mother and child is disrupted by the third term of the father'.[7] But Ronald does not, I think, figure as Father. He is, as Mrs Kerr says, her 'little boy', and the threat that he poses to Sydney is not that of an adult lover asserting his exclusive sexual possession of Mother: rather, he threatens to *replace* Sydney at Mrs Kerr's breast, as the new baby whose arrival precipitates the weaning of the older child. Separation does not introduce a third person into the baby's model of the relational world: it leaves the two-person structure of the dyad unchanged, while radically transforming its nature, at least from the point of view of the displaced child. Where once harmony reigned between a bountiful mother and a devoted infant, there is now, for the disallowed, cancelled-out baby, only terrible pain and incomprehension, paradise transmogrified into Hell.

A key feature of the weaning dyad is thus a dramatic divergence of feeling and intention between Mother, whom we may make out to be trying her best to persuade her child of the merits of solid food, and Baby, who is liable to regard the new comestibles with horror and alarm. Bowen's most detailed analysis of these radically incommensurable perspectives appears in Chapter 17: 'Pâtisserie', which focuses upon a conversation at a local café that Mrs Kerr insists upon patronising during the course of a morning walk with Sydney, not long after Ronald's arrival at the Hotel. At this point in the story, Ronald has for several days been monopolising his mother's attention, and the walk represents a concession on Mrs Kerr's part to the wounded feelings of her formerly favoured young friend. It is however with no intention of revoking her relegation of Sydney that Mrs Kerr leads the way onto the terrace of the patisserie. For this is a place of compulsory re-education, where the baby who longs for breastmilk will be instructed in the necessity of eating cake. The patisserie is hailed by Mrs Kerr with a mystifyingly effusive 'Do look, Sydney – how civilized!' 'How greedy!' Sydney replies, unable to understand Mrs Kerr's enthusiasm; to her, the café seems merely a decadent cul-de-sac, and she has been 'trying to direct her friend to the older end of the town, where she would at least find nothing but fruit shops' (H 127). In Sydney's view the patisserie is a literally fruitless dead-end; in place of the trustworthy nourishment of yesteryear there jostle here only strange, unaccountable pastries. ('Don't go for the coffee kind', Sydney is warned by Victor, an acquaintance from the Hotel, as they fill their plates at the counter: 'they look first-rate but they're hollow. Do you mind if I take the last green one? Veronica's fearfully keen on them' [H 129].) According to Mrs Kerr, however, the patisserie represents a state of superior culture, or personal maturation: to Sydney's 'How greedy!' she responds 'Yes, that's just what I mean – how civilized! Anybody can eat at meal-times. Come over – oh, Sydney, we must!' 'But we're not hungry!' Sydney protests, her instinctive confidence in the existence of a shared or collaborative appetite a leftover from the charmed mutuality of the nursing dyad (H 127). Mrs Kerr remains adamant, however, that Sydney must comply with the regime of the patisserie – 'Look, eat one of those little flaky things', Mrs Kerr urges her, 'they look delicious' (H 130) – so although the food seems 'like sawdust' in her mouth Sydney 'eat[s] pastry quickly, in spite of a frightened feeling each time that she might not be able to swallow' (H 131).

The divergence of views between mother and baby is echoed in the infant's ambivalence towards the parent who has imposed separation: love and confidence battle fear and hate for supremacy in the child's feelings about the weaning mother. In Chapter 17 Bowen exploits narrative point of view to demonstrate how the profound distress of the child may produce hostile, even paranoid patterns of thought. Thus much of Mrs Kerr's behaviour at the patisserie – as related, always, from a narrative viewpoint closely identified with Sydney's perception of events – seems calculated to refigure the image of a vulnerable and trusting baby at the breast as something ludicrous, or even blameworthy. As if identifying in the spectacle of a courting couple – Victor and his girlfriend Veronica – exactly such a scene of intimate nourishment, Mrs Kerr remarks to Sydney: 'He is looking at her with the most awful expression, with cream on his chin. Isn't passion debasing?' (H 128) From Sydney's anguished perspective, Mrs Kerr seems bent on a retroactive destruction of the mutuality that Sydney recalls with longing: as Mrs Kerr settles herself at one of the patisserie's tables she says, with a show of delight apparently calculated to conceal but skimpily a devastating implication of neglect, 'I'm so seldom allowed to do this' (H 128). For what seems like the cruellest of Mrs Kerr's gambits in this scene is to suggest that Sydney has hitherto shown herself insufficiently attentive to the question of her older friend's preferences and pleasures, so that the precious identity of feeling from whose loss in the present Sydney is reeling is implicitly thrown into question as a reality of the past as well. Reduced, by her pain and confusion, to an artlessly reproachful simplicity, Sydney says: 'I never knew this *was* your sort of morning. We might often have come here.' 'I suppose', Mrs Kerr replies, 'that I hardly liked to suggest it' (H 128), thereby appearing to give a masterful finishing touch to her self-portrait as a martyr to Sydney's culpable self-absorption.

In the wake of Mrs Kerr's 'rejection' Sydney accepts a proposal of marriage from James Milton, an English clergyman and fellow guest at the hotel. In readings that prioritise the external reality of the novel's fictional world, Petra Rau and Elizabeth Cullingford consider the twenty-two-year-old Sydney – as she would, no doubt, consider herself – as a mature sexual adult from the first.[8] Thus what Cullingford characterises as 'Sydney's frustrated lesbian desire' for Mrs Kerr is, in Rau's analysis of Bowen's literary experimentalism, an exemplary mark of the avant-garde, 'a sign of the real and a signifier of modernity' in Bowen's novel.[9] When Sydney becomes engaged to Milton, Rau can accordingly identify in Bowen's text the lineaments of 'a halfhearted [heterosexual] conversion narrative',[10] the wavering of Sydney's sexual orientation – in Cullingford's view, evidence of 'severe heterosexual panic'[11] – a correlative of Bowen's authorial ambivalence in relation to 'the heterosexual teleology demanded by traditional realist forms such as romance'.[12] But despite the ostentatious masculine prestige of his name, Milton's appeal to Sydney comprises nothing other than his suitability as a replacement for Mrs Kerr, who was, herself, an attempted replacement for a lost maternal original. What is sought in such a replacement is a mother who will repudiate the necessity of separation, a mother who will repudiate the reality of loss itself, driving time backwards to restore the harmony of the nursing dyad: a harmony that Sydney associates with a kind of immortality. Death 'hint[s] itself as something to be imposed on one, the last and most humiliating of those deprivations [Sydney] had begun to experience' (H 99); so Milton, who, as a clergyman, 'did not acknowledge finality anywhere' (H 99), seems ideally placed to revoke this iteration of the maternal No. 'He presented himself [as] an undriven, a comforting figure. She saw him conducting a funeral: voluminous, fluttering, milk-white [. . .] with the expression, a submerged beam, of this having in a cognizant Mind its order. The word "death" used in his presence would have a slow-dying ring to it' (H 100). Milk-white, voluminous, the motherly Milton intimates the maternal Mind of the Maker, a Maker who counterposes to the mortal finitude implied by Mrs Kerr's commitment to development the comforting mirage of a changeless eternity.

The first and third sections of *The House in Paris* focus on a day spent together by Leopold and Henrietta in the house of the novel's title. Leopold has travelled to Paris from his adoptive family's home in Spezia to meet his birth mother, and Henrietta is in transit from her widowed father's house in England to the Riviera home of her grandmother Mrs Arbuthnot. The house in Paris belongs to the formidable Madame Fisher – the French widow of an English naval officer – and her middle-aged daughter Naomi, whom Mrs Arbuthnot had met on holiday many years previously and is now making use of in the organisation of Henrietta's journey across France. The middle section of the novel tells the story of how Leopold came to be conceived, nearly a decade before, by the upper-middle-class Englishwoman Karen Michaelis and the French Jew Max Eberhart, each of whom had been, at the time, engaged to marry other people, Max's fiancée being Naomi Fisher. Karen had first met both Naomi and Max during her finishing year abroad as a paying guest of Madame Fisher's, when she had welcomed Naomi's friendship and been fascinated by Max's reserve. Subsequently Karen had become engaged to Ray Forrestier, an eminently suitable man of her own class and nationality, while Max, who had previously enjoyed an exclusive intimacy with Madame Fisher, had entered into an engagement with her daughter Naomi. Brought together again by Naomi at this time, Karen and Max fall violently in love and conceive Leopold; Max dies shortly afterwards. Karen gives birth to Leopold, gives him up for adoption and marries Ray, who forgives her the affair with Max and wishes to have her child to live with them, although for many years Karen will not hear of it. In the 'Present' sections of the novel Leopold waits in the Fishers' house in Paris for a meeting with Karen, his mother, who has finally expressed a desire to see him again.

The intercutting of Leopold's experience in the present with the tale of his conception ten years before invites us to read his story as a revision of his father's, for just as Leopold yearns for his mother so Max, too, had been deeply attracted to what he himself identified as the maternal quality of his fiancée Naomi. 'When I see how the stony lines of her dress and her entirely unsurprised face moved me', Max says of Naomi, 'I see now that it was the Madonna trick – my nerves tricking my senses with the idea of peace, making someone to make for me an unattackable safe place' (HP 166). Like Leopold, and like Sydney, too, Max had been searching for a mother, a mother who would undo the separation that he has suffered – a separation that is figured here in terms of his prior relationship to Naomi's mother, Madame Fisher. 'It was Mme Fisher he came to talk to', Karen tells her own fiancé, Ray: 'they had a kind of salon all to themselves, just they two' (HP 85). I have looked previously at the way that Sydney's experience of separation results in the transmogrification of her beloved Mrs Kerr into a figure of remarkable cruelty, but this pales in comparison to the monstrousness of Madame Fisher, one of the great maternal grotesques in modern fiction. Mrs Kerr is often to be found arranged picturesquely on a sofa, but Madame Fisher takes this mannered repose to a hyperbolic extreme: she passes the entirety of the first and third sections of the novel in bed – theatrically proximate to death, she nevertheless exercises an iron control over the household by means of her aggressively measured tapping on the floor with a stick – and she achieves for the performance of her decisive role in the melodramatic climax of Section Two a similarly violent and moribund passivity.

At this point in the story Max has betrayed his fiancée Naomi by falling in love with her richer, prettier, luckier friend Karen, whom he has decided to marry. This turn of events may be understood, I think, in terms of an unconscious transition, on Max's part, from denying separation to identifying with the mother who carries it out – for by consummating his relationship with Karen, Max cuts himself off from Naomi, the woman whom he had been looking to for a restoration of infantile dyadic security. There is thus a sense in which Max, tormented by the pain of separation, a pain that evidently cannot be effectively remedied by denial, seeks to exchange for the powerlessness of the abandoned baby the malign potency of the mother who abandons. This account of Max's behaviour is endorsed, I think we may see, by Madame Fisher herself, who 'commend[s] him', as she puts it, for throwing over Naomi in favour of Karen (HP 191). Having hoped, perhaps, that Madame Fisher would condemn him for abandoning her daughter, and thereby call into question the necessity of the separation that she has imposed, Max encounters instead, in her approval of his decision, an intensely unwelcome confirmation that there can be no revoking of individuation. Almost immediately he leaves the room, and the house, and Naomi re-enters the drawing-room in search of Madame Fisher. Here is Naomi's account, to Karen, of what she, Naomi, would see:

> My mother was there. She was as though she had fallen across the sofa, with eyes half shut and no colour in her face, but I looked at her with no pity. [. . .] I saw then that all her life her power had never properly used itself, and that now it had used itself she was like the dead, like someone killed in a victory. Her lips were stiff and she could not speak at first; then she said: 'Go after him,' and when I still stood there she said: 'You fool, he is dying.' I thought she meant in the spirit. But she moved herself on the sofa and, with a frown like she has when someone spills wine or ink, made me look at the mantelpiece. [. . .] I saw his blood splashed on the marble, on the parquet where he had stood and in a trail to the door, smeared where I had trodden without knowing. I saw his penknife with the long blade open, fallen between where he had stood and where my mother sat. She said: 'He cut his wrist across, through the artery, to hurt me.' [. . .] When Max came out our street must have been empty [. . .] He must have stood a minute on our doorstep; then, holding his wrist and muffling it, for there was no trace of blood in the street, crossed the street to the mouth of that alley between the two studio walls. At the end of that he fell down. As no trace led us there, when we came to him it was too late, which was as he wished. (HP 189–90)

The overblown dreadfulness of Max's suicide corresponds closely to the overblown dreadfulness of Madame Fisher, for in killing himself Max acts simultaneously to express and to put an end to the suffering of separation, and to punish and destroy the maternal author of his plight. Opening up in his wrist an unstanchable wound, Max gives bodily form to the trauma of separation, his death by exsanguination a literalisation of his desperate psychic state. Bowen offers us here a Grand Guignol representation of the weaning dyad, a two-person bloodbath of pain, incomprehension and rage. That it evokes simultaneously a macabre scene of postcoital exhaustion – a woman, the ravished object of a sexual conquest, fainting on a sofa 'like someone killed in a victory' while her seducer, sated and spent, staggers away in search of oblivion, having distributed his vital fluids liberally throughout the house – should not surprise us, as we have noted already the intense sexual fantasies of union that Bowen's characters oppose to the unbearable reality of separation.

Although it will be evident that the tone of this novel is very different from that of *The Hotel*, both the logic and the staging of Max's death are remarkably reminiscent of the second pivotal episode in Sydney's story – Chapter 23: 'Next Corner'. This chapter focuses on a day trip made at Tessa's behest; she thinks 'it would be so nice for James to get to know Sydney's friend Mrs Kerr really well before they went back to England, so she planned a surprise on her own account, hired a car for the afternoon and invited Mrs Kerr and Milton to drive with herself and Sydney up to a village high in the hills' (H 175). There they will enjoy a remarkable view; '[t]here would be also a church with a very dark, old-looking painting, and a pâtisserie kept by a lady from Nice where they gave you an excellent tea' (H 175).

The mountain village seems designed to exemplify the hell that is the post-separation dyad. The patisserie, of course, reiterates the scene of torturous consumption that we have explored previously. The church, its air 'stale with the incense of years, the breath of long-dead congregations' (H 176), is a kind of tomb, a grave for the painting, or for the subject of the painting, a painting that is 'so dark that it might have been anything' (H 175–6). Bowen does not specify directly what the painting depicts, but Tessa's focus on the represented visage of the subject – 'There's something *about* that face . . . [sic] I know there's something about the expression' – and her perception of the picture in terms of 'possible beauty stored up in secrecy' (H 176) imply very strongly that it is a Madonna, for the twinned ideas of beauty and of death are associated throughout the novel with Ronald's image of his mother. In an earlier scene, for example, Mrs Kerr retreats into an afternoon nap 'in the attitude of the Beata Beatrix' and we see Ronald '[go] back through his memory, past his admiration for Rossetti, to the day when at six years old he had called his mother "My Beautiful"' (H 110). The symbolic knotting-together of maternal beauty and a startlingly seductive deathliness appears also in *The House in Paris*: Henrietta 'f[inds] in [Madame Fisher's] smile a perplexingness she had once been told was beauty and learnt to recognise by some pause in herself. The smile was pungent, extraordinary, as deep as darkness and as dazzling as light' (HP 38).

Finally, the spectacular elevated view from the village seems a correlative of the terror of abandonment, for the mountain looks out upon a 'void', a vertiginous inhospitable environment that renders in terms of emptiness the emotional desolation of the infant's world in the wake of separation. And thus Sydney, like Max, begins to envisage a *coup de théâtre* that would simultaneously end her own suffering, destroy the woman responsible for hurting her, objectify her feeling that she and her tormentor are hopelessly lost to each other already, and effect between them, nevertheless, a kind of erotic reunion in death. As the party drives back down the mountain road at the end of the day, Sydney 'concentrate[s] her whole will and imagination' on the idea that the car will run over the edge and plunge its occupants to an orgasmic extinction.

> 'If it could be the next corner,' she thought, 'we should go over clean – there is that clear drop. Let it be the next corner [. . .] We mustn't go over too quickly,' she thought, 'there must be time to say something.' Under the rug her hand found out Mrs Kerr's sleeve and rested there ever so lightly. She racked her brain for all there would be to say, then relinquished the effort.

At all events there would be a moment to look at each other, just to look at each other: that would be best. (H 178–9)

What, then, can possibly redeem this terrible state: this terrible, normal, inevitable state of the dyad after separation? The joyful culmination of *The House in Paris* answers my question with splendid clarity and emphasis, for what Bowen dramatises here is her understanding that what can redeem this state – indeed, what *should* redeem this state – is the intervention of Father, whose specific responsibility it is to refigure separation as a mandate of external law. As Bowen conceives of it, Father's role is thus double-faced, or paradoxical: he limits the real and imaginary agency of both mother and child and, by so doing, frees both of them to experience again a happy mutual love. To play such a part, Father must wield a special authority; it has to be evident that he is more powerful than Mother and Baby, if he is to release them both from the dyadic hell of their own manufacture.

From the age of two, after the death of his first foster mother, Leopold has been brought up by a trio of 'relations by adoption', 'his aunts Sally and Marian and his uncle Dee'. 'Uncle Dee, incredibly, was the husband of Aunt Marian', and yet Marian and Dee – and Sally too – have wilfully eschewed the identities of Mother and Father and thereby vitiated their own attempt to parent the child, who has remained, despite their adoption – and because of it – essentially orphaned (HP 21). The 'solicitous' and yet inadequate care supplied by the pseudo-sibling Grant-Moody trio is characterised by an effeminacy that, while doing nothing to compensate Leopold for the absence of a mother, seems especially hostile to the qualities that a father might be expected to display. In the early years of the adoption, Leopold and the Grant-Moodys had lived in Rome, a city that 'became the image of [Leopold's] ambition, communicating its pride to him so violently and immediately that antiquity went for nothing: the hills and columns seemed to be made for himself. To have been born became to be on the scale of emperors and popes, to be conspicuous everywhere, like the startling white Vittorio

Emmanuele monument. He was, in fact, full of the bastard's pride' (HP 21): a pride that was to be deflated, as if on purpose, by the adults' decision to move to Spezia, where '[Leopold's] spirit became crustacean under douches of culture and mild philosophic chat from his Uncle Dee, who was cultured rather than erudite' (HP 21). Consciously, Leopold longs for nothing except reunion with Karen, but Bowen nonetheless suggests in the eight-year-old boy some cloudy intuition of the crucial paternal function that could enable this ambition to be achieved. Without knowing why, Leopold yearns for the vertical, the columnar, the conspicuous, the monumental: his readiness to desert the Grant-Moodys, I think, has at least as much to do with their hostility towards the emblematically phallic qualities of an archetypal father as with their reluctance to mother him properly. In the moment before he decisively disallows their claim upon him in his mind, he sees, among other images of his childhood by the 'nibbling blue edge of the sea that drowned Shelley' (HP 21), 'the row of red plasticine figures he had kept out for days on his windowsill because they had kidded him plasticine sunbaked hard, and the one vague shape he had modelled that had dismayed Uncle Dee and disappeared in the night' (HP 34).

The arrival of Ray Forrestier, Karen's husband, at the house in Paris literalises the redemptive role of Father in Bowen's understanding of psychosexual development. In the story of Leopold and Karen we see the potential for a repetition of the story of Max and Madame Fisher, for just as Madame Fisher renounced the dyadic salon of two that she and Max had shared, so too Karen has imposed separation on her son, in the dramatic form of giving him up first for fostering and then for adoption. And just as the elder woman reigns supreme over her household from her commanding position of moribund immobility, so Karen, having set up in her son the expectation that he and she will meet in Paris, sends word that she will not come and instead takes to her bed in Versailles, prostrate and despotic. Correspondingly, Leopold seems set fair to suffer some version of his father's terrible fate, for although 'Max does not leave a suicide note' – as Gildersleeve mordantly remarks – '[he] does leave his unborn son, and might then be said to haunt the present in the form of his son.'[13] But Ray is no Captain Fisher, uselessly dead at his marital post. Rising to the challenge posed by his wife's theatrical collapse, and by her vetoing of the meeting with her son, Ray sets out alone to meet Leopold in Paris, ascertains that the boy is keen to live with his mother, informs Naomi of his decision, takes Leopold away from the Fishers' house, and telephones to Versailles to inform Karen of his actions, in just a couple of hours of impressively concentrated activity. And this does not exhaust his capacities: he also contributes some competent paternal facilitation to the cause of Henrietta's transit southwards. At the same time as removing his step-son from the virtual clutches of Madame Fisher, Ray delivers Henrietta to her train in good time and moreover takes care to equip her with everything that she might need on the next stage of her journey: 'a bottle of Vichy in a twist of pink paper', 'three outsize packets of Suchard, a carton of grapes, and two rolls with ham clapped inside them that she had fancied the look of and Ray had bought for her at the buffet' (HP 246). He even adds entertainment, and a souvenir, 'plung[ing] back' at the last moment to buy Henrietta 'an armful of American picture papers, and a bronze paper-weight, with the Eiffel Tower on it' (HP 247). 'I love it', she says, 'scarlet with pleasure'.

'It should be clear', Bowen's narrator remarks,

> that Ray looked like any of these tall Englishmen who stand back in train corridors to let foreigners pass to meals or to the lavatory, in a dark grey suit with a just visible stripe, light blue shirt, deep blue tie with a just visible stripe, a signet ring of some dull stone, trimmed spade-shaped nails, a composed unclear romantic evenly coloured face with structure behind it, a slight moustache two tones darker – and, if you look down, deeply polished brown shoes. He was the Englishman's age: about thirty-six. To make marriage with Karen entirely possible he had exchanged the [diplomatic] career he had once projected for business, which makes for a more private private life. In business he had done well. (HP 222)

In context this reads as a wholly unsatirical description. In grateful contrast to Madame Fisher and to his own wife in her state of – it is to be hoped – temporary hysteria, Ray strikes a figure of quietly heroic upper-middle-class normality, an intrusion into the novel's Gothic psychodrama of a character from a quite different literary genre, in psychological terms the maturational antidote to the gruesome spectre of Mother in the wake of separation.[14] It is very important that Ray is guided by principle, not by emotion: without warming at all towards Leopold, 'little brittle Jewish boy with the thin neck, putting a hand at once wherever you looked' (HP 225), Ray acts to reunite the mother and son because he knows that it is the correct thing to do. Impressed by Ray's willingness to discount the Grant-Moodys, Neil Corcoran argues that '[t]he characterization of Ray must [. . .] give us pause in any decision that Elizabeth Bowen is politically an essentially conservative novelist: his responsibility is exercised by the breaking of social constraint and taboo, by an act of transgression.'[15] But I think that symbolic law is exactly what Ray represents, and what, in his assumption of paternal responsibility for Leopold (and, briefly, for Henrietta), he acts to instantiate, as against the culpable failure and refusal of the Grant-Moody 'aunts' and 'uncle' – something that is apparent to Leopold and Henrietta almost at once. 'He's married to my mother', Leopold says of Ray: 'Then he's your step-father?' Henrietta asks. 'Leopold hesitated, he said quickly, "Yes"' (HP 236). The happy ending that Bowen organises for Leopold, Karen and Ray has nothing about it of the fairy-tale: it is guaranteed not by sentiment or idealisation but by a kind of disinterested moral law, and is therefore distinguished by a wonderfully trustworthy imperviousness to personal foibles and quotidian irritation alike. 'You will notice', Ray says to his new son, in his head, in what constitutes a resounding affirmation of his paternal commitment to the child,

> we talk where I can talk. You will not quote Mme Fisher, you will not kick me in taxis, you will not shout in houses where they are ill. You will wear a civilian cap, not snub little girls and

not get under my feet. There will be many things that you will not like. There are many things that I do not like about you.' (HP 249–50)

*The Hotel*, too, engineers for its heroine an authentically happy ending, which is associated with the imposition of a salutary limitation upon Sydney's real and imaginary power closely akin to Ray's curbing of his step-son's egotism, theatricality and disdain for the authority of adults. We return to the Mediterranean mountain, and to the hired car transporting Sydney, Milton, Mrs Kerr and Tessa back to the Hotel after their day-excursion. The car is zipping swiftly around the hairpin bends, and Sydney is willing a fatal accident. 'Let it be the next corner', she repeats in her head, the grammatical form of her thought associating her mental state with the divine omnipotence of the original fiat ('Let there be light') and with the potential vehicle of the party's destruction – the car is a Fiat, a detail that the text has by this point specified several times. Ahead of the party in the car, but as yet out of sight, the road is blocked by 'a long wagon of timber jammed crossways' and a melee of 'shouting men [and] backing, terrified horses' (H 179). Nothing seems capable of interrupting this 'climactic "death drive"', as Gildersleeve, in a nice literalisation of the Freudian term, calls the seemingly headlong descent:[16] all that is needed for the Fiat to bring about the enactment of Sydney's murderous and suicidal will is for the driver of the car to notice too late the obstacle ahead on the narrow and precipitous road. But in fact, even as Sydney longs for death at '[t]he next corner . . . [sic] the *next* corner', '[r]ound the next, barely round it, the brakes jarred, the car swayed on locked wheels and stopped dead' (H 179). In an action that corresponds very closely to the arrival of Ray Forrestier at the house in Paris, the unnamed local driver of the Fiat – 'a brigandish individual in a check cap' (H 178) – intervenes in the killing-ground of the dyad, opposing to Sydney's limitless despair and rage his own vocational competence and reliability. 'Our fellow *can* drive', Milton remarks, gratefully, to Sydney. It's a very strange moment in the novel: Milton observes that Sydney is 'what people describe as "upset"' (H 179), but he can have no understanding that her upset is a response to the thwarting of her wish that the entire party should be literally, and calamitously, upset and dashed to nothing on the rocks below. 'She looked over the side of the car down into the valley: a kind of farewell. It was a long way below – the depth of it would never be forgotten' (H 180). Milton, Tessa and Mrs Kerr get out to have a look at the impasse ahead, leaving Sydney alone in the car.[17]

What happens next has a revelatory quality and a profound, if uncanny, undertone of joy, bound up with a sense of unprecedented vision and a positively painful access of vitality.

> They were having – up here – a later view of the sun than their friends down below; by now the tennis courts would be silent, the sea fading, the earliest lights coming out pale and exotic in hotels whose walls still had an afterglow. Here the sun was still full on the village, level on peak behind peak; the gold only gave way reluctantly to a mild rose that chilled and abated and was transfused by shadows mounting up like smoke out of the valley. This isolation above the regular approach of night connected itself in her mind with her present shocked sense of having been flung back on to living. [. . .] Above, in this unnatural, endless prolongation of the daylight she for the first time felt life sharply, life as keen as death to bite upon the consciousness, pressed inexorably upon her, held to her throat like a knife. Dazed by the realization of their import she stared at her hands, at her body, at the hills round her.
> Later she had scrambled from the car and was running down the hill on her stiff legs unsteadily, calling to James. (H 180)

What Sydney – 'protected by some kind of exaltation' (H 181) – has to tell James Milton is that she has realised that their engagement is, of course, utterly misconceived.

> I think we have been asleep here; you know in a dream how quickly and lightly shapes move, they have no weight, nothing offers them any resistance [. . .] You and me – how could we ever have thought of it? It was just a dream. (H 182)

In the final lines of *The House in Paris*, Bowen figures the child's emergence from the oneiric enclosure of the maternal dyad into the world of paternal triangulation as a kind of re-birth. 'The air tasted of night and Leopold shivered once. "Cold?" "No." No, he was not cold; he had been someone drawing a first breath. Ray had not seen Karen's child in bright light before; now he saw light strike the dilated pupils of Leopold's eyes' (HP 250). In just the same way we may understand Sydney to be experiencing, as never before, 'the shock of being alive' (H 182), the hired chauffeur having effected the kind of virtual obstetric delivery, and deliverance, that Ray will later perform for Leopold. '[R]unning [. . .] on her stiff legs unsteadily', Sydney has the look of a young animal, a newborn creature unpractised in ambulation and yet eager to be afoot: a foal, perhaps, or a baby giraffe – not a human infant, certainly, confined by muscular incapacity to the exclusive world of the dyad. Such a birth, or re-birth, is a redemptive re-structuring of the subject's relation to reality, at once revivifying everything that had been negated by the trauma of separation and allowing it to be apprehended as fully alive for the first time. If the nursing dyad is a mirage of immortality, and the state of separation an experience at once of killing, of dying, and of feeling that everything, the self included, is already dead, the world instituted by triangulation is a place in which mortality is recognised as the enabling condition of human subjectivity, or, to put it another way, a place in which 'life' and 'death', and 'life' and 'knife', no longer represent mutually oppositional forces or states. 'I had no idea we were as real as this', Sydney says to Milton. 'I'd never realized it mattered so much' (H 182).

It's easy to miss the happy ending of Bowen's first novel, because the text's imitative loyalty to the point of view of the weaned child in the dyad persists into the final episode of the Sydney story, the departure from the hotel of Milton (accompanied by Ronald) a few hours before Sydney herself, and Tessa, are due to leave. This has made it difficult for readers to grasp the transformational effect of the chauffeur's intervention in Sydney's omnipotence and despair.[18] Andrew Bennett, for example, has recently written of the novel's 'plot or non-plot, an anti-narrative [. . .] in which several people meet in a hotel and then [. . .] after nothing very much has happened, leave to go their separate ways', while Sinéad Mooney describes *The Hotel* as 'a narrative where stasis is everywhere preferred over forward movement'.[19] Although neither characterisation does justice to Bowen's text in its symbolic totality, both may be applied most effectively to its stubbornly unchanging narrative procedures, habits of story-telling by which Bowen dramatises at the level of form that resistance to separation, that emotional petrifaction, from which the story's heroine Sydney has herself at last been released. Unable to focus on what is different, revitalised and new, the narrative here is preoccupied instead with the excruciating social spectacle of the broken engagement, with the mortification of the rejected suitor, and with the prurient sympathy of the hotel's other residents, who gather to wave off the departing guests. Sydney herself is not at first to be observed; at last, 'looking unnatural and urban in a dark-coloured travelling-dress', she comes downstairs to shake hands with Milton, '[h]er manner [. . .] strained and unwomanly' (H 196). As Maud Ellmann has pointed out, Sydney's 'favourite accessory' is 'a flame-red scarf, bound around her forehead like a bandage or streaming from her neck like blood';[20] it is an image with which Sydney is repeatedly associated in the earlier parts of the text, and it may be seen to foreshadow, I think, the catastrophic bleeding that will end Max's life in the alleyway across the street from Madame Fisher's house in Paris. Thus in this final appearance of Sydney's the absence of her scarf, and the dark colour of her travelling dress, together suggest that the previously unstoppable flow of 'flame-red' blood has ceased with the institution of symbolic law, the wound of separation scabbing over nicely and allowing the skin beneath to heal. For from the point of view of the revelation on the mountain, the acute social awkwardness of the scene of departure is essentially unimportant: it is only embarrassment, after all, a temporary superficial discomfort that has to be got through before the promise of the future can be embraced. Where will Sydney go next? What will she find when she gets there? Who will she meet, what will she do, who, indeed, will it turn out that she is to be? The world is all before her, where to choose.

## Section Two: Trauma and Psychosis

Bowen's substantial and technically masterful short story 'Ivy Gripped the Steps' (1945) begins with a proliferation of images that together offer complex information about the developmental history of the story's middle-aged protagonist Gavin Doddington. The story starts, and finishes, with Gavin's return to Southstone, at the end of the Second World War, after an absence of more than thirty years: in his childhood, before the First World War, he had visited the wealthy south coast town three times as the guest of a beautiful young widow – Mrs Nicholson, his mother's friend – for the sake of his uncertain health, which had delayed his admission to prep school. '[Gavin] had been eight' – Leopold's age – 'when he met [Mrs Nicholson], ten' – Henrietta's age – 'when she died', in 1912.[21] After Mrs Nicholson's death Gavin had stayed away from the town – as if by choice – for three decades, until, in the summer of 1940, his voluntary exile had been superseded by law: 'Southstone had been declared in the front line', many of its residents had been evicted, their houses had been requisitioned by the military, and travel into the town had been forbidden. But in the September of 1944, with 'the silencing of the guns across the Channel' (I 687), Southstone is opened again to civilians: and

> the lifting of the official ban on the area had had the effect of bringing [Gavin] straight back – why? When what one has refused is put out of reach, when what one has avoided becomes forbidden, some lessening of the inhibition may well occur. The ban had so acted on his reluctance that, when the one was removed, the other came away with it – as a scab, adhering, comes off with a wad of lint. The transmutation, due to the fall of France, of his '*I* cannot go back to Southstone' into '*One* cannot go there' must have been salutary, or, at least, exteriorizing. (I 688)

This passage offers us a notably explicit and virtually theoretical statement of an important stage in the account of development whose logic is to be discerned in analyses of subjectivity across the full range of Bowen's fictional and non-fictional writing alike. Bowen's narrative voice specifies here a difference between 'inhibition' and prohibition, a difference between, on the one hand, a person's avoidance of a once-loved place that has become detestable, and, on the other hand, the imposition by an external authority of a ban upon that place, a ban whose 'salutary' effect is to restore the original desirability of what has been ruled out of bounds. Inhibition is one possible reaction to the experience of separation at Mother's hands; prohibition, by contrast, results from the refiguration – Bowen's term is 'transmutation' – of that experience by Father's outlawing of certain kinds and degrees of intimacy in the relation between mother and child. Taking up again her metaphoric association of the dyad, post-separation, with an unstanchable wound, and of the happy results of paternal triangulation with the cessation of bleeding and the healing up of the skin, Bowen compares the effect of symbolic prohibition on the injured mutual love of mother and child to the action of a dressing – a wad of lint, secured with a piece of sticking-plaster – that is applied externally to a site of epidermal trauma to promote its recovery and repair. If Southstone is Mother, and Gavin's inveterate rejection of the town his response to the agony of separation at her hands, it is the paternal authority of the British Army that both mandates the separation as a necessity of war *and* restores Southstone to Gavin as a place that he would want again to visit. Although he has had to wait much longer than Leopold or even than Sydney, Gavin, too, would thus appear to have experienced at last the kind of redemptive paternal intervention that we have observed in the happy endings arranged for Bowen's central characters in *The Hotel* and *The House in Paris*.

And yet the extraordinary image that dominates the first pages of the story, and that gives the text its title – the image of a rank growth of ivy half-covering the former home of the long-dead Mrs Nicholson – suggests that the retardation of Father's intervention has presented a secondary problem in the life of Gavin Doddington; the primary, or prior, difficulty that afflicts Bowen's protagonist is identified as an inadequate experience of separation itself, for the obscurely distasteful image, I think, figures the relationship between the middle-aged man and the 'mother' long since consigned to the grave in terms of an endless bout of breastfeeding, a bout uninterrupted even by Mrs Nicholson's death more than thirty years before. Notwithstanding the extinction of its host, the parasite has continued to feed:

> Ivy gripped and sucked at the flight of steps, down which with such a deceptive wildness it seemed to be flowing like a cascade. Ivy matted the door at the top and amassed in bushes above and below the porch. More, it had covered, or one might feel consumed, one entire half of the high, double-fronted house [. . .] One was left to guess at the size and the number of windows hidden by looking at those in the other side. But these, though in sight, had been made effectively sightless: sheets of some dark composition that looked like metal were sealed closely into their frames [. . .] To crown all, the ivy was now in fruit, clustered over with fleshy pale green berries. There was something brutal about its fecundity. [. . .] Had not reason insisted that the lost windows must, like their fellows, have been made fast, so that the suckers for all their seeking voracity could not enter, one could have convinced oneself that the ivy must be feeding on something inside the house. (I 686)

The problem here, then, is not that the maternal object has been lost (the normal, if temporary, outcome of separation, in Bowen's view) and the process of its restoration held up, abnormally, for thirty years; the problem is that the maternal object *never has been lost*, and thus Gavin, lacking an adequate model of separation, can apprehend neither the mortal finitude of life itself – as exemplified by the literal fact of Mrs Nicholson's death – nor its symbolic redemption in the form of that transformative détente with reality that we have seen exhilarate Sydney on the mountain road. If Father's function is to redeem the death that separation has brought into the world, the strength or weakness with which he discharges his duty will show as moot insofar as the 'child' in question has failed to be persuaded of mortality. In Bowen's understanding, then, Father's debilitation matters little to an infant whose voracious attachment to a maternal eternity has not been effectually interrupted.

The first focus of my attention in this section of the chapter is Bowen's exploration of Mother's relationship to the separation that it falls to her to enact in the earliest life of her baby: the separation that Bowen presents as an intrinsic component of human experience, whether it is encountered in the form of weaning, or bedtime, or any other embodiment of a limit on, or interruption to, the child's access to its beloved mother. We have looked previously at the strength and disinterestedness of the paternal authority that can refigure separation as a mandate of external law. Here, I want to examine the question – equally important in Bowen's work – of the requisite quality of the *maternal* No. In some ways this is a more difficult capability to conceptualise, and, perhaps, to assume, as it involves a limitation not only of other people's omnipotence – as when Father steps in to outlaw certain kinds and degrees of intimacy between his wife and his child – but of one's own. As Bowen understands it, when a mother says No to her baby she is simultaneously saying No to herself, for the trauma of separation wounds both halves of the dyad.

We might then feel an enhanced respect for Mrs Kerr if we compare her assumption of responsibility for the deprivational aspects of mothering to the evasion practised by other mothers in Bowen's writing: women such as Lilian Nicholson, for example, who balks at the work of separating Gavin from herself, preferring instead to delegate responsibility to her maid Rockham, who, as Lilian tells Gavin's mother, is 'good with children' (I 689). During the first of Gavin's three stays with Mrs Nicholson, '[i]t was Rockham who worked out the daily programme, devised to keep the little boy out of Madam's way [. . .] It was by Rockham that, every morning, he was taken down to play by the sea' (I 693). Gavin hates his subjection to the proxy maternal No, experiencing 'a literal feeling of degradation [in] this descent from the plateau to the cliff's foot', and spending 'most of the time', once down on the beach, standing 'with his back to [the sea], shading his eyes and staring up at the heights' (I 693); and Mrs Nicholson appears to hate it too, as when, coming into

Gavin's room to say goodnight before departing for a dinner party, she finds him '[p]ropped upright against his pillows, gripping his glass of milk', an eloquent image of resistance to the separation enforced by his hostess's servant.

> 'Perhaps,' [Mrs Nicholson] suggested humbly, 'you'll go to sleep? They all say it is right for you, going to bed so early, but I wish it did not make days so short. – I must go. [. . .] Just once, one evening perhaps, you could stay up late. Do you think it would matter? I'll ask Rockham.' (I 693)

Deferring to her maid as 'the arbiter', leaving Rockham 'to exercise anything so nearly as harsh as authority', Lilian outsources the maternal No in much the same way as does Florence Bowen, Elizabeth's mother, as described in *Seven Winters*.

> She explained to me candidly that she kept a governess because she did not wish to scold me herself. To have had to keep saying 'Do this,' 'Don't do that,' and 'No,' to me would have been, as she saw it, a peril to everything. So, to interpose between my mother and me, to prevent our spending the best part of our days together, was the curious function of every governess. It was not that there were more pressing claims on my mother's time: she was not a worldly woman (though she did like pleasure) and my father was out the greater part of the day. When she was not with me she thought of me constantly, and planned ways in which we could meet and could be alone. (SW 488–9)

There are two features of this passage that I particularly want to highlight. For a start, I want to draw attention to Florence's apparent discomfort in relation to her own power as Elizabeth's mother, for the conception of the maternal role that is indicated here is at once authoritarian and aversive. In Florence's gloomy view, the predominant activity of mothering seems to consist of 'scold[ing]' – the relentless, punitive giving out of orders which expressly disallow the child's preferences or desire. There's no Yes in this vision, no imagination of Mother as anything more than a heartless disciplinarian, as if Florence herself were a weaned child whose pain and distrust have yet to be refigured and redeemed by the intervention of Father. Appalled and betrayed, as it appears, by her own experience of separation, and yet resigned, as it also appears, to its inevitability, Florence shifts responsibility for the unpleasant task to a paid maternal substitute. But the authority exercised by a governess over her employer's child is at best provisional, subject always to the possibility of protest, attack or countermanding by the child's mother. Thus even as Florence tasks another woman with the responsibility of 'interpos[ing]' between herself and her daughter, she ensures the contractual and socioeconomic subordination of No to Yes, setting up a governess as an agent of separation as if to fatally undermine its existential necessity, and thereby suggesting in herself, and encouraging in Elizabeth, a fantasy of uninterrupted dyadic union. During the first seven years of Elizabeth's life – as during the first of Gavin's stays with Mrs Nicholson – separation is thus instituted, but only in a weak and eminently contestable form.

Secondly, I want to draw attention to the confidence with which Bowen pronounces here upon her mother's experience of the separation that she has so reluctantly established: 'When she was not with me she thought of me constantly, and planned ways in which we could meet and could be alone.' It is a confidence that Bowen problematises in her account of Gavin's limited capacity for imagining those aspects of Mrs Nicholson's life to which he is not privy: 'In even the affairs of her own house Mrs Nicholson was not heard giving an order [. . .] Yet the effect she gave was not of idleness but of preoccupation: what she did with her days Gavin did not ask himself – when he did ask himself, later, it was too late' (I 693). For what Gavin prefers not to dwell upon is his hostess's enjoyment of a lively social life, the highlight of which is her prolonged campaign to seduce one Admiral Concannon, who lives, with his wife and high-school-age daughters, in the same part of Southstone as Lilian. There is thus a certain tricksiness in Mrs Nicholson's attitude towards separation, for although she affects to challenge its necessity – and thereby preserves her idealisation in Gavin's eyes – she also profits richly from the sexual opportunities provided by its frequent and regular imposition. It is therefore not sufficient to say that Mother suffers from separation as much, or in the same way, as does her child, for as Bowen makes clear in 'Ivy Gripped the Steps' the instituting of the maternal No guarantees the possibility of a private life for Mother. Another way of putting this would be to say that Mother's reluctance to say no to her child is modified by the force of her desire for someone or something that is not Baby, a desire that challenges her absorption in the two-person passion of the dyad and thereby strengthens her in carrying out the separation for which she might otherwise have little stomach.

Thus it is very important, in Bowen's view, that Mother's desire should be piqued and secured by something in the world outside the nursery, for without this competing claim upon her attention she is unlikely to be able to provide a reliable experience of separation for her child – although this is not, it need hardly be said, a provision for which any child in Bowen's work will feel gratitude at the time. Indeed, the child's anguish at separation is likely to increase in proportion to the evidence that Mother's actions are motivated in part by her desire for anyone or anything other than her child. We have observed in both Gavin and the narrator of *Seven Winters* a protective obtuseness in relation to the possibility that Mother's desire might be magnetised by something outside the dyad; we may recall also the acute pain caused Sydney by Mrs Kerr's assertion of a love for patisseries. But whether such an object of desire takes the form of a continental café, or of a plausible love interest, Bowen places great stress on its function of supporting the crucial experience of separation in the dyad.

In 'Ivy Gripped the Steps' the role falls to Admiral Concannon, whose suitability for the job, during Gavin's first stay in Southstone, remains an open question. On the one hand, '[h]is voice and step had become familiar, among the few nocturnal sounds of the avenue, some time before Gavin had seen his face; for he escorted Mrs Nicholson home from parties to which she had been wilful enough to walk. Looking out one night, after the hall door shut, Gavin had seen the head of a cigarette, immobile, pulsating sharply under the dark trees', an image that makes a strong, if not conclusive, claim for the Admiral's virile attractions (I 695). On the other hand, however, his masculine charisma is devalued by his being retired, which might put us in mind of Madame Fisher's husband, the defunct naval officer, or of the dead father of the boy Casabianca, whose fatal adherence to the deck of his father's burning ship was pictured, as we have noted, in a painting on the wall of Bowen's childhood nursery in Dublin. The Admiral goes no more to sea, and cuts a far from heroic figure as, accompanying Mrs Nicholson on a morning walk upon the Promenade, 'intent on spearing on the tip of his cane a straying fragment of paper', 'he crosse[s] to a little basket [. . .] and knock[s] the fragment into it off his cane', before 'burst[ing] out: "I should like to know what this place is coming to – we shall have trippers next!"' (I 696)

In her autobiographical writings Bowen characterises the father of her own early childhood as a figure of seriously compromised prestige. She identifies this, in part, as a consequence of Henry's quixotic attempt to assert his independence of ancestral convention, highlighting, in *Bowen's Court*, the pointed defiance of her father's decision to pursue a professional career, a course that flouted the traditions of his class and mutinied against the judgment of his own father. Elizabeth's grandfather, Robert Cole Bowen, had taken the view that 'Fate had selected Henry's profession for him: he was to be Henry Cole Bowen of Bowen's Court, landowner'; but Elizabeth's father, 'after years of lonely reflection, [had decided] that the law was his calling, and he must follow it' (BC 375). 'He loved Bowen's Court, was prepared to inherit it and hoped to serve it in every way, but he would not pretend to himself or Robert that either his interests or his duties ended with the estate' (BC 375–6). Enraged, grandfather Robert began a terrible campaign against his son's future leadership of the family and its fortunes:

> Bowen's Court being entailed upon the eldest son, Henry could not be disinherited. Robert, however, could and did do a good deal to hamper Henry's succession: in the will he drew up he disposed of what he was free to dispose of, and it would have

been a tax on even Robert's genius to run Bowen's Court with any hopes of advantage on the means that Henry was to enjoy. (Make your pile at the Bar then, may have been Robert's taunt.) In fact, if not the destruction the headlong decline of Bowen's Court seems to have been implicit in Robert's will: in the dark in which he now increasingly dwelled he planned the destruction of his life's work [. . .] I think of the Giotto figure of *Anger*, the figure tearing, clawing its own breast. (BC 376)

It was, then, to a Bowen's Court considerably reduced in financial resources that Henry succeeded in 1888; as master of the estate Elizabeth's father was wounded from the start, condemned to failure, a predicament dramatised and exaggerated in the figures of numerous pathos-ridden landowners in Bowen's work – landowners such as Gavin Doddington's parents, for example,

> poor gentry [. . .] at a period when poverty could not be laughed away. Their lot was less enviable than that of any of their employees or tenants, whose faces, naked in their dejection, and voices pitched to complaints they could at least utter, had disconcerted Gavin, since babyhood, at the Hall door. (I 692)

But despite Henry Bowen's cleaving instead – and so calamitously, from the point of view of his inheritance – to the rival authority of the law, Elizabeth's father appears to have cut, as a professional man in town, a figure of at best ambiguous success. In the chapter of *Seven Winters* called 'Brass Plates', Bowen notes that in South Dublin, the area of the city between 15 Herbert Place and the centre, 'each door [. . .] bore its polished brass plate':

> Daughter of a professional neighbourhood, I took this brass plate announcing its owner's name to be the *sine qua non* of any gentleman's house. Just as the tombstone says '*Here Lies*' the plate on the front door (in my view) said '*Here Lives*.' Failure to write one's name on one's door seemed to me the

admission of nonentity. The householder with the anonymous door must resign himself to being overlooked by the world – to being passed by by the postman, unfed by tradesmen, guestless, unsought by friends – and his family dwelt in the shadow of this disgrace [. . .] At the top of the Herbert Place front steps, waiting for the front door to be opened (for my governess never carried a latchkey) I would trace with my finger my father's name. This was not an act of filial piety only; it gave him an objective reality, which I shared. (SW 493–4)

It is not only as a landowner that Henry Bowen, in his daughter's eyes, is debilitated: as a lawyer, too, he is – in his daughter's imagination – a dead man walking, for even as Bowen emphasises her father's power to assert himself in the world her association of the professional gentleman's house with his grave ironises exactly the potency or 'objective reality' that the nameplate seems to endorse. And the hint of an essential fragility in Bowen's father is borne out by the terse and troubling end to which she brings the account of her early childhood. 'How', Bowen asks, in the final paragraph of *Seven Winters*,

shall I write '*The End*' to a book which is about the essence of a beginning? When I was seven years old, Herbert Place was given up: my father's mental illness had to be fought alone; my mother and I were ordered to England. (SW 512)

Elsewhere in her autobiographical writings Bowen discusses at greater length her father's breakdown (Henry's illness was believed to express an inherited mental vulnerability: another variety of weakness passed down the paternal line) but this single sentence is the only explicit reference to it in the book whose temporal reach it nonetheless delimits.

Thus it is that the era of Elizabeth's earliest childhood – a period characterised, as we have seen, by her mother's only uncertainly manifest commitment to separation – is brought to a conclusion not by Father's decisive institution of symbolic prohibition but rather by the dramatic breakdown of his already weak authority, and by the near-extinction of the image of Henry from the daily lives of his family. Advised – so Bowen claims – that their absence would conduce to Henry's recovery, Florence and Elizabeth moved, in 1906, to the Kent coast, while Henry remained in Ireland, some of the time under psychiatric care, until his health began to improve. '[B]efore I was twelve years old', Bowen reports,

> he was well again. He could come back to us – or we could go back to him. But my mother and I did not return to Ireland to live. [. . .] Our complete family life renewed itself in the series of visits my father made to Hythe: between these visits he stayed in Dublin, where he was resuming practice as a barrister. (BC 422)

This dispensation was not to last for long, however, as Florence Bowen – who had become ill in the last years of Henry's convalescence – died of cancer in the summer of 1912, one month after Elizabeth's thirteenth birthday. 'I had', Bowen writes in *Pictures and Conversations*, 'what I see can go with total bereavement, a sense of disfigurement, mortification, disgrace'.[22]

Bowen offers a striking fictional exploration of the consequences of the addition of paternal failure to the pre-existing problem of a weak maternal No in the second of Gavin's visits to Southstone. Gavin is met at the station by Mrs Nicholson herself, because her maid is ill, and for the same reason Gavin is spared those 'odious drops to the beach', his bedtime becomes later and later, and 'more than once or twice' he is allowed to dine downstairs. 'Rockham's cold had imperilled Rockham's prestige: as intervener or arbiter she could be counted out' (I 699). At the same time, the task of representing *paternal* power, which had previously been confided to the courtly, not unglamorous Admiral, is re-assigned to the frankly inadequate figure of one Massingham, a local bachelor invited to partner Mrs Nicholson at a dinner party held by the Concannons. At the last moment Massingham 'drop[s] out' (I 699), felled by an influenza that seems likely to be the same as that afflicting Rockham (although, as a servant, her illness is designated merely as 'a nasty cold' [I 698]). 'What a pity', Lilian cries, upon hearing of Massingham's defection, 'I don't care for lopsided parties' – and then makes a suggestion 'so completely outrageous' that it entirely unmans the Admiral's capacity to contest it: '[W]hy not ask somebody else?' she inquires. '[I]nvite Gavin!' (I 699).

The dinner party, as Mrs Nicholson puts it, scornfully, to Gavin, has been arranged 'for no other reason but to show off [the Concannons'] marriage' (I 701). It is an attempt to impress upon Lilian the authority of those social structures that she has already, in her flirtation with the Admiral, shown herself apt to undermine, an attempt to repressively re-assimilate and rehabilitate the rogue widow as the consort of an appropriate man. But Lilian's scandalous importation of an eight- or nine-year-old child into the studied theatrical rite of the dinner party poses a challenge of a wholly different order to that of her previous assays upon the Admiral's uxorious virtue, for it radically repudiates the triangular structuration represented by the Concannons' marriage in favour of a dyadic sexuality that threatens to collapse the hierarchical settlements of family and society alike. 'For this dinner-party lost all point if it were not *de rigueur*. The Concannon daughters, even (big girls, but with hair still down their backs) had, as not qualified for it, been sent out for the evening', which gives the measure of 'Mrs Nicholson's caprice in bringing a little boy' (I 700). And yet the 'effrontery' of her act is not exhausted by her companion's anomalous juvenility, for an equally provocative aspect of Gavin's inclusion is an uncanny and precocious sexualisation of the child, who is described as 'squiring' the beautiful woman whom we know to be the same age as his own mother (I 699). Mrs Nicholson's is what the psychoanalytic language of the 1940s might characterise as a profoundly *incestuous* act, an attack on generational difference and on psychosocial structure that might today draw comparisons with what contemporary psychotherapy terms child sexual abuse. A notable effect upon Gavin is to seed and breed in him a limitless and destructive cynicism.

> It, the party, had been balanced up and up on itself like a house of cards: built, it remained as precarious. Now the structure trembled, down to its base, from one contemptuous flip at its

top story [...] Gavin perceived that night what he was not to forget: the helplessness, in the last resort, of society – which he was never, later, to be able to think of as a force.' (I 700)

The finer details of Lilian's assault upon the sociosymbolic order may remind us again, by contrast, of *The Hotel*'s maternal hate-figure Mrs Kerr, who, despite the seemingly total absence of paternal distraction, so properly refused to accede to Sydney's desire for exactly such a restoration of dyadic union and insisted instead upon 'weaning'. We have seen how, in that early novel, Bowen transfuses into Sydney's purchasing of carnations for Mrs Kerr the full enigmatic force of an infant's attachment to the breastfeeding mother: the episode is recalled by a scene at the florist's in Southstone, a florist's whose suggestive juxtaposition of '[d]elayed late autumn and forced early spring flowers' seems like an image of the developmental perversion and intergenerational confusion that Bowen associates with the addition of paternal failure to an equivocal experience of separation (I 698). Here it is that Mrs Nicholson – out shopping with Gavin on the morning of the Concannons' dinner – comes upon the Admiral 'selecting flowers and fruit' for the party and, learning of Massingham's debilitation, engineers the invitation of Gavin in his place; and here it is, too, that Lilian countermands Mrs Concannon's request for white chrysanthemums and insists on presenting the Admiral instead with 'all the scarlet carnations that were in reach' (I 699). Naturally, the carnations turn out to be 'slightly but strikingly "off" the red of the [lamp] shade' above the festal board, 'but pre-eminently flattering in their contrast to Mrs Nicholson's orchid *glacé* gown' (I 700), for Lilian's primary gambit at the party is to compel everyone's attention to her body, and, in particular, to her eyes and to her décolletage, which is highlighted, as by a beacon or a target, by her jewellery: the 'sapphire darkness [of her eyes], with that of the sapphire pendant she was wearing, was struck into by the Concannons' electric light' (I 700). Lilian is not described as saying a word during the course of the meal, the narrative noting instead how 'her glance', with 'its leisurely, not quite attentive play', 'contain[s]' Gavin, who is seated opposite her across the table; and how she entrances also the two gentlemen sitting on each side of her:

> More and more, as course followed course, these two showed how highly they rated their good fortune – indeed, the censure around the rest of the table only acted for them, like heat drawing out scent, to heighten the headiness of her immediate aura. Like the quick stuff of her dress her delinquency, even, gave out a sort of shimmer: while she, neither arch nor indolent, turned from one to the other her look – if you like, melting; for it dissolved her pupils, which had never been so dilated, dark, as tonight. In this look, as dinner proceeded, the two flies, ceasing to struggle, drowned. [. . .] Silent between the flies' wives, hypnotized by the rise and fall of Mrs Nicholson's pendant, Gavin ate on and on. (I 701)

Conversation is not an important part of Mrs Nicholson's appeal here, because the experience that her behaviour evokes is the prelinguistic beginnings of a baby's life at the mother's breast, eating 'on and on', eyes fixed on the mother's face and on the upper part of her chest, the infant's sucking and swallowing harmonised with the breathing of the body from which he feeds. It's interesting that smell is so predominant, and so seductive, although nothing is said of the taste or texture of the food itself, as if the external reality of the Concannons' pointedly sophisticated dishes is suppressed in the service of an overwhelmingly regressive fantasy of feasting on breast milk. As complex dinner-party food seems to melt back into the liquid simplicity of milk, so the psychosocial sophistication of Lilian's neighbours at table dissolves in the deliquescent pools of her eyes, twin watering-holes in which a thirsty creature may drown; as if, like the Scylla and Charybdis of Odysseus's ocean, Mrs Nicholson's 'maternal' eyes offered to the sailor's searching gaze the promise of an exquisite extinction to the infantile longing for home.

Mrs Nicholson's all-out attempt to revoke separation gives way soon enough, however, to the developmental programme championed by the society that she has endeavoured to discredit.

'After that midwinter visit there were two changes: Mrs Nicholson went abroad, Gavin went to school' – this last a move that signals, on the Doddingtons' part, a decisive commitment to the symbolic weaning of their son in an institution of formal education, the Spartan regime of the prep school a rebuke to the wet-nurse-like indulgences of Lilian's luxurious establishment (I 702).[23] During this visit – which will turn out to have been Gavin's final stay as Lilian's guest – Mrs Nicholson, though reluctantly, does at last submit to the necessity of separation, a submission that is represented symbolically, I think, by the nature of her response to an appeal from the Concannons that she should support the Southstone branch of the Awaken Britannia League, whose political position is associated, in Bowen's story, with the Admiral's insistence that 'we should be preparing to fight [Germany], for the reason that she is preparing to fight us' (I 696). In the third section of this chapter I will look in more detail at Bowen's mining of the symbolic resources of global politics, in particular world war, in order to figure and explore the turmoil of individual psychological development. Here, it is enough to observe that 'Ivy Gripped the Steps' sets up a parallel between the Concannons' enthusiasm for the Awaken Britannia League and their commitment to the developmental trajectory that Mrs Nicholson has sought to sabotage, and that Mrs Nicholson's hostility to the League is somehow congruous with her repudiation of the necessity of weaning. In essence, the disagreement is over the question of separation and its effects in the maternal dyad, the Admiral implicitly insisting that, because separation is unavoidable, so too is the experience of conflict, as against Lilian's refusal to countenance the inevitability of any such deterioration in the mutual adoration of mother and child. 'You forget the way we behave now, and there's no other way', Mrs Nicholson tells the Admiral. 'Civilized countries are polite to each other, just as you and I are to the people we know [. . .] I should not dream of suspecting *any* civilized country!' (I 696). Thus when at last Lilian agrees to send cakes from her kitchen to the inaugural meeting of the League we may see in her act a grudging submission to the developmental necessity of separation, the cakes at once an attempt to distract the League's supporters from the Admiral's predictions of war and yet at the same time an implicit concession to the authority of his analysis. '[C]ake, don't you think, makes everything so much nicer?' Lilian remarks to the Concannons. 'You can't offer people nothing but disagreeable ideas' (I 704).

In Bowen's writing, children's reactions to the experience of separation are frequently emblematised by the contrasting figures of the puppy and the monkey. To be precise, a character's first fully conscious apprehension of a momentous and agonising disruption in the relationship with his or her mother is often marked by a sudden metaphorical identification with the image of a little dog, whereas a symbolic association with the figure of a monkey denotes, by contrast, a character's attempt to deny the reality of separation. In Bowen's first novel *The Hotel*, for example, Sydney is for a moment mystified by Mrs Kerr's remark to her, as they pass on the stairs, the morning after the arrival of Mrs Kerr's son Ronald: 'Well? [. . .] Isn't it rather a nice puppy?' (H 89) '"What puppy?" Sydney sa[ys] blankly, looking up from a few steps below her. "My Ronald. Isn't it *rather* a nice – " "Oh yes, very"', Sydney replies, interrupting her friend as if, once her meaning has become clear, the characterisation of Mrs Kerr's object of maternal care as a canine baby is too painful for Sydney to hear a second time, as it simultaneously confronts her with an image of her own dependence and confirms her in her frightened and angry perception of Mrs Kerr – Mrs Cur – as a real bitch. Later that morning Sydney accedes to the wish of an eleven-year-old child, Cordelia, to accompany her on a walk, despite having already agreed to spend the morning alone with James Milton. 'Milton was waiting below in the lounge and his face did fall perceptibly as Sydney at last appearing at the turn of the stair indicated Cordelia, less in tow than towing, capering round possessively': good manners prevent Milton from protesting against this arrangement, but, 'as Cordelia passed out behind Sydney with the self-assurance of a pet monkey he looked daggers at her profile' (H 91). Hesitating between denial and deprivation, Sydney thus achieves simultaneously a symbolic objectification of her monkey-self (Cordelia) and her puppy-self (Milton), while enacting in her respective relation to each the figure of the mother before and after the institution of separation.

In 'Ivy Gripped the Steps' the figuring of the infant prior to separation as a monkey occurs in the context of the Concannons' dinner party, the party at which, as we have seen, Lilian works so hard to reverse the developmental sophistication of the male guests. 'It was without a word that, at the end of the evening, the Admiral saw Mrs Nicholson to her carriage – Gavin, like an afterthought or a monkey, nipping in under his host's arm extended to hold open the carriage door' (I 701). Thus we can pinpoint the precise moment at which Gavin is forced to know himself as the juvenile victim of maternal rejection by the replacement of the monkey by the puppy. It is the last night of Gavin's third stay with Mrs Nicholson, and the Admiral has come round to collect the cakes that her cook has made for the Awaken Britannia League. Trying not to acknowledge that his beloved hostess has conceded the necessity of separation, Gavin seeks to escape the Admiral's visit by hiding in his room, but Rockham sends him back downstairs, and as he approaches the drawing-room he overhears the Admiral reproaching Mrs Nicholson for 'making a ninnie of that unfortunate boy'. 'Who, poor little funny Gavin?' Lilian replies: 'Must I have nothing? – I have no little dog' (I 707). For the child outside the drawing-room door the verbal image delivers new insight into Mrs Nicholson's mind and operates as the developmental gateway to a world of almost unbearable anguish.

Separation inaugurated by Mother, it now falls to Father – in Bowen's view – to refigure it as the mandate of an external law, thereby at once confirming its necessity and rendering it tolerable to the child. We know that Gavin has seen the head of the Admiral's cigarette, 'immobile, pulsating sharply' in the darkness of the street outside Mrs Nicholson's door (I 695): the question now is whether the Admiral can make good on this promise of potency, refiguring the separation of Lilian and Gavin in terms of his own sexual command of the woman who represents Mother. As Gavin enters the drawing-room he sees the Admiral and his hostess 'standing before the fire. Of this, not a glint had room to appear between the figures of the antagonists' – an encouraging sign indeed, for

> if they had not, throughout, been speaking from this distance, the Admiral must have taken a step forward. But this, on his part, must have been, and must be, all – his head was averted from her, his shoulders were braced back, and behind his back he imprisoned one of his own wrists in a handcuff grip that shifted only to tighten. (I 708)

At this crucial moment, then, the Admiral's cigarette is nowhere to be seen. Instead of consummating his relationship with Mrs Nicholson, the Admiral refuses to do so, and thereby fails to reconfigure for Mrs Nicholson's filial admirer the two-person trauma of separation as the triangular crisis of prohibition. The result is the decades-long persistence in Gavin of that agonising state of destruction and destructiveness that we have observed in Sydney on the mountain road, before the salutary intervention of the hired chauffeur. Thus when Gavin next returns to Southstone – thirty years later, in the final days of the Second World War – the visit has nothing about it of a 'pilgrimage', but represents, rather, a 'tour of annihilation' (I 689, 708). He makes his way purposively to the florist's shop at which he had assisted Mrs Nicholson in the buying of carnations for the Concannons' dinner party; he finds it destroyed by bombing, but this in no way satisfies or softens his violent feelings.

> When time takes our revenges out of our hands it is, usually, to execute them more slowly: her vindictiveness, more thorough than ours, might satisfy us, if, in the course of her slowness, we did not forget. In this case, however, she had worked in the less than a second of detonation. Gavin Doddington paused where there was no florist – was he not, none the less, entitled to draw a line through this? (I 709)

Mother is dead already – she has caused her own death, and mine as well – and yet, 'none the less', I want to kill her, too.

In Bowen's signature story of developmental derailment, then, the 'death' in the maternal dyad that is caused by separation and that, in the proper course of things, is reconfigured by the intervention of external law, fails to be so redeemed and comes to be represented by Mother's *literal* death and by the continuingly murderous and deathly feelings of her desperate child. There is thus a powerful suggestion in such a story that Mother's death, and the symbolic death of her child, too, should be understood as in some sense Father's fault.

In Bowen's short story 'The Visitor', a pre-prep-school-age boy, Roger, and his two younger sisters are sent to stay with neighbours while their mother dies at home. Roger's father is literally present, but he lacks a crucial capability that is associated in the story with the fatal decline of his wife:

> Father didn't go to work now but walked about the house and garden, [. . .] lighting cigarettes and throwing them away again. Sometimes he would search anxiously for the cigarette he had thrown away, and when he picked it up would look at it and sigh desolately to find it had gone quite out.[24]

Just as Admiral Concannon's cigarette, at the climactic moment, is nowhere to be seen, so too Roger's father lacks virility, his claim on Roger's mother less that of an adult man than of another little child. 'Roger disliked people who were ridiculous, and he had never cared to look long at his father. Father had dark-brown hair, all fluffy like a baby's, that stood out away from his head' (V 128). Roger's father might remind us, I think, of the lamentably ineffectual Uncle Dee of *The House in Paris*; and just as Leopold, in the midst of his implacable longing for his mother, seems to intuit the need for exactly that 'paternal' intervention that is eventually provided by Ray Forrestier, so too Roger appears to be searching for some external voice of law. Roger is staying in the house of the Miss Emerys, a pair of unmarried sisters, who avoid at all costs any mention of the terrible reason for his visit; in contrast to their evasiveness the story counterposes the image of a clock, a very big one, perhaps a stationmaster's clock, given the Miss Emerys by a relation. It had no expression in its voice; it neither urged one on nor restrained one, simply commented quite impartially upon the flight of time. Sixty of these ticks went to make a minute, neither more nor less than sixty, and the hands of the clock would be pointing to an hour and a minute when they came to tell Roger what he was expecting to hear. (V 125)

A steadying embodiment of symbolic regulation, the clock enables Roger to tolerate the idea of his mother's mortality, whereas the Miss Emerys' well-meaning denial of reality can neither prevent the death of Roger's mother nor support him in surviving it.[25]

Of course the clock, too, can do nothing to prevent Roger's mother from dying; she is suffering from a real disease, a disease that sounds very much like the illness that kills Gavin's Mrs Nicholson in 1912, which is itself reminiscent of the cancer that killed Florence Bowen in that same year. But I think that what's important to understand here is the difference between a bereavement that comes as a trauma, and a bereavement that comes as a crisis. Bowen's work suggests, that is, that the impact of a mother's death upon her child is an index of her child's developmental history and state. She explores this idea most explicitly in her early story 'Coming Home', which describes the reaction of its thirteen-year-old protagonist Rosalind to finding her mother absent when she returns home at the end of her school day. Rosalind's family situation might remind us of the psychic conditions prevailing during Gavin's second visit to Southstone, for, as an only child and with her father dead, Rosalind's access to her mother might seem to be uninterrupted both by separation and by paternal prohibition:

> Other people's mothers had terrible little babies: they ran quickly in and out to go to them, or they had smoky husbands who came in and sat, with big feet. There was something so distracted about other people's mothers. But Darlingest, so exclusively one's own . . . [sic][26]

But in fact I think we may be confident that Rosalind's mother – very unlike the Mrs Nicholson of Gavin's second visit – has indeed undertaken responsibility for separation, for when she returns home, only a little after Rosalind, she brings with her a paper bag full of macaroons for the pair to share at tea. Thus it makes sense to understand Rosalind's idealisation of her mother, and of the unbroken intimacy between them, as a fragile defence against the trauma of separation, a trauma which has persisted in the absence of a father capable of importing and imposing the more bearable form of the three-position crisis. For Rosalind's reaction to her mother's unexpected absence is the reaction of a baby to the experience of separation: she feels that her mother has died, and that, moreover, she herself – Rosalind – is somehow responsible for the death. Darlingest of course is not dead, and Rosalind has not killed her: but she dies in Rosalind's mind, at once its victim and its persecutor, because, as we have seen, in Bowen's analysis this is what separation feels like.

> She would never see Darlingest again [. . .] She heard herself making a high, whining noise at the back of her throat, *like a puppy*, felt her swollen face distorted by another paroxysm. 'I can't bear it, I can't bear it. What have I done? I did love her, I did so awfully love her [. . .] I was angry and she died. I killed her.' (CH 98; my italics)

Because separation comes to the child in the dyad as death, to the child whose experience of separation has not yet been re-presented as a mandate of external law *death comes as separation*: unbearable, unthinkable, and on its own terms unredeemable.

Yet the proposition that, in essence, it is Father's fault if Mother dies for good – if her first 'death', the death of separation, persists untransformed by paternal re-presentation, a predicament that may be exemplified by a second death, a death at once real and symbolic of itself – does not complete our exploration of Bowen's signature story of developmental perversion, for, as we observed in the opening images of 'Ivy Gripped the Steps', the trauma of separation in the dyad may co-exist with

Development 69

an at least equally intransigent refusal, or inability, to register on any terms the mortal facts of life. For even as the middle-aged Gavin tours the scenes of Southstone's destruction, the ivy clinging imperturbably to the carcase of Mrs Nicholson's shut-up and abandoned house continues to feed as if oblivious to the extinction of its host. There is thus a sense in which the perpetual deathliness of Gavin's emotional state – the morbidity of the weaned child prior to triangulation – is at once paralleled, imitated and contested by a primary *ignorance* of death, and of the limitations of human intimacy and of human agency that death both exemplifies and represents. Whereas we have noticed in Rosalind, for example, a defensive idealisation of the mother who has in fact taken responsibility for separation – an idealisation that we might also identify in Roger, and Leopold, and Sydney, and that corresponds to the terrible force of Gavin's hostility towards Mrs Nicholson in the wake of her eventual symbolic weaning of him – we may make out in the image of the ivy feeding on the dead house a depiction of an overgrown baby who in the absence of an adequate experience of loss has neither the need nor the capacity to deny it. The word that I want to use to refer to this state of mind is 'psychosis'. The term is used across a wide range of psychological and psychoanalytic discourses to indicate a partial or complete absence of cognitive relation to reality. The psychotic person is not in touch with truth, cannot recognise the real conditions of being. There is thus an intrinsic loneliness in the experience of psychosis; it is a state of radical alienation from self and other alike. We may see something of this predicament in the seeming paradox of the adult Gavin's relentless sociability and unbreachable loneliness. He makes his 1944 visit to Southstone alone, although, '[a]morist since his 'teens, he had not often set off on a holiday uncompanioned' (I 689), and he makes, at the story's end, an unsuccessful attempt to pick up an Auxiliary Territorial Service (ATS) girl in the street. This compulsive yet strangely unmeaning promiscuity – like the 'brutal [. . .] fecundity' of the ivy (I 686) – suggests a sexuality whose basic structure and assumptions have survived intact from the earliest days of the maternal dyad, Gavin's voracious fixation on Mother and his inability to comprehend the mortal finitude of her existence two sides of a single infantile coin. If, in Bowen's view, Mother's death results from Father's failure to confirm and reconfigure separation, Mother's *inability* to die – her uncanny, even inhuman alienation from death – results rather from the failure of separation itself, an experience that Father can helpfully promote but which can only be inaugurated by Mother herself, for as the primary experience of loss it necessarily occurs in the primary relationship of care.

In Bowen's fictional protagonist Gavin Doddington, the strange complicity of the symptoms of these different stages and states of developmental failure is to be observed in the ATS girl's view of the man whose come-on she rebuffs. 'She had seen' – in Gavin Doddington – 'the face of somebody dead who was still there – "old" because of the presence, under an icy screen, of a whole stopped mechanism for feeling' (I 711). 'Somebody dead who was still there', or, at least, 'somebody dead', is an image of the trauma of separation, a deathliness as yet unredeemed by paternal intervention; the 'icy screen' implies the potential for further and different experience, as the idea of a frozen thing suggests a state that is blessedly vulnerable to external transformation. On the other hand, the inhuman persistence of the 'still there', and the implication that feeling itself derives from or is generated by a mechanical device, speak of a psychotic alienation from the time-bound reality of human culture and from its mortal, bodily support. Deathlessness thus shadows deathliness, at once its nemesis and its twin.

## Section Three: *The Heat of the Day*

In this third and final section of the chapter I want to show how an understanding of Bowen's signature story of complex developmental failure can illuminate *The Heat of the Day* (1948), arguably Bowen's masterpiece and certainly, with *The Last September* (1929), one of the two best known and most highly regarded of her novels today. Most of the action takes place in the early autumn of 1942, with a kind of informal coda set in September 1944 – the date, also, of the frame narrative in 'Ivy

Gripped the Steps'. Stella Rodney, an attractive upper-middle-class divorcee employed, in London, in 'secret, exacting, not unimportant' war work, is visited repeatedly by a man called Harrison who identifies himself as a state security agent and offers to protect her lover, Robert Kelway, from arrest as a spy if she, Stella, will consent to become Harrison's lover instead.[27] Over a period of two months, Stella tests the accusation that Robert is a traitor by going with him to visit the Kelway family home – Holme Dene, the haute-bourgeois Arts-and-Crafts lair of the redoubtable Muttikins, Robert's mother – and by questioning him directly. At first Robert denies the charge, but when eventually he thinks that he is about to be arrested he tells Stella the truth – he has indeed been passing state secrets to the enemy – and, endeavouring to evade capture, either leaps or falls to his death from the roof of Stella's top-floor flat. Of two subplots, one concerns Stella's twenty-year-old son, Roderick, a conscript, who has recently inherited an estate in Ireland from a male relative on his dead father's side; the other concerns the daily lives of a pair of working-class women friends, one of whom, Louie, becomes pregnant as a result of her promiscuous sexual behaviour in the absence of her husband Tom, who is fighting overseas.

What I want to show is that Bowen's novel is essentially double, and that its doubleness is homologous to that specific formation of subjectivity that Bowen identifies as the cumulative result of ambivalent separation and paternal breakdown. *The Heat of the Day* is composed of, or inhabited by, two versions of itself, versions which, reflecting different stages of development, show as mutually incompatible without ever figuring a simple, symmetrical opposition. Thus *The Heat of the Day* offers a dynamic illustration of that same representational or ontological duality that we have observed already in the protagonist of 'Ivy Gripped the Steps', for in the content and in the form of this novel we may make out the simultaneous symbolic articulation of divergent and asymmetrical developmental malformations.

I take as my starting-point the topic of Robert Kelway's war wound and the limp associated with it: the topic will prompt us to turn immediately to the big question – touched on in the previous section of the chapter – of how Bowen's texts align geopolitics with the psychodrama of individual development, for Robert's injury correlates historical referents with psychological significance. Robert and Stella first met

> in September 1940, when Robert, discharged from hospital after a Dunkirk wound, came to the War Office. The damage was to a knee; it had left its trace on his walk in an inequality which could be called a limp; he was not likely again to see active service. That honourable queerness about his gait varied: at times he could control it out of existence, at others he fairly pitched along with an impatient exaggeration of lameness further exaggerated by his height. The variation, [Stella] had discovered, had like that in a stammer a psychic cause – it was a matter of whether he did or did not, that day, feel like a wounded man. (HD 90)

Thus Robert's injury both memorialises a notorious episode of military and naval failure – in August 1940, British, French and Belgian forces in the Low Countries were beaten back to the Channel by the German army and bombed from the air while they waited on the beaches of Dunkirk for evacuation by sea – and at the same time locates in that historical event a psychological meaning, as the day-to-day variation in Robert's limp 'ha[s] like that in a stammer a psychic cause'. How, then, are we to parse the developmental, or psychobiographical, significance of Robert's disability? – for Stella's recognition that the variation in the limp is psychologically expressive does not begin to identify the precise determinants of Robert's fluctuating experience of himself as a wounded man.[28]

We have noted already how, in 'Ivy Gripped the Steps', the question of whether or not a European war is in the offing articulates the disagreement between Admiral Concannon and Mrs Nicholson over the necessity of separation and the inevitability of the dyadic conflict to which separation gives rise. Its embedded narrative set a couple of years before the outbreak of the First World War, but with a frame narrative set in 1944 and a first publication date of 1945, 'Ivy Gripped the Steps' mobilises the ironical resources of recent and contemporary history to endorse, in retrospect, the Admiral's prognostications of war – prognostications evidently not exhausted by the First World War – and the conception of psychological development that implicitly underpins his views, and to critique, rather severely, what is presented as the fey and disingenuous nature of Lilian's resistance to Admiral Concannon's geopolitical realism – a resistance that is all of a piece with her cavalier and mischievous parenting practices. 'Civilized countries are polite to each other', Mrs Nicholson says to the Admiral, in a formulation that we noted in the previous section of the chapter,

> just as you and I are to the people we know, and uncivilized countries are put down – but, if one thinks, there are beautifully few of those. Even savages really prefer wearing hats and coats. Once people wear hats and coats and can turn on electric light, they would no more want to be silly than you or I do. (I 696)

'Silly' is the term that Lilian uses to deride other people's hostility. 'I should not dream of suspecting *any* civilized country!' she continues; she means that she would not credit the suggestion that Germany wants to be 'silly', the proposition, that is to say, that Germany has bellicose intentions in relation to other powers. To the Admiral's specification of Germany as the enemy-in-preparation she ripostes, 'more nearly definitely than usual': 'I have never been happier anywhere' – for as we learn in the opening pages of the story, Lilian had spent her finishing year in Dresden.

We might recall at this point Mrs Kerr's endeavours to interest Sydney in the 'civilized' practice of patisserie-eating during the course of her symbolic weaning: the comparison will help us to identify in Lilian's historico-evolutionary utopianism some of the self-interested evasiveness that is discernible in her outsourcing of responsibility for separation to her maid Rockham – except that in this instance the aggression and bad feeling that attend the process of weaning, or 'civilization', are not so much side-stepped as flatly denied. Speaking like a mother who has imposed separation without being willing to acknowledge the dyadic violence thereby stirred up, Mrs Nicholson not only maintains that weaned children ('civilized countries') never manifest hostility, but implies also that as children actually *like* to be weaned ('savages really prefer wearing hats and coats') the absence of hostility from their behaviour reflects an absence of conflict in the dyad. In this context, Mrs Nicholson's enthusiasm for Germany strikes an intriguingly filial note: 'I have never been happier anywhere.' Is this a defensive idealisation on the part of a woman who – as we have seen – is tactically unwilling to acknowledge the reality of conflict in the primary relationship of care? Or does it indicate that in some part of her mind Lilian recalls the original harmony of the dyad before separation, and that, therefore, her denial of conflict expresses an authentic, albeit partial, ignorance of its reality? Either way, it seems to me that there is something very suggestive, if indeterminate, in Lilian's loyalty to Germany in the context of her relationship to the idea and the experience of separation.

In fact we may observe that throughout Bowen's writing Germany is strongly associated with motherhood, its powers and its responsibilities. When, in *The House in Paris*, Karen Michaelis discovers that she is pregnant with Max's child, she hides herself in Germany; her own mother joins her there, for some 'terrible weeks' in which Leopold is born and the relationship between Mrs Michaelis and her daughter is irretrievably damaged (HP 229); for the first two years of Leopold's life he is fostered by a German friend of Naomi's, 'a lady with a family of her own', whose sudden death leads to Leopold's adoption by the Grant-Moodys and exile in Italy (HP 214); and after years of resisting Ray's pleas that they should recover her son, years of travel in France, Venice, New York, it is 'one afternoon in Berlin' that Karen 'stop[s] at a street corner' and says to her husband: 'Ray, I should like to see Leopold somehow [. . .] Do you think it could be arranged?' (HP 230)

In *The House in Paris* nobody *says* anything about Germany, but characters' behaviour in the country is always suggestive.

## Development 75

Characters in Bowen's first novel *The Hotel* are more explicit, their attitudes, feelings and ideas about Germany offering the reader a sure means of gauging these fictional subjects' psychic position in relation to the figure of the mother. Germany is the geographic location and the epistemological focus of Ronald's earnest study-holiday immediately prior to his visit to Mrs Kerr in the Riviera hotel. 'It does please me so', Mrs Kerr tells her son, 'that you've come down to me from Germany, given up Germany. I hope it didn't cost a lot?' Taking this as a reference to money, Ronald remains silent, embarrassed, until his mother corrects his misapprehension. 'I meant in *development*. Pictures. Music' (H 107) – at which characterisation of his interests Ronald demurs, claiming that such things were 'purely secondary' considerations (H 107), the primary purpose of his stay in Germany being to study the country's economic problems. Later in the conversation, however, he somewhat self-contradictorily takes issue with his mother's description of his attitude towards personal relationships as 'hygienic and bald': '"I suppose," he said, as though he were speaking to her in the dark and had to guess her position, "that you think I don't like things to be beautiful"' (H 109). Shortly after this exchange his mother closes her eyes for a siesta, subsiding, as we have noted previously, into a likeness of the Beata Beatrix and reminding Ronald of how he had, as a child of six, addressed his mother as 'My Beautiful' (H 110).

Mrs Kerr, as we know, is commendably committed to separation, and we have seen the pain this causes Sydney in the absence of paternal intervention; Ronald's father, too, is dead, and the ambivalence of Ronald's feelings in relation to the beautiful things of Germany suggests that the fatherly capability of his guardian – a figure to whom only cursory reference is made by Ronald and his mother – leaves something to be desired. By Bowen's lights, it is in an important sense due to the weakness of these paternal figures that Ronald at twenty has yet to recover fully from the trauma of separation, which manifests itself as much in his unhappiness in Germany, where he experienced 'a childish feeling of homelessness' and had 'been lonely in Munich and bored in Dresden, while several people had been rude to him in Berlin' (H 108), as in the chariness, self-pity and tentative hostility that we may observe in Ronald during the course of this conversation with Mrs Kerr.[29]

> He felt impelled to ask his mother some fantastic question: 'What do I mean to you?' or 'What part do I play in your life?' or even (a final outrage), 'Do you care for me?' (This he could not remember that she had ever avowed.) (H 108)

Thus the problem of the Rentenmark reiterates the problem of a dead father and the problem, also, of an inadequate guardian: each is an example or a representative of a failed or failing symbolic technology – a currency, a psychic structure, a system of legally mandated paternal authority – by which it should, properly, be possible to gain and regain access to the lovely, beloved and loving figure of Mother. The incoherence of Ronald's feelings towards Mrs Kerr corresponds to the 'economic confusion' besetting the German population (H 107), the inadequacy of the paternal function that legislates Ronald's access to his mother the precise psychic counterpart to the instability of the financial and institutional structures by which, in Bowen's novel of 1927, the Weimar Republic is endeavouring to regulate the German people's relation to their country in the years after the First World War.

Across the full span of her writing life, Bowen conceives of war as dyadic: war between Germany and England functions as a geopolitical elaboration of the conflict that erupts between mother and child upon the inauguration of separation. The resolution of war by a process of national and international reconfiguration thus allegorises the maturational necessity of triangulation in the course of psychological development. We observed previously that *The Hotel* exploits the symbolic potential of the unsatisfactory political settlement in 1920s Germany to reflect upon the uneasy relationship between Mrs Kerr and her son, and in the previous section of the chapter we saw that *The House in Paris* (1935) explores via the figure of a volatile Continental culture intervened upon by a representative of the English class system the salvific action of the symbolic order upon the maternal dyad after separation. In 'Ivy Gripped the Steps' (1945), the First World War, its twenty-year aftermath, and the starting up again of hostilities in 1939 demonstrate figuratively the psychological consequences of Admiral Concannon's unwillingness to assert his sexual authority over Mrs Nicholson, while the prohibition by the military authorities of Southstone to civilians following the fall of France in 1940 indicates in symbolic terms that a failure of paternal function may, even after prolonged mutual destruction on the part of mother and child, eventually be made good. I want now to add to these observations a recognition that Bowen makes use of the historiographic and political redefinition of the Great War as the first of two consecutive conflicts to objectify the traumatic structure of her own childhood, because by virtue of what is characterised in 'Ivy Gripped the Steps' as the origins of the Second World War in the First, Bowen can figure in geopolitical terms both the temporal and the causal relationship that in her analysis obtains between her father's breakdown when she was seven, and the psychic destruction of her mother that found external form in the tragedy of Florence's death six years later. Thus in Bowen's writing from 1939 and after, both European wars figure the agonistic experience of separation, but it is only the Second World War, conceived as a continuation of the earlier war, that functions as a trope for irreparable annihilation.[30] In *Pictures and Conversations*, for example, Bowen describes the late summer of 1912 in terms that explicitly link the experience of waiting for her mother to die with the period immediately before the beginning of an aerial attack:

> That September the evenings at Hythe [. . .] were stuffy and bodeful. The sorts of evenings which later one associated with the thrumming of a bomber, circling, coming brutally nearer each time. [Florence] died, at Clyne House, on the – of the month. I was staying next door. (PC 48–9)

Bowen's conflation of the angel of death with an enemy warplane evokes specifically the kind of war in which civilians cower helplessly in domestic buildings while hostile aircraft circle overhead – not, I think, the conflict that broke out only two years after Florence died, but the Second World War, during which Bowen herself experienced, in London, the bombing of a great civilian centre.

By now it will have become possible to recognise in Robert Kelway's limp, as in the disaster of Dunkirk and in the tragedy of Florence Bowen's death, an image of the delayed, inevitable, and catastrophic consequences of paternal deficit. 'I was born wounded', Robert tells Stella, at almost the end of the novel: 'my father's son. Dunkirk was waiting there in us – what a race! A class without a middle, a race without a country. Unwhole. Never earthed in' (HD 272). Of course, in condemning British military incompetence Robert does not intend to suggest that his injury was literally inflicted by his own side, and yet there is nothing irrational in his attribution of blame to the British state for a disability deriving originally from a wound from a German gun. For in Robert's analysis of the culpability of the British state for the lasting damage done him by the enemy's attack we may recognise in geopolitical dress Bowen's account of the paternal responsibility to intervene in the battleground of the dyad after separation, and to bind up the wounds sustained by both warring parties. Robert's limp is not the inevitable consequence of an injury at Mother's hands, but gives evidence rather of an unsatisfactory process of healing, for which Father must shoulder the blame.

Such an account of Robert Kelway thus identifies in *The Heat of the Day* a story concerning the trauma of separation in the absence of adequate symbolic redemption. Perhaps the most exciting interpretative consequence of this formulation is the opportunity to cast a newly sceptical eye upon the figure of Muttikins, a mother whose exquisite awfulness exceeds even the standard set by Madame Fisher. The earlier monster's baneful flamboyance edges perilously close to the merely hammy when compared to the dream-dense toxicity of the Kelway mamma, a figure of 'miniature daunting beauty' (HD 109).

> [W]hy *should* she speak? – she had all she needed: the self-contained mystery of herself. Her lack of wish for communication showed in her contemptuous use of words. The lounge

became what it was from being the repository of her nature; it was the indoors she selected, she consecrated – indeed, she had no reason to go out. By sitting here where she sat, and by sometimes looking, by sometimes even not looking, across the furnished lawn, she projected Holme Dene: this was a bewitched wood. If her power came to an end at the white gate, so did the world. (HD 109–10)

The absolute frightfulness of Muttikins is a truth universally acknowledged in the history of critical responses to this novel; but I want to suggest that in light of Bowen's implicit understanding of development, the logic of which is as discernible in this text as it is throughout Bowen's work, we might think afresh about the meaning of Muttikins's hatefulness – think, that is, about the specific subject position or developmental stage from which Muttikins is to be perceived as hateful. Muttikins has been very deeply loved by her children (Robert and his sisters Ernestine and Amabelle): like Darlingest, she has earned a shamelessly affectionate and wallowingly undignified pet-name, a name whose fond intimations of Teutonic maternity ('Mutti' is German for 'Mummy') make absolutely clear – given the wartime setting of this novel – the relation between love and loathing in the dyad. What I want to suggest is that Muttikins – like Darlingest, like Mrs Kerr – has taken responsibility for weaning; and that, without subsequent paternal reconfiguration of the dyad as a triangle, her children's inevitable trauma has persisted untransformed, the originally adored mother now feared and hated as a monster of aggression. Thus it is that the Germany of pictures and music (as Mrs Kerr characterises it), the place of which Lilian Nicholson avers: 'I have never been happier anywhere' (I 696), the location of Leopold's birth and of his first two years with a properly maternal foster-mother, comes to be perceived instead as the brutal instigator of a massively destructive global war. Indeed it is by exactly so much as 'Germany' was her children's darling, indeed their *darlingest*, that she will now appear as the author of a shockingly hostile deprivation. Towards the end of *The Heat of the Day* we see Robert, visiting Mrs Kelway and

Ernestine at Holme Dene, muse upon the house in which he stands. Closely aligned, at this point, with Robert's perspective, the narrative voice remarks: '[U]pstairs life, since the war, had [. . .] condensed itself into very few rooms – swastika-arms of passage leading to nothing, stripped of carpet, bulbs gone from the light-sockets, were flanked by doors with their keys turned' (HD 258). What strips out the carpet, banishes the lightbulbs, locks up the bedroom doors? What transmogrifies German beauty into German belligerence? What makes the difference between Mummy and a Nazi? Separation.

To complete this first reading of the novel I want to explore the significance of Robert's treachery, and its relation to the manner of his death, questions that I will approach via the richly suggestive episode of Stella's one visit to Holme Dene with Robert. Arriving by train in his home town, Robert displays in his steering of Stella across the station a 'sort of rapid somnambulism' (HD 104) that will remind us of the oneiric quality of life in the maternal dyad in *The Hotel* and *The House in Paris*; as we have noted already Holme Dene is a 'project[ion]' of Muttikins's, a 'bewitched wood' (HD 110). It should not surprise us, then, that in the afternoon's encounter between Stella, Robert, Muttikins, Ernestine, Anne and Peter – these last the primary-school-age children of Amabelle, herself confined for the duration of the war to India – the question of access to food, and to resources more generally, is of central importance. For the ostentatious Puritanism of the Kelway ménage speaks eloquently of the rigours of weaning. Muttikins's monologues advert repeatedly to 'the fuel shortage', the reason, she explains, that she does not indulge in unnecessary travel or heat more than one room on the ground floor of Holme Dene; Ernestine, her mother claims, 'does not feel the cold, from moving about so much that she seldom takes off her hat', but we might wonder if both the incessant motion and the constant retention of her outdoor clothes were not rather indications that Muttikins's lieutenant is in fact cold all the time (HD 113). The seven-year-old Peter shares his grandmother's enthusiasm for the topic of scarcity, rebuking the visitors sternly for what he perceives as their ineffectual approach to the conservation of energy: 'Uncle Robert, you didn't save your taxi much petrol by getting out of it at the gate; it had to go on more than a mile down the road before it could turn; when it drives up to here it can quite easily turn in front of the door' (HD 112). In contrast to his sister, nine-year-old Anne, whose total submission to the miseries of separation is signalled sadly by the 'pink plastic brooch representing a dog [. . .] pinned to [her] chest', Peter appears to be adapting himself to the regime at Holme Dene by identifying with its aggression. '[S]porting an armlet with cryptic letters', Muttikins's grandson is more Hitler Youth than pitiful puppy, but the contrast works to indicate the continuity of these sibling subjectivities, and their common origins in the experience of deprivation at Mother's hands.

And so we come again to the perennial question raised by Bowen's work in presence of the bleak spectacle of the dyad after separation: can Father refigure a frightening restriction on resources as a system of regulation which guarantees a reliable supply? In fact I want to show that tea-time at Holme Dene offers the opportunity to assess not one but several different versions of symbolic law, each of which demonstrates its efficaciousness primarily in terms of the feelings and behaviours to which it gives rise in those characters with whom it is particularly associated in the scene.

The weakest form of paternal regulation on display pertains to the use of fuel. Neither Mrs Kelway or her grandson explicitly acknowledges the historical reality of wartime fuel rationing; Mrs Kelway speaks of having been 'told' of the fuel shortage (HD 113), and of having been 'asked not to travel for no reason' (HD 109), but such a request by the state falls far short of the mandatory regulation that would figure in this context a robust operation of symbolic law, with the result that the individual consumer appears to be made responsible for operationalising a perverse self-deprivation that can easily extend into the aggressive policing of others.

In contrast, the existence of a state system of food rationing is writ large across the Kelway tea-table: 'each one of the family had his or her own [butter] ration placed before his or her own plate in a differently coloured china shell' (HD 111). The modest but by no means negligible capability of this form of symbolic law is demonstrated by the perfectly adequate meal that materialises under its mandate: in addition to the butter, and to 'a japanned tray of tea things opposite Mrs Kelway', Robert, Stella and the family sit down to 'buns, a loaf, an uncut cake which had the look of being of long standing, and an inviting pot of damson jam' (HD 111). However, it would appear that rationing, too, leaves something to be desired, for as a system that legislates desire it betrays at the Holme Dene tea-table some significant failures. At this point it may be helpful to recall Bowen's understanding of development in its literal or original terms. After weaning, Mother is liable to look like a monster in the eyes of her desperate, desolate child; when Father intervenes to refigure separation as a mandate of external law, a precious consequence of his action is to restore Mother's desirability, and Baby's desire. The 'inviting pot of damson jam' upon the Holme Dene tea-table thus gives evidence of some competent symbolic regulation, as it speaks of a happy relationship between an attractive object and an appetitive would-be consumer. Similarly, the individual china dishes at each place, each holding one person's butter ration for the week, are certainly appealing; less happily, however, they signal an inverse relationship between desire and the possibility of its satisfaction. 'Today was the delusive opening of the rationing week; the results of intemperance, as the week drew on, would be to be judged' (HD 111).

And then there is the figure of the cake, which, as we know – in light of Mrs Kerr's patisserie, Darlingest's macaroons, and the cakes made in Mrs Nicholson's kitchen for the Awaken Britannia League – is likely to function in Bowen's writing as a special repository of significance in the drama of the weaning dyad. Whereas both the damson jam and the butter look as if they would be nice to eat, with the difference between them that the foregrounded scarcity of the butter makes appetite – whether indulged or resisted – an essentially bittersweet experience, the cake, with its 'look of being of long standing', appears to have remained uncut because nobody wants it. Here, a maternal object, in the form of an item of food, has been made available for consumption without any apparent restriction on quantity, but the regulatory system that has in this respect succeeded has failed at the same time to stimulate and encourage the potential consumers' desire. Thus the ample, undesirable cake poses a virtually existential hazard to the people gathered around the tea-table, for by disabling the experience of appetite the cake threatens to forestall the activity of eating. 'You wouldn't think it was time we bought a new cake?' Robert asks Ernestine; as he speaks he is 'trying to knife the cake', a gesture of rage and despair in the face of the weaning mother that may remind us of Sydney's destructive daydream about a car crash (*The Hotel*) or of Max's vindictive suicide in *The House in Paris*. 'But that one has not been eaten', Ernestine objects; 'I'm sure Mrs Rodney will take us as she finds us.' 'Happily for Mrs Rodney', Robert responds, 'she does not eat cake', which astonishes Anne, but Ernestine is swift to point the moral: 'Mrs Rodney is free not to eat cake if she doesn't want to: that is just what I mean by the difference between England and Germany.' Sadistically excited by the tragic choice thus adumbrated, the choice between voluntary starvation and coerced survival, Peter, 'wriggling inside his jersey', adds: 'The Nazis would *force* her to eat cake' (HD 113).

That the visitors from London remain unpersuaded of the efficaciousness of the state regulation of resources is made clear by their marked detachment from its protocols: 'Dear me', Robert remarks, without much contrition or plausible affectation of it, 'Mrs Rodney and I forgot about bringing our own butter' (HD 111). Instead, both Stella and Robert trust to the operations of the market. In Stella's case, it is a legal market, a system that competes, it would appear successfully, with the scarcity-management techniques of the state: 'Stella's solitary Londoner's footloose habits of living, in and out of restaurants, had kept from her many of the realities of the home front' (HD 111).[31] But the impressive supply-side capacity of restaurants has evidently not acted to encourage in Stella much of an enthusiasm for meals: upon seeing the butter rations set out at Holme Dene, '[s]he said hurriedly that she did not eat tea' (HD 111), a claim whose truthfulness would later appear to be confirmed by Robert's revelation, so startling to Anne, that Stella does not eat cake. Robert, too, eschews the state regulation of supply in favour of the operations of the market, but he relies on a different commercial system to the one made use of by Stella – a system whose superior symbolic capability is evidenced by the frankness of Robert's appetite, his evident relish for a meal. It is, however, emphatically and unnegotiably illegal. 'Robert helped himself to a bun, which he split open in order to spread thickly with damson jam. "Oh I say!" expostulated his nephew, Peter, speaking for the first time' (this is the reader's first sight of Amabelle's children). 'The girl, Anne, remarked: "Do you do that in London? You must use a lot of jam, a most awful lot." "Black market," said Robert, out of the side of his mouth' (HD 111). Dreadfully upset, because Robert is her favourite of the Kelways, Anne says: 'Uncle Robert, suppose you end up in prison!' 'In that case', Robert replies, 'you'll have to come and visit me', a prospect that nearly reduces his niece to tears (HD 112).

What I want to argue is that Robert's willingness to make use of the black market (for I do not think that he is merely teasing or joking at this moment) exactly parallels his actions in passing state secrets to the Third Reich. Because he loves and needs his mother, and because she has spoiled herself for him by instituting separation, Robert plots for a father who can restore his mother to him as a loved, loving and lovable object – a father who, in the terms of Bowen's carb-rich metaphor, can re-enchant the cake upon the Kelway table, supply butter without apparent limit, and guarantee that there will always be jam for tea. '[W]hy are you against this country?' Stella asks him when, at nearly the end of the book, Robert thinks that he is about to be arrested and flees to Stella's flat for a final tryst, during which he confirms that Harrison's allegations have been correct. 'Country?' Robert replies. 'This, where we are', Stella explains. 'I don't see what you mean – ', Robert says, 'what *do* you mean? Country? – there are no more countries left. What country have you and I outside this room? Exhausted shadows, dragging themselves out again to fight – and how long are they going to drag the fight out?' (HD 267). Robert voices eloquently here the war-weariness of the child in the dyad after separation, and highlights also a corresponding draining of emotional value, of felt vitality, from the figure of the mother in the eyes of the child that she has weaned: 'Country? – there are no more countries left.' Thus Stella's question profoundly misrecognises the logic of Robert's politics: in radical contrast to the us-versus-them patriotism implicit in Stella's conception of treachery, Robert has been scheming for the institution of a transnational or global order by which such mutual destructiveness may be rectified and resolved. '[H]ow long are they going to drag the fight out? We have come out at the far side of that.' 'We?' Stella asks. 'We', Robert explains, 'who are ready for the next thing' – the next thing that Robert understands to be triangulation. For the only hope of definitively stopping the war is the institution of symbolic law, the reconfiguration of the war-torn dyad by the introduction into it of a third term – not the German state in its present historical actuality, but the ideal fascist order that is, in Robert's view, prefigured by the Third Reich. 'So you are with the enemy', Stella remarks some pages later. 'Naturally they're the enemy', Robert responds: 'they're facing us with what has got to be the conclusion. They won't last, but *it* will' (HD 273; my italics). Moments later, Stella tries again; the two-position logic of her thought remains unchanged. 'It's not just that they're the enemy, but that they're horrible – specious, unthinkable, grotesque.' 'Oh *they*', Robert responds: ' – evidently! But you judge *it* by them' (HD 274; second italics mine). Modelling here the patriot as a child of the dyad, Stella thinks in twos, while Robert's conceptual commitment to threeness ('we', 'they' and 'it') equates in this context to a treacherous supranationalism or political globalisation.

Thus we may discern in the scene a strong resemblance to the conclusion of *The House in Paris*, and perceive in the character of Robert Kelway a reiteration of the stepfather-and-son pairing of Ray Forrestier and Leopold. Like Leopold, who modelled a Plasticine phallus and hoped that it would bake hard in the sun (HP 34), Robert wishfully looks to the as-yet unrealised figure of international fascism for an instantiation of paternal authority. 'We must have something to envisage', he tells Stella, 'and we must act, and there must be law. We must have law – if necessary let it break us: to have been broken is to have been something.' 'But law – ' Stella objects, 'that's just what you break.' 'Nothing I can break is law!' Robert responds (HD 269), a resounding articulation of the faith in a transcendent moral order that we have seen expressed also in Ray Forrestier's readiness to carry out what he himself recognises would be identified, from the less exalted perspective of the British, French or Italian police forces, as a kidnapping of Leopold from his legal guardians, the Grant-Moodys: 'You know', Ray says to Leopold, 'till things get fixed up – if they ever do get fixed up – this amounts to stealing you?' (HP 233) Indeed both novels relish and exploit for thrills the hyperbolic transgressiveness of their respective heroes' actions – child-snatching, treason – while at the same time characterising the extreme technical illegality of those actions as an index of their essential virtue, their ardent conformity to a superior system of values, their homage to an absolute morality.

We may recall at this point Bowen's use of the image of a monkey to indicate that a child is trying to deny the reality of separation and resist, more broadly, the reality that separation exemplifies and represents, for both Robert and Ray deploy this symbolic resource to distinguish their own actions from any such infantile refusal of what is and what has to be. When Ray is shown into the salon of the house in Paris he notices '[a] plush monkey propped up on the sofa, [and] ask[s] himself if this hideous toy could be Leopold's'. Aware of the presence in the house of another child, Henrietta, Ray 'strongly wishe[s] to believe the monkey hers' (as indeed it is), and shortly afterwards displaces the monkey from its seat 'with a quiet savageness' (HP: 220–3). 'You think, in me this was simply wanting to get my hand on the controls?' Robert says to Stella. 'Well, it's not', he insists, 'it's not a question of that. Who wants to monkey about? To feel control is enough. It's a very much bigger thing to be under orders' (HD 273), his simian imagery drawing on the metaphorics of Bowen's fiction at large to bolster the account that he is advancing of himself as the honourable agent of a salvific geopolitical maturation. Robert is distinctly reminiscent of Ray in appearance, too: both men are tall and fair; both are, as it is termed in the earlier novel, 'the Englishman's age: about thirty-six' (HP 222). Ray's name – with its intimation of the daylight rationality that should break in upon the cave-like enclosure of the dyad: the sun that Leopold counted on to fortify his Plasticine models – finds its echo or resemblance in 'the most curious of the qualities [Robert] should have, candescence' (HD 98). 'You may not like it, but it's the beginning of a day. A day on our scale', Robert tells Stella (HD 274), his imagery and his phrasing recalling at once Ray's responsibility for the symbolic re-birth of his wife's son and his sense of that child, Leopold, as the embodiment of a moral imperative. '[T]he child commanded tonight', Ray thinks to himself as he stands with Leopold beneath the 'strong arc lamps' of a taxi rank; 'I have acted on his scale' (HP 250).

But despite Robert's best efforts he proves unable to engineer for himself the kind of paternal rescue successfully staged for Leopold by Ray, or by the unnamed chauffeur of the Fiat for the equally desperate Sydney Warren in Bowen's first novel, *The Hotel*. Instead, Robert meets his end in the form of what the novel describes as a 'fall or leap from the roof' of Stella's flat (HD 291). Whether we construe his death as an accident in the course of an attempt to evade arrest by the British authorities, or speculate that he may have killed himself in preference to being captured alive, Robert's downfall as an agent of the Third Reich is symptomatic of the world-historical failure of Father Fascism: later that day 'news broke [of] the Allied landings in North Africa' and of Montgomery's Order of the Day to the Eighth Army, 'We have completely smashed the German and Italian armies' (HD 291). Shortly after this, the novel launches into a breathless, popular-journalism-type account of the progress of the war in the succeeding years, narrated as if from the perspective of the Allies and attending in particular to the experience of the mass audience addressed by newsreels: 'The wiping out of Monte Cassino caused an uncertain breath to be drawn in cinemas: all this was going to be necessary, and more' (HD 308). It is not the first time that Bowen's text has intermitted its focus on the lives of a few highly distinctive fictional characters: earlier intermissions take the form of historical or philosophical meditations upon the relationship between the individual subject and the national or international community of people and politics. But it is, very strikingly, the only such passage in which we may observe a failure of triangulation enacted at the level of textual form, for the novel now lapses from the secure third-person narration that otherwise obtains throughout into a disconcerting first-person plural narration, accompanied by a dyadic chauvinism: 'As early as January [1944] we broke the Gustav Line [. . .] February, in Italy we encircled ten enemy divisions' (HD 308).

And yet such an account of the novel leaves too much unaccounted for: the story of paternal failure to redeem separation is a compelling plot but it is, as I have indicated, only one plot of two that inhabit and make up *The Heat of the Day*. The other plot, by contrast, pertains rather to an original failure of separation and thus tends to deprioritise or foreclose altogether the question of symbolic law. Father is only ever a secondary figure in this story: the prime mover has to be Mother, whose responsibility it is to incorporate into her relationship with her baby the reality of separation. I have suggested that it is Muttikins's willingness to undertake this task that leads – in the absence of subsequent paternal re-presentation – to her demonisation in the eyes of her son. It is a willingness that is to be detected also in Stella Rodney, whose relationship with *her* own son, Roderick, suggests an at least equally rigorous weaning. Unexpectedly granted a short period of leave from the army, Roderick arrives at Stella's flat with expressively little expectation that his mother will feed him: '"[Y]ou wouldn't," Roderick venture[s], "have any cake?" "Absolutely none,"' Stella replies, before managing to unearth from her kitchen three 'musty' biscuits to serve up with coffee, this last giving signs of being the only form of food preparation with which she is very familiar (HD 53).

However, the wider symbolic implications of Roderick's arrival, and the place of the episode within the design of the novel as a whole, seem radically at odds with Stella's demonstrated austerity as a mother. For the visit is not only the homecoming of a son. It is also a tryst of some kind, a soldier's late-night assignation at the suggestively secluded flat of a suggestively independent woman: 'This did not look like home', Roderick reflects, upon first coming in; 'but it looked like something – possibly a story' (HD 47). The hastily arranged appointment – 'Roderick', we are told, 'never came to the flat without giving warning' (HD 46) – is preceded by a visit of Harrison's and succeeded, as Roderick falls asleep, by a telephone call from Robert. In addition to the 'separation mother' version of Stella we may therefore recognise in her a figure of the mother who has *never begun* to wean her child. For the flat is not only an image of a high-class brothel, although its decor certainly makes it that: 'a complete and no doubt valuable set of dark glass pictures of Regency goddesses hung round [the walls]. The feather-etched chintz encasing armchairs and sofa advertised its original delicacy by being these days always a little soiled' (HD 24). It is also, at the most fundamental or literal level of physical structure, an architectural iteration of the maternal dyad: 'In this flat, rooms had no names; there being only two, whichever you were not in was "the other room"' (HD 51). The point is not, I think, that Roderick's mother is like a prostitute, but that Roderick's prostitute is his mother. For the fictional characters of *The Heat of the Day*, sex, I propose, is symbolically continuous with breastfeeding; it is the figurative means by which Bowen's novel evokes and invokes the paradigmatic activity of the maternal dyad in its blissful original harmony.

To thus recognise at the emotional heart of what we might think of as the 'psychosis plot' the figure of the mother who resists or revokes separation will make it possible to understand some striking aspects of the novel that make no sense in the context of the 'separation trauma plot'. I will conclude my discussion with another look at Robert Kelway, whose doubleness articulates in the form of a fictional character the intriguing dual structure of Bowen's novel as a whole. First, though, I want to address the question of the remarkable symbolic violence perpetrated by Muttikins and by Stella Rodney against virtually every representative of paternal authority who crosses their paths, a violence that would be inexplicable if we were to limit our account of either woman to the model of the weaning mother. For the weaning mother has no reason to attack the figure of Father; on the contrary, as we have seen, an attractive paternal presence may make it easier for Mother to insist upon separation, and Father's subsequent reconfiguration of the dyad as a triangle will reconstitute – and legitimate for the first time – the very love-affair between mother and child that it simultaneously outlaws. Yet both Mrs Kelway and Mrs Rodney are repeatedly characterised as Delilahs *de nos jours*, perverse seductresses who deploy their sexual attractions to further a project of attacking and delegitimating representatives of paternal power.

Because virtually all critics have succumbed to Robert's loathing of his mamma, it will not be surprising for me to draw attention to the dark fantasies nursed by Robert on the subject of his parents' marriage, fantasies that revolve around the idea that Mrs Kelway, to speak symbolically, castrated her husband. 'In all but one sense he was impotent', Robert says to Stella, of his father, during their visit together to Holme Dene; 'that was what came out in his relationship to me. What I think must have happened to him I cannot[,] while we're in this house, say' (HD 119). And it will be similarly uncontroversial to highlight the expressive function of the Kelway family home in relation to its diminutive mistress. 'Chiefly [. . .] a man-eating house', '[c]onceived to please and appease middle-class ladies' (HD 257), Holme Dene is a kind of architectural vagina dentata that inculpates Muttikins as the author of her husband's symbolic mutilation. 'Lock-shorn' – here is the hand of Delilah –

> without the bodily prestige of either a soldier or a manual worker, as incapable of knocking anyone about as he was of bellowing, Mr Kelway had been to be watched seeing out at Holme Dene the last two years of an existence which had become derisory. (HD 257)

On the other hand, there is nothing routine about drawing attention to Stella's no less merciless attacks on the manhood of the men around her, as Bowen's critics have tended to give the attractive Mrs Rodney a tremendously easy ride.[32] In the case of Victor Rodney, Stella's ex-husband, who left her for his nurse and died not long after his divorce from Stella had been finalised, it may be easy to sympathise with the long-term dishonesty with which Stella has elected to protect herself: rather than appear as the victim of her husband's infidelity, she has encouraged in her family and friends a false understanding of the break-up as the result of sexual transgressions on her own part. Thus Stella has avenged herself for her husband's rejection by 'castrating' him in the eyes of the world – an act whose combination of mendaciousness and destructiveness upsets Roderick very deeply when it is revealed to him by another member of the family. 'But it *was* my father' is almost the only protest that he is able – or needs – to make when he raises with Stella the topic of her denial of the facts (HD 220).

In contrast, it is hard to see what justification might be advanced for a similar act of Stella's on the occasion of Roderick's late-night arrival to stay at his mother's Weymouth Street flat. While Stella makes coffee, and digs out the meagre trio of musty biscuits, Roderick has a bath, and then takes to the 'more formal' of the two sofas in the sitting-room; in the absence of a spare bed, Roderick will sleep on this imposing piece of furniture, 'brocade-covered, heaped at each end with cushions', and 'long enough for a person, even of some stature, to be able to lie on it full length' (HD 24). In line with the figure of the mother who quite properly deprives her child of unlimited access to her body, this arrangement separates Roderick from Stella at night, and yet – in line with the 'psychosis plot' – the scene strongly associates Roderick's sofa with his mother's bed. For a start, Roderick is clad in his mother's lover's clothing – a dressing-gown of Robert's handed to Roderick by his mother when he gets out of the bath. Roderick settles himself immediately as if for sleep, 'sw[i]ng[ing] his legs up on the sofa', 'test[ing] it out for length', and 'refold[ing] the dressing-gown round his body' (HD 52). 'What are you doing?' he calls to his mother, 'I've more or less gone to bed' – an interestingly ambiguous remark to which Stella responds by bringing in the coffee and joining him on the sofa, sitting by his feet. 'Now we're in the same boat', Roderick remarks. 'What? – how?' his mother says, 'starting', as if there is something troubling or bizarre in the idea, which Roderick immediately repeats: 'This is like being opposite one another in a boat on a river.' *'Have we ever been in a boat on a river – have we?'* Stella replies, which seems a strange question for a mother to put to her son (HD 52–3).

The image of mother and son on a sofa – a sofa that may also be a bed, or a boat – commands a distinguished place in Bowen's writing as an eloquent and sometimes very elaborate metaphor for the state of the relationship obtaining between the two people thus pictured. A couple of examples from Bowen's first novel *The Hotel* display striking tonal similarities to the scene in Stella's flat. In the first, the occasion of the conversation between Mrs Kerr and her son about Ronald's experience of Germany, we may notice a sense of virtually erotic anticipation in mother and son alike, for

> the novelty of being together made each seeking out of one another unique. A meeting was in the nature of a rendezvous, and the *mise en scène* queerly important. The isolation of rendezvous made indifferent such publicity as that of a bench, a waiting-room, or this rigid sofa pasted square to the wall of a [hotel] drawing-room. As they sat here, Ronald exulted. (H 105)

But in light of Mrs Kerr's by now well-documented commitment to separation it will come as no surprise that this indefinite spectre of sexual possibility never materialises, and subsequent episodes upon the sofa instead showcase Mrs Kerr's attempts to encourage her son to leave her. Towards the end of the novel, and seated, this time, upon the sofa in her hotel bedroom, 'I don't begin to be lonely just yet', Mrs Kerr reassures Ronald; '"– here's such a charming letter, an invitation, from those Emmerys in Paris [. . .] So you, my dear, can run away to Sicily." She tugged gently at a fold of her tea-gown on which he happened to be sitting and swept him away from her with a gesture, as though he were a little boy again and she were sending him off to bed' (H 189).

For Roderick, too, the early promise of the sofa-bed in Stella's spectral bordello gives way all too swiftly to the deflations and disappointments of separation. 'The reality of the fancy' – Roderick's conceit that he and his mother are together in a boat –

> was better than the unreality of the room. In a boat you were happy to be suspended in nothing but light, air, water, opposite another face. On a sofa you could be surrounded by what was lacking. Though this particular sofa backed on a wall and stood on a carpet, it was without environment; it might have been some derelict piece of furniture exposed on a pavement after an air raid or washed up by a flood on some unknown shore. (H 54–5)

Well may he feel that '[h]is return to his mother cried out for something better' (H 55).

And yet, even as the passage seems to insist upon the reality of separation, Bowen's metaphors call up the very vision of dyadic union that they seem designed to see off. Certainly we may recognise in the picture of a 'derelict piece of furniture exposed on a pavement after an air raid' a desolate interlude in the conflict triggered by separation; indeed, as it refers to civilian experiences of the Second World War, we might judge that the image comprehends also the adamant critique of paternal failure that we have seen to be central to the 'trauma plot' of *The Heat of the Day*. But with the metamorphosis of the air raid into a flood, and of the pavement into 'some unknown shore', the sofa of separation transmutes into Noah's Ark, the vessel constructed at God's command to ensure the survival of the righteous and thereby maintain, affirm and enhance the bond between Noah and his creator. The image might thus remind us of one of the pictures on the walls of Elizabeth's nursery at 15 Herbert Place, the scene of 'a baby in a wooden cradle float[ing] smilingly on an immense flood, stretching out its two hands to a guardian cat that sat upright on the quilt at the cradle's foot'

(SW 472). Previously, I linked this uncanny nursery picture to the story of Moses, and argued that its troubling vision of abandonment incorporates an at least equally powerful fantasy of dyadic harmony. We may now enhance our understanding of the painting, and of Bowen's zoological lexicon, by identifying the precise symbolic charge of that 'guardian cat'. We have seen that the child who seeks to elude separation is often compared to a monkey. I want now to specify that the maternal counterpart of the monkey – the mother who precedes, denies or resists separation – is often envisaged as a cat, a cat stationed upon an ambiguous piece of furniture – sofa, cradle, mother's bed. In 'Ivy Gripped the Steps', Gavin's second visit to Southstone begins with Lilian's collecting of him, at midwinter, from the station; it is the visit devoted, on his hostess's part, to the systematic revocation of the separation that Gavin, too, would wish to deny. After their drive home in the cold, they ascend to the hot, scented drawing-room. '[Mrs Nicholson] dropped her muff on the sofa, and Gavin', who has been fantasising about her incessantly for months, 'stroked it – "It's like a cat," he said quickly, as she turned round. "Shall I have a cat?" she said. "Would you like me to have a cat?"' (I 698). The sexual imagination suggested in this scene is startling: it at once contrasts and conflates Mrs Nicholson's pussy and a little boy's pet.

Strikingly different in tone yet if possible even more emotionally charged is Bowen's use of the trope to envisage her own mother in the earliest months of Florence's first pregnancy; we will need to recall, at this point, that Florence and Henry assumed that their child would be a boy, and that they would christen him Robert – although in the event the baby would prove to be a girl, Elizabeth. As through the eyes of a Mrs Gates, a close family friend, *Bowen's Court* presents its reader with the joyful scene of Florence Bowen meditating upon the birth to come, 'elated and serious, on the drawing-room sofa, with her Persian cat Tory (after Queen Victoria) curled up in her skirts: she was eating her way through a large number of raisins, which she had been told would be good for Robert and her' (BC 404). Surely the *ne plus ultra* of Bowen's representations of a perfect original union, and a profoundly humorous creation to boot, the image of Florence, Robert and Tory on the sofa mischievously evokes the composite iconography of the Trinity to rework it in emphatically maternal and domestic terms: Mother-to-be, unborn Son and feline Ghost. The picture of a paternal God upon his throne is thus conjured up only to be at once displaced by a vision of a fertility goddess upon a drawing-room sofa, for the scene calls to mind medieval portrayals of the pregnant Madonna (the 'Madonna del Parto'), and achieves, moreover, a comparison of that resplendent icon of semi-pagan maternity with the ultra-respectable figure of a prolific British queen, the bourgeois Great Mother of the Victorian nineteenth century. Into the bargain, the virtual visual ensemble manages to suggest that both the Empress of India and the Mother of God are, in the nicest possible way, right old cats.

We take a moment to observe that Stella Rodney will be companioned, during her final appearance in *The Heat of the Day*, by a cat which she is trying to comfort in an air-raid – and then return to the late-night scene in the Weymouth Street flat of Roderick on the sofa with his mother. I have drawn attention to the incestuous quality of the scene, which supports an account of Stella as a mother who has not separated herself from her child: I want now to highlight Stella's extraordinary hostility towards the paternal pretensions of both her son and her lover in this scene, a symbolic violence which constitutes, I think, conclusive evidence of the psychotic component of Mrs Rodney, the version or 'plot' of Stella, as it were, that cannot be understood in the context of the separation trauma story. This will in consequence allow us to return to the figure of Robert Kelway with a more complete view of his characterological and motivational duality.

Naked except for Robert's dressing-gown, and beginning to manifest signs of a cold, Roderick searches beneath the sofa cushions for a handkerchief; finding nothing,

> [h]e dived his hand into the slippery pocket of the dressing-gown; in which, audibly, it came upon at least *something*. Stella and he both heard the tired crackle of paper – paper long ago

folded, pulped by age in its folds, limp from being in silk near a body's warmth. The sound from that pocket of Robert's made Stella start: her eyes, with an uncontrollable vehemence, interrogated her son's. 'Correspondence?' Roderick vaguely said: he fished out the paper, lay holding and staring at it, noncommittally twiddled it round and round. (HD 62)

The first thing to notice about this scene is that it is doubly figurative. For a start, it explores, from a cognitive position implicitly sympathetic to Stella, the question of Roderick's attitude towards his mother's sexuality. 'Up to now, with that evasiveness a division between any two loves makes natural, [Stella] had never come to the point of asking herself what Roderick thought, or did not think, of herself and Robert' (HD 63). The episode thus evokes a scene of sexual education in a familial context; Roderick is like a young child scrutinising his parents' relationship.

Like an ignorant looker-on at some famous game, trying to grasp the score and get the hang of the rules, [Roderick] was watching to see what she would now do – expecting, evidently, to learn how far the prerogative of love went. He was waiting to see if this paper from Robert's pocket did count, was to be counted, as also hers. (HD 62)

Linked to this is the question, of course, of Roderick's own sexuality and its proper place in relation to his mother: as he 'fishe[s] out the paper' and '[lies] holding and staring at it, noncommittally twiddl[ing] it round and round', he looks very much like a little boy experimentally masturbating, exploring the sexual capability of his body in a way that seems imaginatively authorised by the idea of his father's penis, and not too absorbed in the interesting sensations to keep half an eye on his mother's reaction to his behaviour. Thus Stella's immediate response – '"It's not yours," she sharply said. "Put it back"' – seems fully in accordance with the mother of the separation story. Father is allowed to enjoy his penis in Mother's presence, but Baby certainly isn't.

At the same time, the passage investigates Stella's feelings in relation to Harrison's claim that her lover is spying for the enemy. The paper may constitute evidence of Robert's treachery, which is, of course, the other way of explaining Stella's reaction to Roderick's inadvertent discovery of it. Stella loves Robert: of course she wants him to be safe, and so, as Roderick suggests to her that she should, she takes charge of the paper from her son. It is at this point that we may observe the displacement of one maternal figure by another – the displacement, that is, of the mother who weans by the mother who does not wean: Stella, no longer protective of the symbol of her lover's virility but 'terrified of the paper' (HD 63), 'ma[kes] ready to tear it up' (HD 62). For the figure of Father, so welcome to the mother who weans, represents to the mother who does *not* wean the necessity of the separation that she sets herself against; and as we have established, Robert's passing of state secrets to the Third Reich expresses precisely his yearning for a plausible instantiation of paternal authority – in the world, in his family, and in his mind. If Roderick has located the fascist phallus in the pocket of Robert's dressing-gown, the mother of the psychosis plot will want to destroy it immediately. As if sensing the threat to Robert, and the threat to himself that such a threat would represent, Roderick now becomes increasingly concerned with the possible value of the paper – '[I]sn't what Robert's at quite important?' he asks (HD 62) – while Stella, in contrast, seeks to deny the paper's significance: 'It can't be anything much', she says. 'I am sure', her son tells her, 'you ought to have a look at it.' 'Are you?' she says 'derisively' – a word of which the reader may subsequently be reminded by the description of Mr Kelway's 'derisory' existence at Holme Dene. '[A]ware of Roderick's eyes upon her', Stella 'hold[s] the twice-folded paper, dingy along its edges, pincer-nipped between her fingers and thumbs': again we see the likeness of Delilah's castrating hand (HD 62). Shortly after this she 'unfold[s] the sheet of paper' and

>glanc[es] through what was written on it in a semi-abstracted, calm, quite businesslike way. 'Nothing at all,' she said, 'as we might have known.' Idly, she tore it across once, still more idly

tore it across again, then stood up to brush the pieces from her dress to the floor. (HD 64)

Stella's ruthless assault on this symbol of her lover's paternal authority recalls not only Muttikins's supposed 'castration' of the hapless Mr Kelway but, in an even closer parallel, Mrs Kelway's furious rejection of Robert's masculinity too, as when, in the final display of Kelway family values at Holme Dene, she indicates her outrage in face of her son's attempt to assume the symbolic role of Father. 'Again [Robert] had taken up his stand – this time, it might really be, ominously – on the rug between his sister and mother': it is a literal enactment of triangulation, Robert intervening in the maternal dyad figured here by Muttikins and another of her children, Ernestine. 'He had placed himself' – as his own father had signally failed to do –

> where it was impossible not to see him; and Mrs Kelway, admitting this, glanced his way – as unflinchingly as if he had drawn a gun. She appeared to measure his height, from the feet up. Then: 'He talks like a man,' she said, contracting her little shoulders. (HD 261)

In light of the double identity of Stella and of Muttikins, each woman figuring both the mother who imposes separation and the mother who refuses it, and in light also of the incommensurate co-existence, in *The Heat of the Day*, of a story about separation trauma and a story about psychosis, we may now return to the figure of Robert Kelway, and to the final episode of his life, in order to articulate explicitly the version of this character and of his end that diverges radically, though not symmetrically, from the account that I have given of the centrality of paternal deficit in this fictional subject's experience. For the scene of the lovers' ultimate tryst illustrates a truly remarkable duality in Robert's feelings, motivations and behaviour. Hurrying away from Holme Dene, the horrible lair of the mother who has imposed separation, Robert seeks out Stella – another mother who imposes separation – and affirms to her, for the first time, his allegiance to the symbolic law that

Nazism, in his eyes, appears to approximate or prefigure. Here is Robert in character as any child after the inevitable, indeed necessary, trauma of separation. Yet at the same time, Robert's behaviour in these last moments of his life may be read as a demonstration, not of his traumatisation by separation, but of his total inexperience of it: for as we have noted, in the context of Roderick's late-night visit to his mother's flat, sex with Stella is strongly associated with unbroken dyadic union. Thus Robert's hurling of himself into bed in the Weymouth Street flat looks like a virtual continuation of breastfeeding, and highlights the psychotic aspect of both Stella and Muttikins, mothers who will not impose separation. The meaning of Robert's demise is equally equivocal, or double. As if failed by Father Fascism, the Robert who has experienced separation either falls or leaps to his death in a last-ditch attempt to elude the loathed grasp of his abhorred mamma; this death is Father's fault. But the Robert who has not experienced separation is both literally and metaphorically fucked by the 'mother' of the original dyad and consequently sleepwalks to oblivion through a trap-door in Stella's roof: this death is Mother's fault, although it is not so much a death as it is a failing to die, which is to say, a failing to live. 'I do want to make it, I want to make it', Robert tells Stella in the moments before he exits through the landing skylight; 'my ideas, you know, are too good to be merely died for: they want life' (HD 288). It is a hopeful voice, but not, I think, a delusional one; the voice, I would suggest, of a weaned child who has begun to experience, or to believe in the possibility of experiencing, the transformative détente with reality that may be brought about by the intervention of symbolic law. But when, half a page later, Stella asks: 'Where are you expecting to get down again?' Robert's response shows no trace of the nascent capacity for realism that he had displayed just moments before. Here again is the child of the unbroken dyad. 'He repeated: "I want to go by the roof – I don't want to run out; I want you to send me off"' (HD 289). And so she does, at once the mother who brings death into the baby's world, and the mother whose perfect original love guarantees her infant's immortality.

## Notes

1. Bowen, *Seven Winters*, p. 465; hereafter cited as SW.
2. Chapter 3 explores in detail the circumstances of Elizabeth's birth. The crucial fact in the present context is that Florence and Henry Bowen expected their first child to be a boy, whom they intended to call Robert, an established family name.
3. Gildersleeve, *Elizabeth Bowen and the Writing of Trauma*, p. 3.
4. Bowen, *The Hotel*, pp. 14, 143; hereafter cited as H.
5. Bowen, *The House in Paris*, p. 20; hereafter cited as HP.
6. Many of Bowen's texts select a specific flower as a trope to be repeated, reworked and reviewed. Maud Ellmann has drawn attention to the way in which, in *The House in Paris*, 'violets are linked to loss and death', and 'intertwine the characters into a complicity beyond their knowledge or control' (Ellmann, *Elizabeth Bowen: The Shadow Across the Page*, pp. 122, 98).
7. Ellmann, *Elizabeth Bowen: The Shadow Across the Page*, p. 73.
8. Rau, 'Telling it Straight'. Cullingford, '"Something else"'.
9. Cullingford, '"Something else"', p. 280; Rau, 'Telling it Straight', p. 217.
10. Rau, 'Telling it Straight', p. 224.
11. Cullingford, '"Something else"', p. 281.
12. Rau, 'Telling it Straight', p. 224.
13. Gildersleeve, *Elizabeth Bowen and the Writing of Trauma*, p. 62.
14. R. B. Kershner, Jr. describes this novel as '[a] dream narrative masquerading as bourgeois realism', which doesn't take into account Ray Forrestier's role as a figure of developmental and generic transformation but nonetheless captures well the almost hallucinatory quality of those parts of the text dominated by the mother of the dyad; he characterises it also as Bowen's 'most *primary* novel' (Kershner, 'Bowen's Oneiric *House in Paris*', pp. 411, 407).
15. Corcoran, *Elizabeth Bowen: The Enforced Return*, p. 100.
16. Gildersleeve, *Elizabeth Bowen and the Writing of Trauma*, p. 30.

17. The form of Sydney's unwilling redemption should give us confidence in relation to the future that awaits Henrietta Mountjoy with Mrs Arbuthnot in Mentone. 'Henrietta', Bowen's narrator tells us, 'trusted her grandmother breathlessly, as one must trust the driver on the Cornici road' (HP 20). This implies that Mrs Arbuthnot will be able to father her granddaughter, a crucial capacity given Colonel Mountjoy's paternal inadequacy, which paradoxically poses more of a threat to Henrietta's development than does the death of her mother. I explore the coincidence of paternal failure and maternal death in the second section of this chapter.
18. Nicola Darwood's recognition that the return journey to the Hotel features for Sydney a 'moment of anagnorisis' is a rare exception; she does not however explore the episode in any depth (Darwood, *A World of Lost Innocence*, p. 21).
19. Bennett, 'Bowen's Modernism: The Early Novels', p. 33. Mooney, 'Unstable Compounds: Bowen's Beckettian Affinities'p. 240.
20. Ellmann, *Elizabeth Bowen: The Shadow Across the Page*, p. 77.
21. Bowen, 'Ivy Gripped the Steps', p. 688; hereafter cited as I.
22. Bowen, *Pictures and Conversations*, p. 47; hereafter cited as PC.
23. Gavin's new 'schoolboy state' is advertised, on his person, by the replacement of his hitherto customary 'sailor blouse' by a Norfolk jacket (I 703), a costume change that might remind us both of Casabianca's death on his father's ship and of Ray Forrestier's determination to replace with 'a civilian cap' the flamboyant headgear sported by his step-son: 'Leopold had in blazing gold round his cap the fierce name of a battleship' (HP 249–50). In Leopold's case, the little boy's aping of nautical heroism is at once disallowed and rendered gratefully redundant by the hoving into view of an authentic paternal commander, Ray – a role that, on the occasion of Gavin's third visit to Southstone, seems again to fall to Admiral Concannon, after the fiasco of Massingham's failure to squire Mrs Nicholson to the Concannons' dinner party.
24. Bowen, 'The Visitor', p. 128; hereafter cited as V.
25. For more on '[t]he many clocks of Bowen's fiction', see Gildersleeve, *Elizabeth Bowen and the Writing of Trauma*, p. 64.

26. Bowen, 'Coming Home', p. 96; hereafter cited as CH.
27. Bowen, *The Heat of the Day*, p. 26; hereafter cited as HD.
28. We have noted in the Introduction that Bowen herself sought psychological help for a speech impediment: on 3 December 1941 her lover Charles Ritchie noted in his diary that Bowen 'is going to a psychoanalyst to be cured of her stammer which is so much part of her' (Bowen and Ritchie, *Love's Civil War*, p. 26).
29. As Elizabeth Cullingford remarks, 'the comparison of Mrs Kerr to Rossetti's painting of a dead woman (his wife Elizabeth Siddal) used as a model for another dead woman (Dante's Beatrice) suggests that in Ronald's case the normal progress of the Oedipus complex has become pathologically frozen' (Cullingford, '"Something else"', p. 282).
30. Neil Corcoran notes of *The Demon Lover and Other Stories* (1945) that '[t]here is [. . .] some suggestion [. . .] that the First World War persists under the surface of the Second in something of the way in which the origins of sexual neurosis persist in these stories too, a suggestion that the culture itself, as well as individual psychologies, is trapped in a repetitive or serial pattern' (Corcoran, *Elizabeth Bowen: The Enforced Return*, p. 157). The notion of a series, in particular, nicely captures the non-identical nature of, on the one hand, the necessary trauma of separation and, on the other, its abnormal continuation and consolidation in the absence of paternal confirmation. Vera Kreilkamp makes a similar point about the association in Bowen's work of the First World War with the ghostly: 'For Bowen, the First World War exists not only as a dislocating break with the past, but as the century's recurring source of the dead, the maimed and ghostly undead' – although this formulation doesn't allow that Bowen's work might ever entertain the historical possibility of the First World War's political redemption, an outcome that is, I think, at least gestured towards by the exhilarating resolution of the Sydney story in *The Hotel* (Kreilkamp, 'Bowen: Ascendancy Modernist', p. 19). For more on Bowen's perception of the Second World War as a reliving or recurrence of the First World War, see Jordan, *How Will the Heart Endure?*, p. 133 and

Gildersleeve, *Elizabeth Bowen and the Writing of Trauma*, pp. 16–17.
31. In the context of a novel in which war with Germany functions as an allegory of the conflict between a baby and the mother who weans it, the figurative aspect of the term 'home front' rewards attention.
32. To Neil Corcoran, for example, 'her name makes her a bright particular star: she is explicitly a highly independent woman, a cosmopolitan sophisticate and linguist, beautiful and capable' (Corcoran, *Elizabeth Bowen: The Enforced Return*, p. 179); while Jacqueline Rose's confession of her wholesale identification with Stella appears rather to acknowledge the putative problem, in a politically responsible reader, of an all-too-human predilection for Love than to raise any questions about the nature of the novel's primary female protagonist: 'the main problem with *The Heat of the Day* is that, so deep is the reader's sympathy with the romance of the central woman character, Stella, that he or she is in danger, like Stella herself, first of not believing and then frankly not caring that her lover, Robert, might be – as he indeed turns out to be – a Nazi spy' (Rose, 'Bizarre Objects: Hallucination and Modernism', p. 91). Perhaps the most critically consequential of such unquestioning infatuations with Mrs Rodney is Barbara Bellow Watson's: her striking and under-appreciated reading of *The Heat of the Day* as a modern war-time *Hamlet* is damaged at its core by her identification of 'the Hamlet-figure' as Stella, whom she commends as 'a character [. . .] seldom met in fiction: an intelligent, attractive woman about forty, ladylike and thoughtful, not a prude, not a snob' (Watson, 'Variations on an Enigma: Elizabeth Bowen's War Novel', p. 85). Watson notes that Roderick 'might pun as Hamlet does on being too much in the sun. He has a dead father, a kind of stepfather in Robert, and [. . .] becomes a cousin's heir', and – in an exquisitely persuasive detail – that Roderick and the house he inherits are associated with references to a mousetrap (93): but if Roderick is Hamlet – which makes, I think, magnificent sense: although I would want to add that the role of the inadequately fathered son is, in Bowen's

novel, a composite part, performed by the several men who stand in relation to Stella as to their own mothers – then the much-admired queen of Bowen's novel will have to be identified with the faithless self-serving Gertrude, a step that Watson seems unable to take.

# Chapter 2
# Sexuality

On 6 December 1921 the Anglo-Irish Treaty was signed in London by representatives of the British government and of the self-proclaimed Irish Republic. The Treaty brought to a conclusion the Irish War of Independence by providing for the establishment of the Irish Free State, a self-governing dominion within the British Empire. In addition it allowed Northern Ireland to opt out of the Irish Free State – an option which was promptly exercised. Although the Treaty was narrowly ratified by the Dáil Éireann, the de facto Republic's legislative assembly, it was followed, as we read in *Bowen's Court*, 'by the disintegrations of Civil War – the dissentients to the treaty, Republicans, in arms against the Free Staters who had accepted it' (BC 440). In the summer of 1922, 'Republican forces, moving west across County Cork [. . .] established themselves in Mitchelstown Castle, decided not to defend it, burned the castle the evening they moved out. Bowen's Court lay next on the route west: seventy Republicans occupied it' (BC 440–1). The 'guests', as Bowen calls them, with a barely inflected irony, 'were not unexpected', so although Henry Bowen and his second wife, Mary, were away in Dublin, 'those in charge of the house had already done what they could by the time the Republicans marched up the avenue. The family portraits [. . .] left the house in a hurry, for the first time, for a sojourn in a cottage at the end of the woods. Other valuables followed them. The Republicans came in to meet cautious faces, emptied cabinets, bare walls' (BC 441). The occupying forces demonstrated their readiness to defend themselves in their new redoubt, 'los[ing] no time in mining the lower avenue' and 'also ma[king] preparations to blow the house up, in case of surprise attack' (BC 441). But according to Bowen's account their subsequent activities were limited to a daily reconnaissance of the local area, the men apparently being detained at home by the welcome domestic facilities of Bowen's Court, notwithstanding the markedly austere character of the house in its defensively prepared state.

> If the house had never had more numerous, it had also never had quieter visitors. Even prejudice allows it that they behaved like lambs. The young men – they were mostly very young men – were very tired. The bedding was gone from the few beds; the leaders lay on the springs, the others lay on the floor [...] When the men woke up, they read. They were great readers, and especially were they attracted by the works of Kipling: a complete set of these, in flexible scarlet leather, with gilt elephants' heads, had been given to Mary, and were available. (BC 441–2)

The occupation lasted barely four days before it was abruptly terminated by the arrival at the house of Elizabeth Bowen's Aunt Sarah, who wished to break the journey from Cork to her home in Mitchelstown with an overnight stay at Bowen's Court. Informed by the housekeeper that the Republicans were in possession 'and that she had better fly', Aunt Sarah 'replied that that was nonsense: this was her brother's house'. The Republican forces being out, Aunt Sarah, 'entering with her usual firmness', 'ordered that her room should be got ready [and] made an inspection of the house' (BC 442).

> She did not, she admits, find things in a bad state: propriety seemed to have governed everyone's habits. Nothing had been 'commandeered' but the keys – and in some cases the locks – of all the presses, and, though this only appeared later, a pair of leather gaiters of Henry VI's.[1] Aunt Sarah went round picking up the volumes of Kipling that lay face down on the floors or beside the beds. She then sat down to consider, to the last phrase, exactly what she should say to the Republicans. But they never came back. (BC 442–3)

'For what reason', Bowen writes, 'and where they went next, I do not know, and suppose that I never shall', although she notes her aunt's opinion that, when the Republicans heard of her arrival, 'the "nice feeling" she did not cease to attribute to Irishmen deterred them from return' (BC 443).

Thus restored to the Bowens, the house would survive the death of Henry Bowen in 1930 and pass into the hands of Elizabeth, an event that she describes, with a distinctly warning note, at the beginning of the 1963 Afterword to *Bowen's Court*. (The book as first published in 1942 had concluded with a description of Henry's funeral.) 'I was the first woman heir', Bowen emphasises; 'already I had changed my father's name for my husband's. We had no children' (BC 448). Nonetheless she reports that she and her husband Alan Cameron were committed to maintaining Bowen's Court and to spending as much time there as was compatible with Cameron's working life in England, and that, upon his retirement, the couple left England in January 1952 to live year-round at Bowen's Court. But in August 1952 Alan Cameron died suddenly, leaving Elizabeth to try 'to carry on the place, and the life which went with it there, alone' (BC 458). This proved impossible, and by 1959, Bowen writes, 'it had become inevitable that I should sell Bowen's Court' (BC 459).

> The buyer was a County Cork man, a neighbour. He already was farming tracts of land, and had the means wherewith to develop mine, and horses to put in the stables. It cheered me also to think that his handsome children would soon be running about the rooms – for it was, I believe, his honest intention, when first he bought the place from me, to inhabit the house. But in the end he did not find that practicable, and who is to blame him? He thought at one time, I understand, of compromising by taking off the top storey (I am glad he did not). Finally, he decided that there was nothing for it but to demolish the house entirely. So it was done. (BC 459)

'Loss has not been entire', however, Bowen claims in the final paragraph of her Afterword: 'When I think of Bowen's Court, there it is. And when others who knew it think of it, there it is, also', an assertion which includes the readers of Bowen's historical narrative in the circle of people in whose minds the house continues to live in spite of its material eradication, for the book begins, as Bowen points out here, with a room-to-room description of Bowen's Court left, in the 1963 reissue of the text, defiantly in the present tense. 'I can only say', Bowen writes in her Afterword, 'that *I* saw no reason to transpose it into the past. There is a sort of perpetuity about livingness, and it is part of the character of Bowen's Court to be, in sometimes its silent way, very much alive' (BC 459).

It is a resounding claim with which to conclude the book, an affirmation of the text's power to preserve and transmit to the future the legacy that Elizabeth Bowen had been unable to secure as a real material presence in the landscape of County Cork. And yet the image of a transcendent Bowen's Court, unharmed and intact, does not entirely obliterate from the mind's eye of the reader a vivid vision of the house as a prime potential target of the kind of politically motivated immolation which destroyed Mitchelstown Castle in 1922 and which figures prominently also in Bowen's view of the 1921 War of Independence. 'Between the armed Irish and the British troops in the country', Bowen writes of this slightly earlier period of conflict,

> reprisals and counter-reprisals – tragic policy – raged. Fire followed shootings, then fires fires. In the same spring night in 1921, three Anglo-Irish houses in our immediate neighbourhood – Rockmills, Ballywalter, Convamore – were burnt by the Irish. The British riposted by burning, still nearer Bowen's Court, the farms of putative Sinn Feiners – some of whom had been our family's friends. What now? (BC 439)

In Elizabeth Bowen's telling of the tale, Henry Bowen immediately warns his daughter to expect the worst. '"I am afraid,"' he wrote to Elizabeth – then in Italy – '"that, as things are now, there can only be one other development. You must be prepared for the next news, and be brave. I will write at once." I read his letter', Elizabeth notes, 'beside Lake Como, and, looking at the blue water, taught myself to imagine Bowen's Court in flames' (BC 440). In the event, 'Bowen's Court stayed untouched' (BC 440) – as it would survive also its subsequent occupation by Republican forces in the summer of 1922. But the image of the house in flames figures repeatedly in Bowen's fictional texts, its claim upon her imagination contesting the mental predominance of the inviolate Bowen's Court of cherished memory. Indeed in her 1952 Preface to *The Last September* (1929), a novel set during the War of Independence and concluding with the torching, by Republican forces, of three fictional houses, including one modelled on Bowen's Court, Bowen ascribes an overweening emotional primacy to the projected vision of her home on fire, a fantasy whose power is unaffected by the writer's recognition of the real building's survival of the political violence of the early 1920s. 'I [was] the child of the house from which Danielstown derives', she writes: 'Bowen's Court survived – nevertheless, so often in my mind's eye did I see it burning that the terrible last event in *The Last September* is more real than anything I have lived through.'[2]

My primary interpretative contention in this chapter is that the image of the Big House, or 'place', as Bowen often calls it – which is to say, the large country residence of an Anglo-Irish landowning family – plays a central role in the representation of Bowen's understanding of sexuality. Across a wide range of Bowen's fictional and nonfictional works, the Big House figures as an object of desire in relation to which the sexualities of adults in its vicinity are expressed, negotiated and sustained. The Big House is invariably imbued in Bowen's texts with a maternal quality, because the object of any Bowen character's heart's desire is Mother, in one form or another. The *nature* of that form – the specific version or iteration of Mother that is embodied by the beloved – indicates the particular *structure* of the sexuality that is organised in relation to it. That is to say, Bowen explores, and carefully differentiates between, on the one hand, a sexuality that perpetuates or reproduces the two-person logic of the mother-baby dyad, and, on the other, a triangulated formation of desire, in which a sexual subject is constituted in relation to a maternal object mediated by paternal authority. Therefore it will always be crucial to ask about the precise nature of the maternal original whom any beloved evokes or recalls. Is she the mother of the dyad, or the mother of the triangle? From the point of view of the lover, that is to say, is the beloved the totality of the world (a two-person model), or is she – however resentfully or reluctantly – perceived in relation to a third person, a figure of paternal control?[3]

We may make out with particular clarity the maternal identity of the Big House in the second of the previous vignettes – the story of the accession of Bowen's Court to Elizabeth after her father's death in 1930, and, after the death of Elizabeth's husband in 1952, of the house's purchase and ultimate destruction by the 'County Cork man'. We may observe also that in this example access to the desirable object is crucially facilitated by father-like figures of authority. The feminine character of Bowen's Court is established at first through a parallel with the dependent figure of its 'first woman heir', who, 'already [having] changed [her] father's name for [her] husband's', characterises herself here as an object of exchange between men, her filial and her marital identities alike registering her subordination to a system of patriarchal law, in which context her succession to the family property seems like an unaccountable anomaly or even a mistake. The death of Alan Cameron thus poses an equal and almost structurally identical threat to Bowen's Court and to Mrs Alan Cameron, as the house's female proprietor is apparently no more able to maintain the property without her husband's support than would the house be able to maintain itself in the absence of an owner, a predicament to which, in this passage, Elizabeth Bowen's tenure seems closely to approximate. As if in an attempt to rescue herself, then, from the haplessness of widowhood, as much as to ensure the future of Bowen's Court, Bowen relinquishes the family home to the virile proprietorship of the 'County Cork man' whose paternal credentials are patent: 'He already was farming tracts of land, and had the means wherewith to develop mine, and horses to put in the stables', and boasts, moreover, a plenitude of 'handsome children' whom Bowen is 'cheered' to imagine 'running about the rooms' (BC 459). Bowen's narrative stays silent on the subject of this man's marital status, presenting him and his children without mention of a wife or mother, so that the transfer of the house to his possession can figure as a kind of second marriage, Bowen's Court now assuming a role of stepmaternal nurture to the children of her new master and anticipating, in turn, the benevolent and fertilising consequences of his good husbandry. If it is shocking that the ultimate exercise of the County Cork man's marital prerogative takes the form of a complete demolition of the building, it is nonetheless an unambiguously lawful act, decided upon after careful deliberation and executed, it is implied, in an orderly and competent fashion. In fact I think we may understand his erasure of the house from material reality as an arresting instance of paternal prohibition, an act, as we have seen in Chapter 1, whose counterintuitive effect is to restore and renew the symbolic vitality of the maternal object. The 'perpetuity [of] livingness' claimed – in the edition of 1963 – for the ancestral dwelling-place at the centre of *Bowen's Court* is thus achieved not in spite of the building's destruction but with the help of it, the house's literal eradication the paradoxical condition of its symbolic transcendence.

Chapter 2 is composed of two sections, a design that reflects what Bowen's work characterises as an important difference between the structure of experience in the dyad and the structure of experience in the triangle. As we will recall from our exploration of psychological development in Chapter 1, it is a difference brought about not by the mother's institution of separation, which, notwithstanding the distress that it causes her child, leaves the two-person structure of the dyad intact, but rather by the subsequent intervention onto the scene of a third person by whose authority the child's possession of Mother is simultaneously prohibited for good and, by that very token, symbolically restored. In the first half of this chapter I shall concern myself with the latter of these psychical formations, exploring

Bowen's understanding of triangulated sexuality. I shall begin by identifying as a key feature of Bowen's account the characterisation of triangulated sexuality as an *affair of roles*: two active (Mother and Father) and one passive or spectatorial (Child). Bowen is greatly interested in adolescence, the period or point of maturation at which the child who has been accustomed to accept his or her exclusion from the sexual interplay of Mother and Father may exchange for a spectatorial role an active part in the adult drama.

The first of the vignettes of Bowen's Court – the account of the house's occupation by Republican forces in 1921 – suggests exactly such a role-related or theatrical conceptualisation of triangulated sexuality, and focuses on the transition, at adolescence, from the playing of a passive to that of an active part in the drama of desire. The triangular context of the episode is clear from the start. Although the master is absent from the house, he has left it well protected by staff who ensure that all the valuable, sensitive contents of the building are safely stowed elsewhere before the arrival of the Republicans; we may recognise another effective agent of Henry Bowen's authority in the figure of Aunt Sarah, too. Correspondingly, although the Republicans' initial intimation of violence may briefly raise the spectre of the volatility of the dyad after separation, their subsequent behaviour in relation to the maternal body of the Big House bespeaks a 'lamb'-like acceptance of the paternal mandate: 'propriety [. . .] governed everyone's habits' (BC 443) and the men's marked devotion to Kipling suggests an enthusiastic investment in the cultural products and imaginative infrastructure of the patriarchal British Empire. In this case, however, the fighters' attempt to assume the powers and responsibilities of Father in relation to the precious maternal place – in Bowen's view, an instance of the standard task of adolescence – is doomed to failure on account of the young men's immaturity. '[T]hey were mostly *very* young men' (BC 441; my italics) and the scene of their mass going-to-bed conjures an image of the house as an impromptu orphanage or school boarding house for a group of rag-tag but lovable urchins. Thus notwithstanding their seizure of the locks and keys of the presses, and of Henry's leather gaiters, the Republican forces prove simply too young to penetrate the inner recesses of Bowen's Court – too young to persuasively don the paternal trousers.

A striking feature of Bowen's thinking that will be apparent throughout the first half of Chapter 2 is the extent to which she entertains a sanguine view of triangulated sexuality: by undertaking, at adolescence, a father-like sexual role, a teenager can be confident of securing a beloved who evokes the mother of the triangle. It is a notably egalitarian account with respect to the question of biological sex: in Bowen's imaginative worlds it is demonstrably possible for girls as well as boys to play the father's part in the essentially theatrical affair of sexuality, to assume, at adolescence, the paternal trousers and by so doing to take possession of the beloved maternal object. The feminine counterpart to this masculine role is in principle equally effective, and it, too, is available to both the male and the female teenagers of Bowen's texts (as we will note with reference to the question of Laurence's gender in *The Last September*). Like the masculine part, the feminine role is in essence dramatic, or theatrical, constituted as the enactment and re-enactment of a performance observed in childhood; and as when male or female adolescents seek to play the masculine part, so too the feminine role is undertaken with the aim of procuring access to the beloved object. But in both cases the beloved object is the mother of the triangle, Father's wife, and the very fact of this identical aim results in a radical difference between the internal structures, if not the imaginative operation, of the two roles. For whereas to assume the masculine part is to take possession of a representation of Mother in the form of a beloved other, for the subject who plays the feminine role the beloved object will materialise *in and as the self*. To play Mother is to function as a representation of one's own beloved, becoming at once the object as well as the subject of one's own desire. Success in the role is not possible without the creative collaboration of Father, whose recognition of Mother in the person of his leading lady is crucial in bringing about that phantasmatic transformation. I will attempt, with reference to *Friends and Relations* (1931) and *The Last September*, a much more substantial explication of the relationship between the feminine role and its masculine counterpart in triangulated sexuality. However, I want at this early moment to signal the exceptional elements of Bowen's thinking about sexuality by acknowledging the striking difficulty of articulating in abstract terms the imaginative operation of triangulated feminine desire as it is explored in the fictional experience of such characters as Lois Farquhar. For the now long-established and widely disseminated language and basic theoretical principles of psychoanalysis will have accustomed literary scholars to the characterisation of a mature masculinity in terms of the playing of a paternal role; though lively and in its own way distinctive, there is likely to be little that is conceptually surprising in the story – to take one example – of the young Republicans' attempt to assume Henry Bowen's leather gaiters. In marked contrast we will need to acknowledge head-on the intellectual challenge posed by Bowen's understanding of triangulated *feminine* sexuality, for the conceptual logic that implicitly underwrites Bowen's explorations of adult feminine desire will show itself immediately as unfamiliar, to say the least. While it is fully commensurable with established psychoanalytic accounts it is not reducible to any existing formulation, or combination of existing ideas. The account of triangulated sexuality that is implicit in Bowen's writing offers us idiosyncratic new ways of thinking about feminine desire in the realm of symbolic law.

In Section Two I shall turn from Bowen's analysis of a role- and rule-based sexuality under the mandate of symbolic law to consider the persistence in Bowen's imagination of a dyadic model of desire. Engaging sympathetically with such an erotic sensibility will thus return us from the psychosexual maturity of a triangulated realm to an earlier stage of development, the world of the two-person dyad before the supervention of paternal law. We may perceive something of this contrast between developmental stages and their associated formations of sexuality in the third of the previous vignettes, in which Bowen's Court stands exposed to the vicissitudes of the War of Independence. Here, I think we may identify the figuration in geopolitical terms of a struggle to displace the psychosexual order by which the mother of the triangle may be accessed in favour of a dyadic formation of desire structured in relation to the mother of the original two-person world. Under attack by Irish forces is the colonial governance of the land, a triangular system by which the access of the Irish population to the territory on which they live and work is regulated by the Anglo-Irish landowning class. The appearance of Bowen's Court in this context, cherished and helplessly feared for by its master Henry and his daughter Elizabeth, identifies the Big House as a kind of political totem, the exemplification and the crowning glory of the mother country under the good husbandry of the Anglo-Irish. But whereas the young men who will subsequently occupy Bowen's Court during the Civil War would seek, rather sweetly, to usurp Henry's position of power in the house, their essentially lawful intentions towards the place closely akin to those of the Bowens' own, the Irishmen fighting for national liberation in the earlier War of Independence are not imagined to want to take possession of the Big House for themselves, but are expected rather to set it on fire, a project that suggests a revolutionary rejection of the triangulated structure of sexual subjectivity on which the colonial order is modelled. For in contrast to the eventual demolition of Bowen's Court in 1960, which Bowen characterises as 'a clean end' (BC 459), the prospect of the house's imminent immolation by Republicans in 1921 arouses 'moral distress' in its lawful owner Henry Bowen (BC 440), and in his daughter a vision so emotionally distressing that she has to 'teach herself' to picture it as a way of reducing its traumatic potential.

In Chapter 1, we looked at the developmental importance of separation in the dyad: an experience that it is the responsibility of the mother to bring about, even though its effects upon her child will unavoidably include terrible pain and incomprehension. In the wake of separation, the child may perceive his or her mother as a figure of grotesque hostility and at the same time as the virtual victim of the child's own retaliatory rage; or the child may try to pretend that no separation has taken place, defensively idealising the mother in lieu of experiencing the anguish that she has caused. A substantial part of my discussion of *The Last September* and also of *The House in Paris*, in the second half of Chapter 2, will focus on the kinds of objects of desire that are produced by these contrasting responses to the trauma of separation: on the one hand architectural instances of devastation and decay, on the other images of buildings or gardens whose uncanny perfection intimates a denial of reality. We may identify both of these types of sexual object as dyadic, because insofar as they register the effects on the beloved of the child's reaction to separation they each recall a period of trauma in the two-person world, prior to its restructuring by the intervention of paternal law. Thus if we make out the presence of such primitive erotic objects alongside or perhaps even in outright competition with the maternal beloved of triangulated sexuality we may usefully recall our exploration in Chapter 1 of how weak paternal function allows for the persistence of dyadic experience in a subject who may in certain respects appear to have accepted the mandate of symbolic law.

I think we may characterise Bowen's account of the threat to her family's property of political arson in 1921 as a story about the challenge posed to the Anglo-Irish Father by a rebellious 'dyad' class bent on the restoration of a two-person relationship between Mother Ireland and her children. Burning down the building would represent a repudiation at once of the roles available in a triangulated socio-political order and of the very totem in relation to which those roles are organised and sustained. Destroying property and property-holding alike, such an act might be thought to make way instead for some sentimental pre-modern vision of agriculture in a landscape as yet unregulated by imperial law. And in light of Henry's powerlessness in face of this regressive insurgency we may certainly make out too the theme of paternal inadequacy, as if the potential triumph of a violent and primitive nationalism in Ireland would be as much the fault of the settler-colonials' weakness as of any endogenous desire in the Irish population for national liberation.

Yet the projected vision of Bowen's Court on fire does not seem to accord with what I have said already about the kinds of maternal object that derive from dyadic experience. Evidently, the burning building is no idealised image of uncanny perfection; and equally it is not an image that records more directly the trauma of separation, for the vision, I think, has a strange vitality that makes it very different from the pictures of architectural desolation and devastation that we will identify, for example, in the figure of the ruined mill building in *The Last September*. Indeed we might wonder whether the image is not associated rather with some irresistible, if inadmissible, excitement, for the virtual picture of a house on fire recurs throughout Bowen's writing, and the stoical self-schooling by the waters of Lake Como – 'I [. . .] taught myself to imagine Bowen's Court in flames' (BC 440) – might be felt to include at least some element of wish fulfilment, however disavowed. What, in short, I want to suggest is that the image recalls, in an almost impossible way, the experience of the child *prior* to separation: a period or variety of experience that we have characterised, in Chapter 1, as psychotic. In this light the problem of Father's inadequate confirmation of separation pales beside the question of Mother's ability to impose it in the first place, the question, that is, of what we have called the maternal No. In the arena of sexuality, an absence or partial failure of separation might register in an experience of desire as a condition at once anarchic and absolute; the beloved object of such a desire would recall the mother who knows no No. In the final pages of Chapter 2, my focus will turn therefore to figures and characters in *Pictures and Conversation*, *The Little Girls*, *Bowen's Court*, 'Ivy Gripped the Steps' and finally back to the final paragraph of *The Last September*, to address the topic of a sexuality that perpetuates or recalls the experience of life in the dyad prior to separation, and explore in more detail the characteristics of the psychotic object of desire.

## Section One: Triangulated Sexuality

Elizabeth Bowen conceives of triangulated sexuality as an affair of roles: two active (Mother and Father) and one passive, or spectatorial (Child). This view is illustrated in the scene which brings to its thrilling if unsatisfactory conclusion the pre-war section of 'Ivy Gripped the Steps'. Reluctantly entering the drawing-room in which he knows he will find his beloved Mrs Nicholson engaged with her married lover Admiral Concannon, Gavin is confronted by an image of the couple's unconsummated sexual relationship in the form of a dramatic tableau:

> Mrs Nicholson, head bent as though to examine the setting of the diamond, was twisting round a ring on her raised left hand – a lace-edged handkerchief, like an abandoned piece of stage property, had been dropped and lay on the hearthrug near the hem of her skirts. She gave the impression of not having moved: if they had not, throughout, been speaking from this distance, the Admiral must have taken a step forward. But this, on his part, must have been, and must be, all – his head was averted from her, his shoulders were braced back, and behind his back he imprisoned one of his own wrists in a handcuff grip that shifted only to tighten. The heat from the fire must have made necessary [. . .] the opening of a window behind the curtains; for, as Gavin advanced into the drawing-room, a burst of applause entered from the theatre, and continued, drowning the music which had begun again. (I 708)

Hardly an advertisement for the erotics of the triangle, identifying, as it does, both the masculine and the feminine roles with experiences of frustration, the scene nonetheless offers an emphatically literal account of adult sexuality as a dramatic two-hander staged before an audience of one. At the age of nine or ten, Gavin is approaching adolescence but still quite properly retains the character of a child, 'advanc[ing] into the drawing-room' without as yet stepping on to the stage to exchange for his spectatorial part an active role in the theatre of adult desire.

Gavin's gender is thus a relatively lightweight construction, as it is for most of the child characters of Bowen's texts: girls and boys are distinguished socially but not psychically, their masculinity or femininity an assemblage of behavioural conventions and signs rather than an articulation of desire. In contrast, the assumption of an active sexual role at adolescence appears to be coterminous with an act of thoroughgoing imaginary identification by which the subject comes to be differentially situated in relation to the object of desire. A crucial feature of Bowen's account of triangulated sexuality is the egalitarian nature of such an identification and its performance: by which I mean that it is demonstrably possible for Bowen's adolescents to assume a sexual role, a gender, that does not accord conventionally with biological sex. We may consider, for example, the fifteen-year-old Theodora Thirdman of *Friends and Relations* (1931). Theodora's relation to the enactment of femininity is uneasy from the start: we get our first view of her at the Studdart-Tilney wedding, her costume anomalous, despite '[h]er mother, with infinite solicitude, ha[ving] chosen her for the occasion a large stiff blue hat', as '[a]ll the grown-up girls present wore droopy hats that cast a transparent shadow across their faces.'[4] Theodora 'determined to persecute Mrs Thirdman for this on the way home', and will subsequently display, as if to insist on her competence in the feminine role, considerable skill in her impersonations, on the telephone, of such representative adult women as one 'Lady Hunter Jervois' and, on another occasion, her own mother. But it is thanks to her aptitude for masculine enactment that she really comes into her own when her parents, newly returned to England after a decade abroad and exhausted by their daughter's appetite for social conquest ('Mother, are we so absolutely *superfluous*? [. . .] Aren't we ever going to begin?' [FR 28]), consign her to a boarding-school in Surrey.

> [Theodora] distinguished herself as a young man in one of the Saturday night plays – these improvised, unrehearsed, in the manner of *commedie dell'arte*. 'You make a marvellous

man,' said Jane and Ludmilla. 'Men walk with their elbows out, women walk with their elbows in,' vouchsafed Theodora. 'I was told that once and it makes all the difference.' (FR 44)

Such a performative identification need not be understood either as a wholly novel invention of adolescence, or as an act of autonomous self-fashioning; it is evident that Theodora's persuasive masculine stylings have been prepared for by her father's way of thinking about her: '"She has a brain," he said [. . .] (the brain his son would have had)' (FR 29), as well as by her mother's noted failure to dress her like all the other girls at the wedding. (Failure – or unconscious choice? Perhaps Theodora's mother, too, has continued to regret the son she didn't have.) But until the paternal sexual role is wholeheartedly assumed by the newly desirous teenager, Theodora's masculinity remains a mere potentiality, a theoretical possibility lightly delineated and awaiting future activation.

The most original feature of Bowen's account of triangulated sexuality is her understanding of the collaborative relation between masculine and feminine roles, and the precise relation of each to the object of desire. Masculine sexuality is an enactment of Father's proprietorial relation to Mother: it is, therefore, at once possessive and constitutive, simultaneously laying claim to the mandated object of triangulated desire and by so doing effecting the imaginative materialisation of such a beloved. *Assuming a paternal sexual role brings into being the object of desire to which it also secures access.* We may study this process in action in the example of the effects of Theodora's 'suggest[ion] that [she and her classmates] should act Don Juan' – this last a watchword, in theatrical terms, for the representation of a hyperbolic masculine sexuality. Theodora's enthusiasm for the paternal role is both seductive and transformative. Her proposal not only prompts a *simulation* of seventeenth-century femininity ('Jenna, who was influential in these matters, was more than agreeable. She tied up her hair in ribbons over the temples like a Velasquez girl's') but also triggers a recognition or discovery in her feminine counterpart of a hitherto unarticulated erotic potentiality, a phantasmatic truth that can now be made manifest for the first time: '[Jenna] had always known she had more passion than she could express' (FR 44). Theodora's swaggering performance of masculinity thus so stimulates Jenna's desire to represent the erotic object of a Don Juan's amorous attentions that Jenna's dramatic enactment of the figure of Doña Anna morphs into a fully performative instantiation of this fictional feminine subjectivity. That this represents a virtually ontological feat is confirmed by Bowen's manner of narrating a conversational exchange between the schoolgirls at bedtime, an exchange in which Jenna is at once conflated with and replaced by the dramatic persona that she had played earlier that evening.

> 'How different you are with no spectacles,' said Doña Anna, lingering by the bathroom door. 'We've never had so much love in a play before,' said Hester, joining them. 'Generally, we just arrange for lovers to go off tenderly. I mean, I do think Theodora's extraordinary.' 'I suppose I can't imagine feeling self-conscious,' said Theodora, straddling a little. 'You tickle my ear when you kiss,' Doña Anna said thoughtfully. 'I do wish you'd hold your breath next time.' (FR 45)

Even after the play is over, and the actors have quit the stage, Theodora's phantasmatic interpellation of Don Juan's object of desire persists in the notional backstage spaces of the virtual theatre – the bathrooms, the most secluded recesses of the school. Where Jenna might be expected to reappear, Doña Anna 'linger[s]' on, affirming the transformational potency of Theodora's bodily and emotional posturing as a man, the phantasmatic power of her masculine 'straddling' to evoke the maternal beloved.

What is to be gained by the assumption of the paternal role may thus easily be identified as access to the mother of the triangle. By enacting Don Juan, a masculine sexual subject may take possession of Doña Anna. But how are we to understand the appeal of the feminine role in the realm of triangulated sexuality? How does undertaking the part of Doña Anna gratify its performer? – for clearly Jenna enjoys being Doña Anna very much, her criticism of Theodora's kissing transparently legible as an enjoyable imaginary re-living of the experience and as a faux-dispassionate instruction that it should be renewed at the next possible opportunity. But whereas Theodora employs her dramatic talents in the service of social conquest – her goal being to capture her classmates' attention and admiration – and thereby confirms the operation of masculine sexuality as the seduction of the beloved other, Jenna's enthusiasm for theatre suggests a much less other-directed satisfaction, a pleasure, that is to say, that is generated by and in relation to the transformations in the performer's self by which the schoolgirl becomes the erotic object of adult desire. Another way of putting this would be to say that Jenna's desire does not seem to take a man, or a masculine woman, as its ultimate object, although such a paternal figure – in the form of Theodora – plays a crucial role in the arousal and gratification of that desire. Rather, I think that Jenna's desire, as much as Theodora's, is for the mother of the triangle, Doña Anna: but whereas in a masculine sexuality such as that assumed by Theodora the role of the lover and the figure of the beloved are distributed between two, differentially gendered actors, in an adult feminine sexuality such as Jenna's the figure of the beloved is made manifest in the self-presence of the feminine performer. Thus it should come as no surprise that the structure of a feminine subject's sexuality does not replicate or mirror that of an adult man's. Whereas masculine men (and masculine women such as Theodora) want women for what they are perceived to be – for what, that is, they represent: Mother – feminine women want father-like men for what they are demonstrably capable of *doing*: for acting, that is, as the almost mage-like agent of an imaginative transformation in the self-experience of the woman herself. In Bowen's conception of adult sexuality, men create Mother and take possession of her, while women, desired by men, *instantiate* her. Controlled, protected and appropriated by men, women become the maternal object of their own heart's desire.

*The Last September* is a novel about war: the war between the British Empire – and its representatives on the ground, the Anglo-Irish Ascendancy – and Irish Republicans for control of the Irish motherland. That is to say, Bowen's 1929 novel draws on the recent political history of Ireland to articulate in symbolic terms a conflict over who is capable of exerting a father-like proprietorship in relation to Mother, a maternal object who is thereby constituted as a feminine subject of desire. It is thus a novel about patriarchy which defines the ultimate question of such a social and psychic order not in terms of men's power, but of women's pleasure – as if at stake in the Irish War of Independence were not, finally, the political supremacy of the Anglo-Irish and their imperial guarantors, but rather the gratification of the disputed territory itself, the almost mystical question of Ireland's self-experience and erotic and ontological satisfaction. Who can give Mother what she wants? The three sections of the novel test in turn the claims of three representative forms of colonial authority: in 'The Arrival of Mr and Mrs Montmorency', the reigning power on the ground, the Anglo-Irish Ascendancy; in 'The Visit of Miss Norton', the upper-middle-class Englishmen of the Home Counties; in 'The Departure of Gerald', the military officers of the British Empire.

In each case, the colonial or imperial father who exercises control over the maternal 'place' – to use Bowen's suggestively comprehensive term for an area of land in its guarded and tended identity as an estate – is set against and in relation to a comparable representative of Irish masculinity. We may thus examine the first of these three colonial figures – Hugo Montmorency, erstwhile proprietor of an Anglo-Irish estate – in the light of his relationship to an elderly Irish tenant farmer with whom Bowen's text associates him. Out walking with a fellow visitor on the Danielstown estate, Hugo is met by 'the white stare of a cottage' that he recognises. 'Dannie Regan lives there', he explains to his companion, Marda Norton:

> he shot out an eye shooting rabbits and now he's losing the sight of the other. I used to go out with him when I was a boy – so high. His mother lives with him – or should still; I haven't heard that she's gone. She must be a hundred and four.[5]

When Dannie emerges from the cottage, 'searching with his one eye', 'helpless and eager', 'trembling', he recognises Hugo from the sound of his voice, but mistakes the identity of the woman by whom he is accompanied. 'And here was the wife he'd brought with him, the beautiful lady [. . .] [H]e took Marda's hand. He declared that she brought back the sight of youth to his eyes' (LS 86). In fact Hugo has left his wife, Francie, back at the house, in order to contrive for himself an ambulatory tête-à-tête with the fascinating Marda: but Dannie's assumption that Hugo's companion must be his wife points at once to the implicitly pedagogical role of the old man – who might be expected to demonstrate to his surrogate son the proper performance of adult masculinity – and to his inability to fulfil it adequately. For Dannie Regan figures here as a kind of incompetent Oedipal father, a poor approximation of the archetypal king who, upon realising that he had married his own mother, gouged out his eyes and achieved a visionary insight. Blinded by his own hand but unrecompensed by any growth of spiritual vision, Dannie Regan lives with his mother without having managed to marry her or – it would seem – anyone else, as if never having aspired to leave his boyhood home.

We may thus make out in the combined figure of Dannie and the ruling-class man who appears here as his symbolic heir an illustration of the effect of paternal weakness on a son's achievement of adult sexuality, for Hugo's marriage to Francie – a major topic of analysis in the novel – appears throughout Bowen's narrative as a virtual repetition of Dannie Regan's relationship with the grotesquely antiquated 'Mrs Regan', the female companion who is Dannie's mother but very pointedly not his wife. Hugo has achieved a perverse notoriety among his Anglo-Irish peers for what might at first seem to be almost the reverse or inverse of Dannie's domestic situation. 'Oh, Hugo and Francie?' Marda exclaims, when, upon arriving at Danielstown, she is apprised of her fellow guests: 'Of course I have heard of them. Isn't she his mother – practically?' (LS 77). But Marda's formulation does not quite get at the essence of the marriage's misconception: the problem is not that Francie is 'practically' – which is to say, symbolically – Hugo's mother, but that Hugo stands in symbolic relation to Francie as does Dannie Regan, literally, to the one-hundred-and-four-year-old Mrs Regan. The problem, that is, concerns the phantasmatic identity of the husband, not that of the wife. In Bowen's implicit understanding of triangulated adult sexuality it is to be expected that a wife will evoke the maternal, will 'be' her husband's mother; what is not appropriate, or adequate, in the same context, is that a husband should behave, in relation to the woman whose bed he shares, like a little boy – that he should 'be' his wife's son.

Both Hugo's irredeemably filial approach to his wife, and his provocative yet impotent predilection for women to whom he is not married, are foreshadowed and explained by what Bowen tells us that Francie has for a long time known about Hugo's childhood relation to his own home – Rockriver – and to Danielstown, a relation that is determined, as we have seen illustrated in the figure of Dannie Regan, by weak paternal function. 'Hugo had stayed at Danielstown as a boy for months together, and knew the place as well as his own house, he told Francie, and certainly liked it better. He had expressed this preference, which had come as a shock to her, when they were first engaged' (LS 14). '[P]ained as by an expression of irreligion', Francie had 'consoled herself, and rehabilitated him secretly, by remembering he had had a step-father and could never have known the meaning of family life', conceiving of her own part in the marriage to come as a project of compensation, of reparation. Bowen, however, insists on the futility of this ambition. '[Francie] intended to make up to him for the deficiencies of his childhood, but, almost immediately after their marriage, Hugo' – in the grip of an abortive plan to emigrate to North America – 'sold Rockriver': 'So when the idea of Canada failed, they had no house, and she, after all, no vocation' (LS 14). Although Bowen thus implies that Francie could, perhaps, have predicted both Hugo's abdication of his husbandly prerogatives and his sterile, would-be infidelities from his virtual abandonment, in childhood, of his proper 'place' in favour of a house that he would never be able to call his own, the novel is nonetheless sympathetic to the predicament to which Francie finds herself condemned by the marriage. Bowen is alert to Francie's frustration at Hugo's determination to be as a son to her, a frustration that Francie feels compelled to tolerate alone. 'They might well say', she reflects of the Naylors, the Montmorencys' hosts at Danielstown,

> she had taken the brilliant young man he'd once been and taught him to watch her, to nurse her and shake out her dresses. And she knew she could, now, never explain [. . .] how Hugo was too much for her altogether. How she had tried, but had not been able, to keep him – first from marrying her, then from giving up Canada, leaving his friends when she had to go to the south of France, or from brushing her hair in the evenings. (LS 18)

Why, it might be asked, *does* Francie tolerate her husband's sexual abandonment of her, if it is not meaningfully of her choosing? The answer, I think, chimes with a notion that sounds throughout this novel about adult women's commitment to representatives of paternal power. The point is not that Francie enjoys her frustration, but that she is not able to imagine forsaking the husband whom she believes to represent the only route or mechanism by which she might, one day, achieve satisfaction. Behind her seemingly irrational or perverse investment in her marriage we may sense, I propose, a more fundamental loyalty on Francie's part: a loyalty to her own desire, and to the prospect – no matter how often postponed – of its ultimate gratification. However, in light of the parallel or reiterative narrative absences from Dannie Regan's cottage of a wife, and from the Rockriver of Hugo's childhood of a mother, it seems perfectly clear that if what Francie wants is to be appropriated by a man who can simultaneously recognise himself as her husband and her as an embodiment of his mother, it seems likely that she will wait in vain.

Such an account of the Montmorencys' marriage is confirmed by its virtually identical reiteration in the relationships of Hugo and Laura, and of Hugo and Lois: the first of these an important episode in the novel's prehistory, the second an essentially imaginary but centrally significant component of the plot of the novel's first section, although Lois's romantic fixation on Hugo, conceived long in advance of his arrival at Danielstown, survives barely a few minutes of contact with him, on account of his failure to perform in relation to Lois as she had hoped that he would. What Lois wants, I think, is quite clear: to be 'recognised' as her own mother, Laura – Laura Farquar, née Naylor, now dead, but by the accounts of the Danielstown party a woman of exceptional force and charisma, volatile, elusive and 'lovely' (LS 11). After the death of her husband Walter Farquar, Laura and the child Lois had lived together in Leamington, during which period Hugo – not yet married to Francie – had conceived an inconclusive passion for Laura, and it is from Hugo in his aspect as her mother's lover that Lois has come to look for so much. Immediately after the Montmorencys' arrival at Danielstown – the event with which the novel begins – Lois finds herself unexpectedly reluctant to follow the guests in to tea in the drawing-room; instead, she lingers on the front steps, projecting desirable conversations between herself and Hugo.

> 'I apologize for the mauve sweet-peas,' she would have liked to be able to say to Mr Montmorency. 'I don't care for the mauve myself. I can't think why I ever picked them; there were plenty of others. But, as a matter of fact, I was nervous.' And – 'Nervous?' she would wish Mr Montmorency to ask her searchingly, 'why?' But she had her reserves, even in imagination; she would never tell him. But she had seen at once that Mr Montmorency, who must be really so subtle, would not take the trouble to understand her. (LS 8)

Lois wants Hugo to treat her as a figure of feminine mystery: she imagines staging herself for him, in conversation, as a titillating object to be 'search[ed]' by his 'subtle' cognitive powers. But he is not interested in penetrating her with his understanding – her 'reserves' are all too crushingly safe from his attentions – for in spite of Lois's hopes it is clear from his first words of arrival at Danielstown that Hugo is not looking for Laura in her daughter.

'"I don't think I should have known you," said Mr Montmorency, who had not seen Lois since she was ten and evidently preferred children' (LS 7). Endeavouring, as always, to make good her husband's deficiencies, Francie interjects immediately: 'Oh, *I* think she's the image of Laura – ', which is kind of her, but doesn't provide Lois with the transformative paternal recognition that could put her in touch with her lost mother. Indeed Lois's early disenchantment with Hugo immediately aligns her with his inveterately disappointed wife, for a reader of Bowen's novel might be prompted by Lois's self-critical musings on the subject of the mauve sweet-peas to observe that Mrs Montmorency's first appearance in the narrative takes the form of 'a wild escape to the wind of her mauve motor-veil' (LS 7). At dinner that evening, it seems possible, during an argument about the activities of local Republican forces, that Hugo might after all be looking for his troublesome deceased paramour in his host's spirited daughter: Lois is 'certain she felt him looking at her while she argued with Uncle Richard about the guns. Seeking a likeness, perhaps. It was this consciousness that had lent her particular fervour' (LS 28). But it comes to nought, by the end of the meal she 'hope[s] nothing more of him' (LS 27), and just a week or so later her foreclosed romance will seem like ancient history: 'She remembered how once she had hoped so much, and how he had been infinitely disobliging. Now she had a tenderness for him, devoid of attraction, as though they had been a couple of widows' (LS 165).

And yet there is a paradoxical sense in which, by failing to appropriate Lois as a representation of her mother, Hugo has in fact treated Laura's daughter to an experience of masculine inadequacy that in some ways closely approximates or reproduces Laura's own – with the difference that whereas Lois is disappointed by Mr Montmorency's anerotic passivity it would seem that her mother had actively encouraged it. 'I once rather had illusions about Mr Montmorency', Lois tells her cousin, Laurence, 'since I was ten':

> 'He came to stay with my mother and me when we were at Leamington. After dinner – I was allowed to sit up – Mother walked out of the house and left us. We were trying chickens at

that time and I dare say she went out to shut them up and then simply stayed in the garden. Mr Montmorency and I talked for some time, then he got solemn and went to sleep all in a moment. I sat and watched him in absolute fascination. You know the way men go to sleep after dinner? Well, that wasn't at all the way he did... Then my mother came, very much refreshed at having been away from us, and said I was a rather bad hostess, and woke Mr Montmorency up. I have thought since, anyone might have said she was a rather bad hostess. But everything she did seemed so natural.' (LS 10–11)

This vignette from Lois's memory of her childhood is suggestively akin to the scene from 'Ivy Gripped the Steps' with which I began this section of the chapter – the dramatic tableau of Mrs Nicholson and her lover enacting their mutual frustration before an audience of one, the nine- or ten-year-old Gavin. Here, too, we are presented with an image of adult sexual dysfunction that threatens to equip its juvenile spectator with a distinctly suboptimal model to operationalise at adolescence. Like Gavin, sent down to the drawing-room explicitly that he might 'see the Admiral', the child Lois has been 'allowed to sit up' as a witness to the encounter between her widowed mother and a putative pretender to the paternal throne. And, as in the later story, what the child on the threshold of adolescence actually observes is a marked failure of the visitor to demonstrate his sexual authority. But whereas the Admiral literally holds himself back from Mrs Nicholson, his standing posture and intimate proximity to her eloquent manifestations of his desire, Mr Montmorency makes no move towards assuming the role of Laura's lover but rather falls asleep, as if modelling his behaviour on the very child to whom he is supposed to be demonstrating the proper function of an adult man. And then there is the question of feminine pleasure itself: for whereas Mrs Nicholson presents, centre stage, a tense and demanding image of the mother's desire for paternal attention, Laura Farquar – very much more disconcertingly – absents herself from the theatre, renouncing her role in the adult drama as if in pursuit of a satisfaction with which the triangular law of the father can have nothing to do. Certainly, Laura does re-enter the room and restores some semblance of the triangulated proprieties – waking Mr Montmorency, critiquing her daughter's attempt to play the hostess – but there linger in Lois's account some wonder, incomprehension, and resentment in relation to her mother's unseen experience outdoors, from which she would return so 'very much refreshed at having been away'.

We will return to the question of Laura's experience in the garden in Section Two of this chapter; for now, it is enough to note that, whatever the significance of Laura's absence from the drawing-room, Hugo's childlike retreat into sleep could hardly put up less of a challenge to his hostess's enigmatic withdrawal.

In considering the case of the second of the representatives of British imperial power – Marda's English fiancé, Leslie Lawe – we will engage again with the trope of the sleeping man, for at the heart of the novel's second section, 'The Visit of Miss Norton', we find the scene of the Danielstown women's encounter with a Republican fighter whom they unintentionally arouse from sleep in a ruined building. In this episode, responsibility for exemplifying adult feminine sexuality is assigned to Marda Norton. Certainly a less volatile figure than Laura Naylor, Miss Norton nonetheless seems to have posed some degree of difficulty in the past for her masculine opposite number in the theatre of triangulated desire: during a previous engagement, Marda lost her fiancé's ring at a Danielstown tennis party but 'wrote afterwards' – as Lois relates to her friend Livvy – 'to say it didn't matter because she had broken off her engagement anyhow and the man said he didn't want the ring, he said he wished it were at the bottom of the sea' (LS 75). In contrast, the current claimant to Marda's hand seems set fair to make a good fist of it. From his 'clipped and traditional garden' in Kent to his 'straight grey gaze' Leslie gives every sign of husbandly capability. 'So much of herself that was fluid', Marda thinks to herself, 'must [. . .] be moulded by his idea of her. Essentials [would be] fixed and localized by their being together – to become as the bricks and wallpaper of a home' (LS 129). Yet by remaining, perhaps a little complacently, in the Garden of England while his betrothed travels alone in Ireland Leslie Lawe may have missed, irreparably, a trick, as the unaccountable

Marda decides not to wear his ring on her visit to Danielstown. Her left hand thus gives no sign of her annexation to Leslie's Kentish demesne and she swiftly accrues a motley gaggle of Anglo-Irish followers, all, in their different ways, thoroughly implausible – Hugo, Laurence, Lois – before, decisively, attracting the interest of a Republican fighter holed up in a derelict mill.

Marda and Lois come across the Irishman during the course of a walk with Hugo, whose sterile crush on the tantalising Miss Norton has by this point built up to an angry intensity. The ruined building seizes the attention of all three; 'the country was full of them', '[t]hose dead mills' – 'never quite stripped and whitened to skeletons' decency: like corpses at their most horrible' (LS 123). Marda is astounded, Lois enjoyably spooked, and Hugo tiresomely quick to point the political moral: '"Another," Hugo declared, "of our national grievances. English law strangled the – "'. His sentence – which probably addresses the nineteenth-century suppression of industrial development in Ireland by protectionist English law – remains unfinished, however, because his companions are anxious to leave him behind. 'Come on', says Marda to Lois, 'I feel demoralized, girlish. Let's hide from Mr Montmorency', and she pulls the younger woman with her into the ruins (LS 123). There they observe 'a man lying face down, arms spread out; a coat rolled into a pillow under his face which twisted sideways a little to let him breathe' (LS 124). Stepping back, as if hoping to leave him undisturbed, Marda crackles some fragments of plaster beneath her heel:

> [T]he man rolled over and sat up, still in the calm of sleep. 'Stay there,' he said, almost persuasively: a pistol bore the persuasion out. They were embarrassed by this curious confrontation. Neither of them had seen a pistol at this angle; it was short-looking, scarcely more than a button. The man sat looking at them with calculating intentness, like a monkey, then got up slowly: the pistol maintained its direction. (LS 124)

I have described *The Last September* as a novel about war. Here, after the narrative's preliminary attention to the pathetic non-combatant figures of the juvenile Hugo and the senescent Dannie Regan, is at last presented a scene of virtual battle: the adversaries, an upper-middle-class Englishman (absent in body but to be presumed to be present in spirit), and a rural Irish rebel; the ground of contention – and the spoils of war – the attractive unmarried Marda Norton. 'Don't be silly', Marda urges the local fighter, 'Go to sleep again', but this man's paternal authority, unlike that of her fiancé's, is not to be evaded. Accustomed to life on big estates, Lois and Marda will be familiar with the look of firearms, as with, we might imagine, the appearance of various male animals' genitalia: but now they see for the first time a weapon – or is it a penis? – pointed straight at them, from which angle it is oddly 'short-looking', the length of its barrel, or shaft, obscured so that all that can be seen is the tip, or eye, the whole instrument thus looking 'scarcely more than a button'. The Irish rebel is thus rather better equipped than is the far-off Leslie to lay down the law on the question of the young women's wilful wandering. 'It is time', he tells Marda and Lois, 'that yourselves gave up walking. If you have nothing better to do, you had better keep in the house while y'have it' (LS 125). The Irishman's exercise of paternal authority is evidently most gratifying to him, and undoubtedly efficacious in its impact on the young women, as, just moments afterwards, his gun goes off, injuring Marda's left hand. 'I seem to have lost some skin', she comments 'resentfully', 'I seem to have lost some pieces of skin' (LS 126).

The first point to note about this episode is that, although it may be characterised as a scene of battle between representatives of rival classes and nations, it does by the same token give evidence of a fundamental agreement between the combatants over the symbolic identity and proper management of the object in dispute. Virginal woman or territory of Ireland, the desirable object represents the mother of triangulated sexuality. Kreilkamp characterises Lois's 'encounters with potential violence against the Big House' – encounters such as this one – as 'liberating', but such a reading would seem to depend upon a presumption that any challenge to the Anglo-Irish Ascendancy must proceed from and represent a radical critique of the colonial governance of Ireland and, by logical extension, of the sexual subordination of women to men.[6] In fact there is nothing revolutionary about the Irish rebel's appropriation of Marda; he seeks merely to beat the English gentleman at his own paternal game, his symbolic defloration of Leslie's betrothed a kind of taunting pre-emptive cuckolding of the imperial father that does nothing to challenge the authority of the triangulated structure of patriarchal social organisation *per se*. 'English law' having strangled Irish industrial production, and English Lawe having arranged to export, to his little Kentish fiefdom, the reproductive potential of an attractive Anglo-Irish woman, the representative of Irish nationalism here demonstrates in miniature the no less patriarchal logic of his project to take back control, to achieve, as Hoogland puts it, Marda Norton's 'definitive subjection to the Law'.[7] Indeed we might perceive an almost tutelary character in the action, the Irish Republican here demonstrating to the Englishman the exercise of paternal sexual authority in a way that recalls Dannie Regan's modelling of impotence to Hugo Montmorency. We might also compare the rebel's appropriation of the Englishman's lady to the rivalrous behaviour of the Republican fighters whom Bowen describes occupying her family's house during the Civil War, their commandeering of the house's keys and locks and of the master's trousers the expression of a near-identical aspiration to stand in the position as of a husband towards the maternal totem of settler-colonial rule – although in that case Republican pretensions to paternal supremacy would dwindle in the face of the Bowens' concerted defence of their 'place'. In each of these examples we may identify a kind of hostile camaraderie in the relations between men of warring tribes, whose efforts are directed primarily towards the taking of spoils, not the injuring of opposing forces. With Marda's assault in the mill Bowen characterises the War of Independence as a politically and psychically conservative turf war, a struggle for paternal control over the materials of production in the form of land, relatively unprocessed agricultural products such as cotton and wool, and the fertile bodies of women.

The second point to note about this episode may be approached by way of the observation that the topic of fertility is raised by Marda herself, Marda the exemplary object – or perhaps rather the exemplary territory, the 'place' – of the rebel's guerrilla husbandry. As she and Lois recover their equilibrium in the minutes after the violent encounter, chatting, with a new intimacy, about the persecutory behaviour of Mr Montmorency, Marda remarks, 'inconsequent: "I hope I shall have some children; I should hate to be barren"' (LS 128). Moments later she says, bitchily, of the hapless Hugo: 'He couldn't be anything's father', a remark which responds most obviously to Lois's expression of relief that Hugo had not been *her* own father, but which also seems to allude to a welcome potency, by contrast, in other representative men, of whom one is surely the cocksure Irish rebel, so lately departed from the scene. It is as if Marda is wondering if she might not already have been impregnated, the efficacy of the Irish fighter's assault on her virginal integrity testified to by the bloody state of her hand and of Lois's handkerchief, with which they have bound up the wound. I think indeed that we may sense in Marda some grudging acceptance of what has just been done to her, maybe even some nascent satisfaction in it, that makes a distinct contrast to her immediate reaction of resentment. Reflecting on her desire to have children – to *become a mother* – Marda may begin to wonder, dimly, whether the Republican's symbolic assault on her virginity might not turn out to have been providential. The episode at the mill thus offers only the most extended elaboration of an idea that we may see entertained throughout the small Anglo-Irish community represented in this novel: the idea, that is, that there might be something salutary, even rather enjoyable, in the experience of being sexually assaulted by Irish Republicans.

At several points in *The Last September* we may observe the Anglo-Irish residents of Danielstown deriving substantial gratification from more or less disguised imaginary scenes of sexual subordination to representatives of their own tenantry. The first of these rape fantasies is to be discerned on the first night of the Montmorencys' visit. Lois forsakes her family in the comfortable, lit-up house to go for a late-night walk in the part of the Danielstown estate in which she can expect to feel afraid – the shrubberies. 'Her fear of the shrubberies tugged at its chain, fear behind reason, fear before her birth; fear like the earliest germ of her life that had stirred in Laura' (LS 33). Several critics have emphasised the phantasmatic importance of Laura Farquhar, Lois's dead mother, in this lonely outdoor scene. Hoogland's observation that 'the intense associations evoked by Laura's memory are connected with Lois's sensual experience of the sound, smell, and feel of nature'[8] has been enhanced by Bennett and Royle's recognition of a specific symbolic linkage in the novel of Laura and laurel bushes: pushing through the laurels in the grounds of Danielstown, Lois is thus 'haunted by the encrypted name of her mother',[9] a reading enriched by Corcoran's identification of the laurel as an icon of war and of victory.[10]

What I want to emphasise is the precise structure of Lois's identification with her mother in this scene. For Lois, the experience of being frightened is somehow suggestive of the experience of being newly pregnant. Fear is compared to a human embryo – '[h]er fear of the shrubberies' is said to be 'like the earliest germ of her life that had stirred in Laura' – so, precisely in order to feel like Laura, she 'eagerly' immerses herself in the dark bushes, putting herself into the place of her mother in hopes of being impregnated with fear. She does not have long to wait before she hears 'steps, hard on the smooth earth; branches slipping against a trench-coat' (LS 33). A masculine figure passes her: seeing his 'resolute profile, powerful as a thought', Lois assumes him to be a Republican engaged in paramilitary planning against imperial dominion. She longs for his recognition – 'not to be known seemed like a doom: extinction' (LS 34) – but, tantalisingly, he is quickly gone. 'Conceivably, she had just surprised life at a significant angle in the shrubbery', Bowen writes, in a sentence that combines the lightest linguistic allusion to conception ('conceivably') with an image of masculine vitality 'at a significant angle' that may remind us of the erect phallic pistol of the rebel in the mill. 'But it was impossible' – Lois feels – 'to speak of this. At a touch from Aunt Myra adventure became literary, to Uncle Richard it suggested an inconvenience; a glance from Mr Montmorency or Laurence would make her encounter sterile' (LS 34–5). Not that other members of Lois's family are insensible to the aggressive charms of local Republicanism. Her uncle 'was delighted, when he heard from the postman, and was able to pass on, how three young women in the Clonmore direction had had their hair cut off by masked men for walking out with the soldiers' (LS 61). Sir Richard's delight, I think, is double-faced, as is this instance of nationalist violence itself. On the one hand, the act of forcibly shearing off women's hair has a repressive, self-righteous character, as against the imputed licentiousness of the local women who have socialised with the enemy; the assault may thus serve as a cautionary tale for the disciplining of Sir Richard's niece, Lois, who has herself, much to her family's displeasure, been entertaining the romantic attentions of one Gerald Lesworth, a young English officer stationed nearby. On the other hand, there is a distinctively sexual quality to the manner in which the punishment is meted out. The vision of masked men overpowering and violating a trio of young women is no less evocative of pornographic tropes than is the picture of feminine decadence to which it responds. Thus we may understand why both Lois's uncle and aunt, and Lois, too, seem to derive considerable if utterly disavowed excitement from picturing Lois herself at the centre of such a scene, for the punitive vision of Lois assaulted and shamed by a posse of masked men is a richly gratifying fantasy of gang rape:

> 'And how would you like it,' Sir Richard said to his niece indignantly, 'if a thing like that were to happen to you?'
> 'I should be bobbed,' said Lois. 'I should take it as a sign. But I have never walked an inch with anyone, not what you would call *out*, Uncle Richard.'
> 'But masked men,' said Lady Naylor, 'would be a very nasty experience for a girl of your age.' Lois said she would prefer the men to be masked; she would be less embarrassed in the event of meeting them afterwards. (LS 61)

## Sexuality 137

We saw previously how Marda's annoyance at being wounded by the rebel fighter's gun modulated with surprising speed into a cloudy acceptance of the injury on account of its potentially fertilising action; here, similarly, we may observe in Lois's speculative reactions to the projected scene of assault a notably sanguine confidence in her ability to go forward from such an experience with equanimity, changed only for the good, her hair thenceforth 'bobbed' in the modern fashion. The only downside that Lois admits, indeed, is the merely social discomfort of the embarrassment that she imagines herself as likely to experience in the event of her encountering her attackers again. Moreover I think we might parse such an embarrassment, on Lois's part, as the not altogether unwilling or unhappy acknowledgment of the undignified lineaments of her own desire – a kind of misrecognised retrospective arousal, a throb of delicious remembered subordination.

We have noted the possibility that Bowen's female characters may assume the paternal role at adolescence; the sadomasochistic fantasies of the Anglo-Irish in *The Last September* confirm the opposite possibility as well, for Lois's cousin Laurence displays his imaginary identification with the mother of the triangle in his enthusiasm for the prospect of Danielstown's being raided by local Republicans in search of arms and ammunition. Instead of sleeping – Laurence's is without question a fully adult sexual sensibility – he lies awake at night, 'long[ing] for the raiders and strain[ing] his ears in the silence [. . .] Once he heard, he thought, a fleet of bicycles in the avenue; he sat up propped on his palms, assembled his attitude, and was prepared to go down and admit the party courteously.' Disappointingly, however, 'there were no bicycles; no one knocked' (LS 106). Can the Irish Republican Army (IRA) do no better than the young men of Laurence's university acquaintance, those Oxford undergraduates – presumably, English – who have similarly failed to claim him for their own? After expressing some disobliging thoughts about his family's politics, Laurence is asked by Hugo why then he chooses to spend his vacations at Danielstown. 'I have no money', Laurence explains, plaintively; 'I was to have gone to Spain this month with a man and last year I should have gone to

Italy with another man, but what do you expect me to go on?' (LS 44) Do these men boast insufficient means to pay Laurence's expenses, or do they simply not desire him enough to want to spend their money on him – is Laurence insufficiently attractive? Welcome reassurance on this point is provided by a scene suggestive of anal rape towards the end of the novel – '[a]n unusual evening', as Bowen's narrative puts it. Out walking, Laurence comes upon three armed men: 'They made him put up his hands and march smartly down the boreen ahead of them' (LS 188). When Laurence realises that they are directing him to the graveyard wall he is 'embarrassed': consciously, he fears that he is about to be shot, but I think we may perceive in the feeling a Lois-like throb of misrecognised arousal, an unconscious excitement about what is to come. Sure enough, his potential killers undress him and position him carefully in a posture of exaggerated vulnerability: 'they asked for his shoes and the loan of his wrist-watch', and, '[p]lacing him with his face close up to the wall they advised him for life's sake not to look round or stir for twenty minutes.' The episode is a thoroughly satisfactory experience for Laurence, even though the men swiftly depart, for their part in Laurence's fantasy is energetically simulated by the local insect population: 'Laurence remained with his forehead against the stone for fifty minutes, horse-flies biting him through the socks', before 'limp[ing] home to dinner and an audience, considerably cheered'. For Laurence, as for Marda and for Lois too, sexual assault at the hands of the Irish would seem, in fantasy, to promise an essentially beneficent experience, leaving its object – if a little bit bloody or swollen – in fine form overall.

> Three days after, [Laurence's] watch was posted back to his Uncle Richard: it was in excellent order and ticked as it was taken out of the package. 'Which just shows,' said Sir Richard, holding the watch to his ear with satisfaction. (LS 189)

The scandal of the Anglo-Irish's flirtation, in fantasy, with the thrilling figure of the Republican rapist, and their corresponding ambivalence in relation to their imperial guarantors, thus highlight at once what Bowen views as the deep-rooted psycho-sexual authority of patriarchal social organisation and the precarious status of those masculine subjects who show themselves, individually, as unable to perform plausibly as Father. Playing Father is indeed a big ask; it means undertaking creative responsibility for the mother of the triangle, in the realm of symbolic law everybody's object of desire. Performance failures are therefore likely to be harshly judged. As long as a woman – we may remember Francie – can imagine no more effective alternative to her current husband, he may continue to occupy the role in peace, no matter how ignominiously. But if a woman or a 'woman' – for example Marda, Lois, or Laurence – begins to suspect that another man might more satisfactorily discharge the rights and responsibilities of Father, her allegiance to her proper suitor or mate will soon show as dangerously labile, as the feminine subject's true loyalty lies not towards any individual man but towards the function that he (or 'he') is required to perform. Thus Bowen's novel draws attention, in historical retrospect, to the threat posed to Anglo-Irish supremacy by their evident incapacity to satisfy Mother Ireland's desire for erotic domination. If the local ruling class cannot perform as required – and this is made only too pathetically clear by the impotence of Hugo Montmorency – and if Hugo's counterpart in English civilian life, Leslie Lawe, is also proved wanting, it will fall to British troops to demonstrate their ability to wear the paternal trousers.

The third section of *The Last September* could be described as a sustained if disaggregated symbolic scene of battle between opposing armies in the war to secure control over the desirous motherland. The army of the British Empire – which we will see execute in this section of the novel an ambitious set-piece manoeuvre with what looks at first like definitive success – is represented front and centre by Gerald Lesworth, Lois's English beau, a young officer garrisoned in the neighbourhood of Danielstown. After Hugo Montmorency and Leslie Lawe, Gerald is the third of the figures of imperial masculinity assessed for their fitness to rule in the course of Bowen's novel, and he demonstrates from the off an excellent understanding of the paternal part that he is to play, and its relation to the object of his possessive and protective attentions. Not for Gerald the absentee-landlordism of Leslie Lawe, footlingly cultivating his garden in Kent while his fiancée wanders unguarded in the southern Irish badlands: the young British officer is stationed on the territory in dispute, his role to instantiate the authority of the empire as of the master and guardian of a desirable 'place'. 'In his world', Bowen writes,

> affections were rare and square – four-square – occurring like houses in a landscape, unrelated and positive, though with sometimes a large bright looming – as of the sunned west face of Danielstown over the tennis courts [. . .] He had sought and was satisfied with a few – he thought final – repositories for his emotions: his mother, country, dog, school, a friend or two, now – crowningly – Lois. Of these he asked only that they should be quiet and positive, not impinged upon, not breaking boundaries from their generous allotment. (LS 40–1)

At the same time, he understands the appropriate lack of symmetry that will distinguish his feeling for the young woman who forms for him a 'repository' or locked box for his emotions – who is at once the home of what he loves, and the mistress of such a home – and her feeling for him: 'A fellow did not expect to be to a girl what a girl was to a fellow – this wasn't modesty, specially, it was an affair of function' (LS 49–50). In Gerald's understanding of triangulated sexuality, as in Bowen's, a 'fellow' and a 'girl' collaborate to secure differently structured access to the beloved maternal object, with whom one of the two lovers – the feminine – is, or becomes, positionally and psychically coincidental, even identical.

The military set-piece to which I have referred is the dance given by Captain and Mrs Rolfe of the Gunners in the married quarters of the British Army garrison at Clonmore. On the one hand, the dance is a figure for the officially sanctioned sexual activities to which such accommodation pays tribute; although the colonel of the regiment 'disapproved tacitly', 'it was not easy to veto what ladies described as "a little fun in the huts"' (LS 141). On the other hand – and by the same token – it is a symbolic offensive in the increasingly violent conflict between the British military guarantors of the political status quo and the republican rebels who oppose them, for the dance is conceived from the start as a wildly provocative demonstration of – so to speak – the imperial phallus. The two Miss Raltes from Castle Ralte report that their own father 'had been more than difficult' about their attendance at the dance: 'He says', Moira Ralte relates, 'that the whole proceeding is not only criminal but lunatic. He says he can't understand the C.O. allowing it, with the country the way it is' (LS 142). But such talk of danger can only heighten the heady sexual promise of the evening, at least for the women of the party, for it offers to settle decisively the question of masculine supremacy. 'We really did think', Moira continues, 'till we got past the gates, [Father] was going to stop us'. 'But we came', adds Cicely, her sister: at which everyone laughs. 'The Miss Raltes had been cast as wild young Irish and rather liked themselves. But they exchanged glances, uneasy. It had not been quite the thing, perhaps, to have laughed at Father' (LS 142) – an excellent example of the feminine disloyalty that we have noted, for Bowen emphasises here the fundamental ruthlessness of women's commitment to the satisfaction of their own desire. In sight of open warfare between imperial and republican forces, the Ralte girls have written off their Anglo-Irish father's authority with barely a moment's contrition, so eager are they to position themselves as trophies for the taking on the edge of the field of battle. Indeed their gratification has already begun. 'We really did think' – I repeat Moira's words – 'he was going to stop us': 'But we came', Cicely finishes – a statement that seems on the face of it gratuitous, and thus hints at other meanings. '[W]e came.'

The crucial event at the dance is Gerald's virtual defloration of Lois – although it is indicated to the reader with such delicacy that it is easy to miss amidst the gaudy delights of the Rolfes' imperial bacchanal. 'The forbidden Irish rebels are the only sexually potent figures in *The Last September*', Kreilkamp writes;[11] 'Lois remains [. . .] virginal from start to finish', Esty concurs.[12] Gerald's act is nonetheless clearly discernible, I think; and, if not actually violent, it is certainly not without force. At the height of the festivities, Lois and Gerald leave the hut together to talk and do other things in the dark. That these other things may not be specified explicitly is indicated by Bowen's registration of an unmeasurable blank in the narrative's time. 'Your arms are so cold', Gerald says to Lois (LS 154). 'He kissed them, inside the elbows. Later: "I like the back of your head," she said with exploring finger-tips.' What happens, and how much time does it take up, between Gerald's kissing of Lois's elbows and Lois's complimenting of the shape of his head? We know only that it is 'later': between the end of one sentence and the beginning of the next, things have been happening and time has been passing, but we cannot specify exactly what and how much. Then we read: 'The soft sound of her dress in the wind became, by some connection of mood, painfully inexplicable to her – the pain was its own, from not being understood. "Gerald, your buttons hurt rather." "My darling – " He let her go, but still, above consciousness, held one of her hands, solemnly. "Shall you really be able to marry me?"' he asks, which makes Lois laugh: 'I don't know till you've asked me', she replies (LS 154). When previously Lois encountered a man in such a state of arousal the weapon whose upward-pointing barrel had reminded her of a button had belonged to an Irish rebel, and the woman whose body came to be punctured was Marda Norton. This time, the importunate 'buttons' belong to an officer of the British Army, and they 'hurt [Lois] rather' and leave her with '[a] tear in her green tulle dress' (LS 166); the colour of the penetrated fabric is scarcely, in this context, to be disregarded. That the experience is momentous is evident upon Lois's return to Danielstown the next day, and, in particular, in her changed perception of her own bedroom.

> What she had done stretched everywhere, like a net. If she had taken a life, the simplest objects could not more have been tinged with consequence. [. . .] 'All the same,' she thought, looking round with patronage at the virginal wallpaper, 'it *is* something definite.' And with curiosity, with complicity almost, she looked at herself in the glass. (LS 162)

We may thus recognise the semi-specified episode in the darkness outside the huts as the moment at which the imperial father at last legitimates his authority, Gerald's sexual and projectedly marital appropriation of the Anglo-Irish Lois at once the culminating action, and, in miniature, the goal, of the larger military offensive represented by the dance; the aim, in fact, on the British side, of the deployment of troops in the rebellious imperial territory of Ireland. For the ultimate effect of Gerald's actions on Lois is to cause her to recognise herself as a desirable 'place', a Big House whose security and very identity depend upon the protective governance of a military master – as we see a couple of days later when Gerald and Lois encounter Hugo in the grounds of Danielstown:

> Lois, encouraged to find that by some growth of womanhood in herself her attitude was already a wife's, at once proud and deprecating, stood there watching Gerald, most grateful for the repose of this intermission and willing that Mr Montmorency should be detained. She knew, from a glance they both gave her, that she must have been startled by some sort of consciousness into beauty, and a particular placidness, a sense of being located, warmed her surroundings, the smooth lawn and heavy trees [. . .] [Gerald] must no doubt some day be a captain, and 'captain's lady' had a ballad-like cadence. She almost took Gerald's arm. (LS171)

'Located' amidst smooth lawns and heavy trees, Lois stands, beautiful and silent, the sinecure of the men's admiring gaze, as Danielstown itself has stood as the backdrop and shelter – and focus and creation – of its inhabitants' activities throughout the course of the text. In this historical novel, however, we may hardly expect that the triumph of the British Army will be allowed to figure as the conclusion of the story: indeed it is only a couple of days after the festivities in the huts that local Republicans ambush a military patrol, shooting Gerald dead and injuring a non-commissioned officer (NCO). And yet in the way that the formal symmetry of this action indicates its continuity with the provocation to which it responds, so that we may identify the dance and the rebels' retaliation as the staggered components of a disaggregated scene of battle, Bowen's novel identifies in the Irish War of Independence a strangely collaborative project, as much identificatory as hostile, sustained between the armies of rival nations. Behind or beneath or beyond the heterosexual performance in the married quarters another dance, as it were, goes forward: a dance between the British Empire and Irish Republicans, a dance between men.

## Section Two: Sexuality and the Dyad

Yet an analysis of *The Last September* that attends exclusively to the novel's articulation, in historical and political form, of the patriarchal operation of triangulated sexuality will fail to engage with much that is evocative and compelling in this text. I will come ultimately to the almost unappreciably strange scene with which the story ends. I want first, however, to look at those architectural and horticultural features of the novel's topography that show themselves to be saturated with the kinds of feelings and ideas that we identified, in Chapter 1, as characteristic of the experience of Bowen's fictional subjects who have suffered separation at the hands of their mothers without the subsequent restorative intervention of paternal law. I want to show that, in Bowen's view, the assumption of an adult role in the drama of desire may be complicated or troubled by the inadequately redeemed trauma of separation, for the sexual appeal of the triangulated object – Father's wife – will naturally be challenged by intimations of the dyad mother lurking close at hand.

That the magnetism of this obscurely insistent figure is in no way neutralised by its traumatogenic aspect is demonstrated by Lois's fascination with the ruined mill, the setting for the encounter between the walking party from Danielstown and the armed republican rebel and an image, I think, of the deathly, deadly mother of the dyad after separation.

> The mill startled them all, staring, light-eyed, ghoulishly, round a bend of the valley. Lois had to come hurrying up to explain how it frightened her. In fact, she wouldn't for worlds go into it but liked going as near as she dared. It was a fear she didn't

want to get over, a kind of deliciousness. Those dead mills – the country was full of them, never quite stripped and whitened to skeletons' decency: like corpses at their most horrible. (LS 122–3)

In her *Elizabeth Bowen and the Writing of Trauma: The Ethics of Survival* (2014), Jessica Gildersleeve identifies the 'horrific ruined mill' as 'a site of trauma in the narrative, in the landscape, and in the novel's sense of an Anglo-Irish heritage'.[13] As such the abject building embodies 'Danielstown's "Other"', and poses by the same token an inter-textual challenge to 'the architectural memorialization and monumentalization represented by [. . .] *Bowen's Court*'.[14] I think this is astute, as is, too, Gildersleeve's further observation that Bowen characterises the Danielstown box-room as a kind of architectural unconscious. Its little window obscured by ivy, this small, 'melancholy' chamber provides a gloomy refuge for Lois when she wishes to avoid the claims of her importunate uncle and aunt: 'The room was too damp for the storage of trunks that were not finished with anyhow; mustiness came from her mother's old vaulted trunks and from a stack of crushed cardboard boxes' (LS 132). If – as Gildersleeve proposes – we understand the box-room as a crypt for the mouldering symbolic remains of Lois's dead mother, we will be able to see that Danielstown itself 'approaches the traumatized architecture of the mill and mimics the structure of the traumatized psyche'.[15] What I think Gildersleeve's reading does not quite capture is the ghoulish thrill that is evidently to be had in the vicinity of the ghoulish mill building; when 'Marda put[s] an arm round [Lois's] waist', Lois enters the decomposing structure 'in an ecstasy at this compulsion': 'Fear heightened her gratification; she welcomed its inrush, letting her look climb the scabby and livid walls to the frightful stare of the sky' (LS 123–4). Lois's reaction to discovering inside the mill a dead crow – a souvenir-sized emblem of the larger rotting body in which it is entombed – emphasises her ready responsiveness to the moribund mother of the dyad. Repeating on a miniature scale the delicious-disgusting quality of the 'scabby and livid' mill, the little decaying bird functions at once as a source of positively enjoyable stimulation and as a suggestive figure for Lois's gratifying apprehension of herself, in this connection, as a kind of delicious-disgusting baby or adorably ill-trained toddler. 'Marda, help', she calls; 'here's a dead crow!' – to which Marda replies, with exciting disdain, merely 'Tchch!' 'But it's very dead!' Lois wails, affectedly-childishly: 'Shuddering exaggeratedly, leaping in a scared way over the nettles, Lois [. . .] made for the dark doorway, eager for comment, contempt, consolation. She was a little idiot – appealing, she felt quite certain, to a particular tenderness' (LS 124).

As we have seen, the episode promptly develops into an important affirmation of patriarchal law: Marda's left hand is punctured by a bullet from the republican fighter's gun and Lois, impressed by the man's sexual authority, thinks to herself: 'I must marry Gerald' (LS 125). 'One won't be girlish again', as Marda puts it; 'I think, as a matter of fact, we were being goatish' – as if the almost campy quality of their initial relation to the mill, with its sexy, comedy-horror allure, were grotesque, even animalistic, in its juvenility (LS 128). 'You know', Lois tells Marda, 'all this has quite stopped any excitement for me about the mill. It's a loss, really. I don't think I'll come down this part of the river again . . . [sic]' (LS 129).

A very similar tussle between the unwholesome lure of the dyadic mother and the claims of a triangulated sexual order is to be discerned in relation to the topos of the Danielstown garden, a large lush enclosure set a little way from the house and entered by a door with a lock: 'deep in its walls, [it] seemed impossibly large, for one could not see to the end of it: it was crossed by espaliers and crowded with apple-trees' (LS 165). It is a place of legendary, even paradigmatic perfection: reflecting on an afternoon's tennis party, Francie – who, as we know, has been deprived of the opportunity for horticulture by her husband's decision to sell off his own family's place – is said by Bowen's narrator 'not [to have] wanted to know if [the guests] thought the garden lovely – the supremacy of Danielstown garden made the opinion irrelevant' (LS 54). If the rotting mill building at a little distance from the Big House offers an image of the desperately blighted mother of the dyad in the wake of separation, the hyperbolically gorgeous garden of Danielstown may be seen as an instance of that defensive idealisation by which a child attempts to deny the reality of the separation that his or her mother has imposed.

From the start, the garden is allocated predominantly to Lois, whose task it is to cut and arrange flowers for the house, and as we have seen in the first section of this chapter – in the context of the example of the mauve sweet-peas – this is an activity symbolically bound up with the young woman's assumption of a triangulated sexuality, her feminine desire for Hugo Montmorency to recognise and misrecognise her as her own mother, Laura Naylor, the woman he once had loved. And yet the security of Lois's commitment to the psycho-sexual mandate of paternal law is repeatedly challenged by Lady Naylor's endeavours to restrict Lois's growing intimacy with another potential 'father', Gerald Lesworth, precisely by means of the claims of the Danielstown garden. During the first part of the tennis party previously mentioned, for example, Lois is nowhere to be seen, as her aunt has 'sent her out to the garden to see about getting in some more [raspberries]' (LS 36); as her friend Livvy remarks, 'it seems too bad she shouldn't see Mr Lesworth' (LS 39). And when Lois does at last appear, '[coming] down the shrubbery path from the garden startled, as if at her own great speed', she is 'flushed and visibly breathless'. Whatever she has been doing, unseen, in the fragrant, fruitful enclosure, it has left her perceptibly aroused and imperfectly dressed, the disarray of her clothes at once expressive and enigmatic: 'A pink unbuttoned cardigan slipped away at the shoulders, she had a hand in both the pockets to keep it on. Her hat flapped back, it rose above her face in surprise, like a wave.' What *has* she been up to in the garden? – there is no sign here of the piercing or penetrating action of a man's phallic buttons, her appearance suggesting rather a rapturous, rosy unbuttoning, amazement and exhilaration; all nature appears complicit, as she with it. 'Behind her the bushes stirred in an almost invisible backwash. Over the laurels, cropped knee-high at the back of the tennis court, her body rose and dipped with her long steps' (LS 40). We might recall here the mysterious defection from the hostess's role of Laura herself, almost a decade earlier, when she abandoned, after dinner, the visiting Hugo to the ten-year-old Lois and disappeared alone into her Leamington garden, from which she would eventually return, as her daughter would observe, 'very much refreshed at having been away' (LS 11).

As in the episode of the adventure at the ruined mill, however, the primitive erotic appeal of Danielstown's garden is eventually superseded – it would appear, decisively – by the demonstration of paternal authority, in this case by Gerald's sexual appropriation, or colonisation, of Lois, at the party at the Clonmore garrison. For on her return the next day to Danielstown, Lois rejects in the uncanny garden, its 'September yellow and scarlets [. . .] metallic in unsunny light', its dahlias, 'orange and wine-coloured, blaz[ing] and gloom[ing]', exactly that developmental retardation or resistance that had before constituted its defensive mystique. 'In yesterday's dusk', Bowen's narrator recalls on Lois's behalf, 'the Square with its flitter of leaves had been all autumnal; smoke was blue in the air and, later, the dark where they kissed' – that is, Lois and Gerald – 'had a sharp intimation of autumn. She loved in autumn a stronger, more shadowy keen spring, sweet shocks of goodbye, transition. Summer meanwhile stayed on inside these walls, forgotten' (LS 165–6). Lois's feelings here are emphatically triangulated in nature. Modest, even in the privacy of her own mind, she may make no reference in thought to Gerald's buttons, but nevertheless faces up squarely to the maturational significance and consequences of the momentous encounter outside the huts: 'The fact was, that though one determined tonight to sit under the lamp and learn verbs' – another of her aunt's prescriptions for thwarting the assumption of an adult sexuality – 'her Italian or German would not dispose of last night, which remained, like the tear in her green tulle dress, to be dealt with practically. [. . .] It was inevitable that she should marry Gerald' (LS 166). As an environment for thinking in, then, and as a representation of the thought that may therein be fostered, the Danielstown garden is to the Square in Clonmore as is the denial of reality in the dyad to its painful but enabling acceptance in the triangle: whereas the second of these cognitive positions underwrites, and is underwritten by, the almost resurrectional capability of paternal prohibition (so that the earliest symptoms of winter, the death of the year, foreshadow the coming of 'a stronger [. . .] spring': a Botticellian vision of the regenerated mother in vernal array), the first of these mindsets refuses to countenance the mortality that is inherent in the seasonal round and thus seems to intimate in spite of its insistence on the eternity of summer an eerie negation of aliveness. 'Summer [. . .] stayed on inside these walls, forgotten.' Grown suddenly ghostly to Lois – her own newly, virtually deflowered state an ironic counterpoint to the flamboyant September blooms before her – the Danielstown garden strikes her as somehow unnatural in its persistence. What had appeared lovely, just days before, is now perceived as a plaintive though unavailing zombie: its 'usual breath [. . .] was cold to her face', the 'branches were quiet as though in anxiety', and 'the flowers appeared to be clamouring vainly, forgotten' (LS 165).

As we know, however, Lois will not, in the event, marry Gerald, or even come to be recognised by the elders of her community as officially affianced to him: out on patrol, only a couple of days after the Clonmore party, Gerald is ambushed by republican fighters, shot and instantly killed. Yet it is not this act of tit-for-tat masculine aggression – the lethal response, by the IRA, to the sexual provocation, emblematised by Gerald's conquest of Lois, of the military bacchanal – that puts an end to the engagement, which had in fact been called off, shortly before the ambush, by Lois and Gerald themselves, each acting under pressure from the skilful Lady Naylor. Why *does* Lois's Aunt Myra refuse to countenance her engagement to Gerald Lesworth? In Section One of this chapter we saw evidence in the Naylors of what Bowen characterises as an Anglo-Irish enthusiasm for the putative sexual authority of the Irish men who forcibly oppose settler-colonial rule: for which reason Gerald's interpretation of Lady Naylor's rejection of his suit might well appear self-evidently correct, as he understands her to be objecting to his lack of manly means. 'You're going to stop it', he exclaims, 'because I'm too young and too poor and not "county" enough – or whatever I ought to be'. As, just moments before, we have witnessed Lois's aunt quizzing the young man on the subject of his family's unsatisfactory social and financial standing, the response with which he is met – '"You have entirely misunderstood me," cried Lady Naylor, hurt' (LS 181) – might thus strike us as a moment of high comedy. But the possibility that Lady Naylor's objections may be truly of a different nature to this, at least in part, has surely been signalled by her earlier attempts to deploy the legendary delights of the Danielstown garden to pre-empt her niece's desire for the English subaltern – a technique that suggests in Lady Naylor a discreet but perhaps not inconsiderable familiarity with the maternal eroticism that Lois, as a ten-year-old child in Leamington, had uncomprehendingly sensed also in the enigmatic Laura. In this light we might focus our attention on another of Myra Naylor's exchanges here with Gerald. When he states: 'As a matter of fact I love Lois', Lady Naylor replies, 'equably', 'Oh yes. But I'm afraid, you know, that she doesn't love you' (LS 179). It is an accusation that might be levelled very effectively at any engagement contracted under paternal law, for in Bowen's work the woman (or man) who assumes a feminine sexual role in such a dispensation is indeed motivated in the ostensible desire for a masculine partner by a longing for the beloved mother that she (or he) thereby impersonates, bodies forth and becomes.[16]

The conflictual ensemble of the garden, the corpse and the mother of the triangle is to be observed also in the Ireland-based passages of *The House in Paris* (1935). Set some few years after the War of Independence, the novel's middle part pays close attention to the domestic milieu of Karen Michaelis's Aunt Violet and her second husband Bill Bent, who live together in a substantial haute-bourgeois Victorian villa – Mount Iris – in a wealthy suburb of Cobh. Under the ancien régime Uncle Bill's family had owned Montebello, a house that sounds very much like Danielstown, and like Bowen's Court; except that, even in the recessed fictional present of 'The Past', the retrospective central section of this tripartite novel, the Big House in question can claim no material existence, but makes its appearance only as a memory and (which is the same thing) in representation.

For Mount Iris is a would-be replacement for Montebello, a scaled-down revenant purchased with the compensation paid by the new republic to the Anglo-Irish owners of houses burned down in the Troubles.

> Ghastly black staring photographs of Montebello hung at Mount Iris outside the bathroom door; downstairs was a photograph of the house as it used to be, in winter, a grey façade of light-reflecting windows, flanked each side by groves of skeleton trees. It could never have been gay or homely. But Rushbrook is full of Protestant gentry, living down misfortunes they once had. None of them, as a matter of fact, had done too badly, or they would not be here, for most of the big villas are miniature 'places' that need some keeping up [. . .] From the harbour, Rushbrook looks like a steep show of doll's-houses; some gothic, some with glass porches, some widely bow-windowed and all bland. Yet this unstrange place was never to lose for Karen a troubling strangeness, a disturbing repose. (HP 69–70)

Here we may observe the careful presentation of multiple images of the dyad mother in ruins – the 'ghastly black staring photographs of Montebello' that hang, in Uncle Bill's new house, outside the bathroom door, as if to recognise, if not to respect, the phantasmatic filthiness or destruction to which they bear witness; while downstairs, in a more public, more accessible part of Mount Iris, is displayed, as it were, the triangulated mother herself, which is to say, a re-presentation of the treasured lost object 'as it used to be'. A bracingly realistic portrayal of Montebello in winter, 'flanked each side by groves of skeleton trees', the photograph does not seek to deny the building's mortal nature, or claim for it an ideal perfection ('It could never have been gay or homely'). Yet by this very token the image works to restore to the place a kind of symbolic vitality, making of it a virtual presence in the political order of the new Irish state and in the minds of its former inhabitants and of viewers of the photograph.

However, the achievements of the symbolic order – represented as much by the photographs of the house in ruins as by the portrait of Montebello in all her austere integrity – are surely to some extent problematised, or ironised, by the cosy, faintly preposterous phenomenon of Mount Iris and its Rushbrook compeers, for the essentially bogus nature of these 'miniature "places"' is registered by their derealising effect on temporal and political actuality: 'The nineteenth-century calm hanging over the colony makes the rest of Ireland a frantic or lonely dream. The bay is sheltered, the gardens full of exotic shrubs that grow nowhere else' (HP 70). Uncanny artefacts of architectural denial, the Rushbrook houses embody an oblique, largely unconscious refusal to recognise the demise of the Anglo-Irish Ascendancy, and a stubborn nestling instead inside an idealised colonial Eden, with an unnaturally accommodating climate and showy, implausible flora that might remind us of the 'blaz[ing] and gloom[ing]' dahlias of the Danielstown garden in September.

Up to this point I have been looking at the challenge posed to the attractiveness of figurations of the mother of the triangle by the persistence on the phantasmatic scene of the mother of the dyad, whether such a figure is characterised primarily by the ruination consequent on the maternal institution of separation or by the eerie, disingenuous perfection conjured up by the child's denial of this desolating reality. We have thus been exploring in Bowen's work what we might think of as a border war or temporal conflict between more primitive and more mature developmental states or stages: at stake, the question of the nature of the sexual project itself. For whether the longed-for object is the mother of the dyad or the mother of the triangle determines the political temporality, as it were, of desire, its operation reactionary or modernising, its sensibility nostalgic or resolutely progressive. Is sexuality a rearguard action of refusal and resistance, or a pioneering project of rediscovery and regeneration? The first of these formations has to recommend it the promise of a one-to-one communion with the subject's first and only true love, but it is a promise that can never be fulfilled; the second, in contrast, can guarantee access to its object, precisely because that object is not the beloved thing-in-itself but a representation of it, of her, the original mother of the dyad irrecoverably transformed by the mediation of symbolic law. But what if Bowen were to entertain the possibility of a third sexual project and a corresponding object of desire? In what remains of this section, and of this chapter, I want to add to my analysis of Bowen's account of desire an exploration of a sexuality pertaining to the dyad *prior* to separation, although, as we will see, the representation of such a sexuality and its object poses exceptionally difficult problems, because the essence of such a psychic formation is at odds with the possibility of representation tout court.

'Origins', the first chapter of Bowen's late unfinished autobiography, selects a topographical mode for its meditation upon the relationship between dyadic and triangulated psychic formations. 'The day this book was begun', Bowen writes – it is the first sentence of *Pictures and Conversations* – 'I went for a walk':

> The part of Kent I am living in has wide views, though also mysterious interstices. It can be considered to have two coastlines: a past, a present – the former looks from below like a ridge of hills, but in fact is the edge of an upland plateau: originally the sea reached to the foot of this. Afterwards, the withdrawal of the sea laid bare salty stretches, formerly its bed; two of the Cinque ports, Hythe, New Romney, consequently found themselves high-and-dry, as did what was left of the Roman harbour under the heights of Lympne . . . [sic] (PC 3)

The modernisation of the coastal landscape is evidently a valued development, as the latter-day formation of the area is secured by expressively substantial precautions against the possibility of geographical retrogression. 'The existing coastline, a long shallow inward curve westward from Folkstone to the far-out shingly projection of Dungeness, is fortified for the greater part of its way by a massive wall, lest the sea change its mind again' (PC 3). Nonetheless Bowen contrasts the landscape of the new dispensation with that of the old in terms that might be felt, if not unambiguously to denigrate the qualities of geographical modernity, then at least to articulate most sympathetically the heady nostalgic appeal of the former coastline in all its superannuated glory:

> Inside the sea-wall, the protected lands keep an illusory look of marine emptiness – widening, west of Hythe, into the spaces of Romney Marsh, known for its sheep, its dykes, its sunsets and its solitary churches. On a clear day, the whole of this area meets the eye: there are no secrets. Not so uphill, inland. The plateau, exposed to gales on its Channel front, has a clement hinterland, undulating and wooded. It is cleft by valleys, down which streams make their way to the sea; and there are also hollows, creases and dips, which, sunk between open-airy pastures and cornfields, are not to be guessed at till you stumble upon them: then, they are enticing, breathless and lush, with their wandering dogpaths and choked thickets. Into a part of such a region, rather to the east, my Saturday morning walk took me – looking for a road I had known sixty years ago. There seemed no reason why it should no longer be there. It was. (PC 3–4)

Already figured forth as a seductive image of Edenic abundance, the lush, alluring landscape of the past will offer up to the beguiled pedestrian exactly the kind of uncanny horticultural enclosure that we have come by now to recognise.

> The May Saturday morning was transiently, slightly hysterically sunny, with a chill undertone. When there had been nothing for some time, I came to – or was come upon, as one might be by an apparition – a garden created by someone in the fertile, leaf-mouldy bed of the cutting. No house was near it, only a shack in which to camp for a night. This less was a garden than a flowering glade, glimmering and sensuous. Young 'weeping' birches trailed veils of foliage golden rather than green; white rhododendrons were in bloom like white lamps in daylight; magnolias dropped upon their chalice buds . . . [sic] (PC 5–6)

'[S]ensuous', isolated and unreal, ravishing, exquisite and 'hysterica[l]', the 'glimmering' garden of denial is counterpointed by not one but two figurations of the dyadic desolation from which, as from a 'fertile, leaf-mouldy bed', this fantasy springs. For '[h]aving ascended past this, the road made later, as ever, a sharp turn in order to cross a bridge': the densely wooded hillside, Bowen has noted already, is criss-crossed by remnants of the South Eastern & Chatham railway, '[t]he bridge's command of the line it was built to span enable[ing] us – once, long ago, as children – to watch the train coming romping out of the distance, loudened by the acoustics of the gulley.' But now the view of the line has been 'blocked by the falling across it of a huge tree, whose deadness accentuated the hush. Weeds sprouting between its torn-up roots, brambles matting its shattered branches, the tree stayed wedged there: nobody's business.' The gargantuan grotesque object appears to trigger in Bowen from '[a]mong [her] pictures of here' the memory of a disturbing image from sixty years before, of which the later figuration of the shattered arboreal corpse thus seems like a traumatic repetition: 'a corpse of another kind: a sheep, come upon by me and another girl. Its body hideously torn open, bowels gushing forth, blood rusting its clotted wool, flies walking about on its open eyes, it lay as though nested in the deep, springy grass edging the road' (PC 6–7).

A perversely elegant dystopian-pastoral assemblage of incongruous psychical artefacts, the passage is perhaps of most interest on account of its abrupt and perplexing termination, whose relation to the girls' experience of seeing the dead sheep is hard to determine and define. Bowen recalls that she and the girl with whom she came upon the rotting animal corpse 'skirted it, sliding glances at it but saying nothing', a reaction recognisably akin to Lois's enjoyable fear of the ruined mill building. But whereas it seemed from Lois's remarks to Marda that she had visited the mill repeatedly before encountering there the armed republican fighter, renewing each time her delicious ambivalent distaste, the ovine corpse is to be seen just once more after this first occasion. 'The day after, in silent, dreadful accord, we went back to look: it was still there – but the next gone, as though it had walked away.' Bowen then draws to her reader's attention the reported sighting of a comparable corpse in her 1964 novel *The Little Girls* – '"I know where there's a wood with a dead sheep in it," Sheikie Beaker announces [. . .], adding, "Some boys showed me"' – before turning or returning her focus to the aspect of the experience that appears to baffle her own comprehension. 'Who, though,' Bowen demands of herself,

> *was* my fellow-conspirator in that entire silence? (We never reported the sheep, being ashamed.) All my companions of that year are as clear as day to me, or at least as yesterday; her only I cannot identify, either by face or name. She is blotted out. (PC 6–7)

I describe this as a returning of focus because what Bowen characterises as the total eradication of her visual and verbal memory of her companion's identity seems to me to reiterate the ostensibly inexplicable disappearance of the animal corpse, 'gone, as though it had walked away', after the girls' two horrified inspections of it. At which – 'She is blotted out' – the autobiographical passage ends.

I want to suggest that we may discern in the passage a typology of mental formations and their corresponding objects figured in terms of the question of the management and disposal of the body after death, as if in a literalisation of the ordinary developmental problem of the subject's relation to mortality. For from the point of view of the child still suffering in the post-separation world of the dyad, the reality of death will appear at once grotesque and obscurely compelling, the equivalent in the realm of thought to a horribly mutilated corpse that the child lacks the capacity to deal with cleanly. In the absence of a cognitive technology of interment and commemoration the child may take refuge in fantasy or hallucination, endeavouring – with only ever partial success – to obscure the sight of the rotting body with the spectre of the glimmering, glittering garden. By contrast, no corpses lie unburied in the thought-world of paternal triangulation. Here reigns instead, as in the low, salty countryside west of Hythe, 'an illusory look of [. . .] emptiness', as if the advent of symbolic law posed the challenge, at least initially, of a certain de-dramatisation of cognition and its object, the revision of the lurid hues and gothic scenes of the field of cognitive activity accompanied by a change in the quality of thought itself in the direction of something less hectic and frenetic, less compulsively reactive. 'On a clear day, the whole of this area meets the eye: there are no secrets.' It is important to recognise nonetheless that the absence of secrets does not mean an absence of objects to think about and enjoy, for the 'spaces' of Romney Marsh in fact contain a plenitude of things natural and man-made – 'its sheep, its dykes, its sunsets and its solitary churches'.

None of this, however, accounts for the apparent vanishing of the rotting sheep, and for the mental 'blott[ing] out' of the face and name of Bowen's young companion in the experience. We may observe a comparably upsetting vanishing or dematerialisation in *The Little Girls*, the novel to which we have seen Bowen, in the course of her topographical narrative, draw attention. The novel is another of Bowen's triptych-style texts, with a recessed central section, as in *The House in Paris*, that supplies the crucial back-story to the narrative's first and third sections, which are set in the fictional present day. In both novels, very little time is imagined to pass between the end of the first section and the beginning of the third: in the earlier novel it is a matter of moments, perhaps only of seconds; in the later, a couple of days or a week at most. And in both novels, the formal breaking off of the first section coincides with a character's receiving of terribly bad news, news that seems likely to entail the drastic failure of a project of recovery or restitution upon whose success that same character has come to depend. Thus Leopold hears from Miss Fisher that '[his] mother' – with whom he is passionately longing to be reunited – 'is not coming; she cannot come' (HP 58), while Dinah learns from Sheila that her desire to '[u]n-bury' the coffer they had, with their friend Clare, interred, fifty years earlier, in the grounds of their day-school, is probably doomed to frustration, as the St. Agatha's premises were destroyed by German shelling of the south coast at the start of the Second World War. 'It's not there', Sheila says of the school, a statement that seems to Dinah and to Clare to suggest an eradication or disappearance of the buried coffer too. '"Into thin air"', Clare remarks, as if in wonder, or shock, quoting from Ariel's speech at the end of *The Tempest*;[17] the comment forms the final sentence of the novel's first section. In the third sections of both novels these 'frightful blow[s]' seem early on to be reversed or repaired, however (LG 150). In place of Leopold's mother, Ray Forrestier arrives at the house in Paris, determined to reunite his wife with her son, while Dinah recommits to her project of disinterment on the grounds that the coffer's burial site may still be discernible despite the building of new houses on the land formerly occupied by St Agatha's. '[N]ew houses, in places with nice views, often have pretty little gardens, don't they? And to make pretty little gardens, one quite often uses fragments of gardens which have been there' (LG 150). But although it will indeed prove possible to locate the little coffin (for the funereal symbolism of the box is patent, Sheila speaking of Dinah's project as a 'digging around for those old bones' [LG 166]), the coffer when opened turns out to be empty, a discovery that seems to effect in Dinah a radical depletion of substantial parts of herself, or perhaps rather of parts of the environment on which Dinah relies in order to locate herself meaningfully in space. Declining Sheila's hospitality in the wake of the coffer's disinterment, Dinah insists, as she puts it, that she 'ha[s] to get back'. 'Your home', Sheila objects, 'won't run away', but 'That's what it *has* done, Sheikie', Dinah replies: 'Everything has. *Now* it has, you see. Nothing's real any more [. . .] We saw there was nothing *there*. So, where am I now?' (LG 163)

Maud Ellmann and, more recently, Jessica Gildersleeve have addressed the topic of the coffer in terms that identify a problem in the nature of the object's burial. '*The Little Girls*', Gildersleeve writes, 'is concerned with the representation of repression and its relation to non-linear temporality and chronology in narrative',[18] while Ellmann similarly compares the interment of the coffer to the faulty psychical procedure of 'incubing', which represents a resistance to the proper work of mourning. Whereas mourning, like burial, requires an acceptance of the reality of loss, incubing follows from a refusal to acknowledge death and therefore causes 'the lost object [to be] entombed alive within the ego'.[19] As my exploration of the topos of the uncanny garden in Bowen's work has indicated, I certainly share these critics' sense of the significance of mechanisms of repression in texts such as *The Little Girls* – in which connection we might pause, at this juncture, to note the ripely nostalgic sensibility of the scene of the novel's beginning and end, Dinah's rural home Applegate, of which the garden, with its blowsy autumnal defiance, evokes an almost parodic contemporary Eden.

> [S]teamy flower-smells filled the air (more, still, that of a lingering August than of September) [. . .] Mauve, puce and cream-pink stock, double, were the most fragrant and most crushingly heavy: more pungent was the blue-bronze straggling profusion of catmint. Magnificently gladioli staggered this way and that [. . .] Roses were on enough into their second blooming to be squandering petals over cushions of pansies [. . .] And everywhere along the serpentine walk

– for the snake lurks already in the lush declivities of this paradise –

> where anything else grew not, dahlias grew: some dwarf, some giant, some corollas like blazons, some close-fluted, some velvet, some porcelain or satin, some darkening, some burning like flame or biting like acid into the faint dusk now being given off by the evening earth. (LG 17)

It is to a cave in the grounds of Applegate that Dinah, at the start of the novel, is preparing to consign a time capsule of her own manufacture, a collection of mementos donated for this purpose by her friends and neighbours; and it is the question of exactly how the cave is to be sealed up to secure its contents for posterity that triggers in Dinah a memory of an earlier act of symbolic interment, the burial in the grounds of St. Agatha's of the famous coffer, fifty years before. Thus we may certainly recognise in Dinah's forgetting and remembering of the original burial an oscillation between repression and its failure, a movement backwards and forwards across the border between a dyadic and a triangulated state of mind. Nonetheless what interests me most about the coffer is not its fifty-year demonstration of the phenomenon of denial but the question of what is figured by the discovery, upon its unburying, that the receptacle is empty. The circumstance is lightly rationalised by the narrator on behalf of the novel's protagonists – 'It was there. It was empty. It had been found' (LG 158) – but no belief in the real existence of the grave's putative robbers is subsequently affected, while the peculiarly disturbing force of the coffer's vacancy is insisted upon by the devastating effect it has on Dinah; she suffers a mysterious accident and retreats into a semi-comatose state, as if deeply depressed. I want, therefore, to focus here not on the nature of the coffer's burial but on the problem of its incalculable contents: what are we to make of the positing, in fiction, of a collection of material items that prove themselves to be capable of a radical dematerialisation – of vanishing, to quote Clare, 'into thin air'? What I want to suggest is that there is something in the nature of the object that is incompatible with its conclusive burial, an element or aspect of its ontological make-up by which it is rendered essentially unstable, radically unaccountable. Like Schroedinger's cat or the person of Jesus Christ, such an object might seem to have submitted itself, in death, to interment, but show on later investigation to have eluded its containment by the tomb, as if figuring in the form of a vanishing corpse an abrogation of the law of mortality itself. An object that behaved in this way might therefore be understood to manifest in itself – at least from time to time – that primary or original absence of a relationship to reality that we identified, in the first chapter of this book, as characteristic of the child's experience in the dyad *before* separation, a state of being that we defined as psychotic.

The possibility of the partially or intermittently psychotic nature of the maternal object is raised repeatedly in Bowen's work via the question of Mother's own desire. Of major importance to the narrative operation of both *The Little Girls* and 'Ivy Gripped the Steps' is the reader's more or less speedy realisation that the beautiful, seemingly celibate widow in each story may in fact have been conducting an affair with a married man in the neighbourhood: Admiral Concannon in the 1945 short story, Major Burkin-Jones in the novel of 1964. Certainly both texts provide ample support for such a reading of their plots and of their formal projects of exploration, discovery and conclusion; in each case, the reader's detection of an active adult sexuality beyond the initial apprehension of the fictions' child protagonists is aligned formally with the protagonists' eventual achievement of psychosexual maturation. In the present-day first section of *The Little Girls*, for example, the now grown-up Sheila casts doubt on her former understanding of the reasons for the departure from Southstone of Dinah and her mother, Mrs Piggott, at the start of the war in 1914. '[D]id she so suddenly leave because of the war, or under a cloud?' Sheila wonders aloud to Clare.

> 'What has dawned on me is, why should it have been the war when she had no father? Supposing,' Sheila proceeded, with growing caution, 'she never did have a father, at the best of times? There they used to be, simply she and her mother, stuck down in that cottagey house with no explanation. Things one may see as a child but not then think anything of seem peculiar later. That drawing-room of theirs smelled like a hothouse, always – who sent those expensive flowers? They never grew them; think of their garden! Then there were those pictures they had which made me giggle (I now see why) hanging right on the wall. Mother'd have had a fit. Her mother wore tea gowns. They had no gong [. . .].' (LG 37)

Sheila's adult re-vision of the 'cottagey house' as the apparent inhabitation of a high-class but flagrant courtesan, a kind of South Coast Lady of the Camellias, enables her to develop in theoretical terms an unrealistically lurid but nonetheless essentially accurate account of the kind of standard, if illicit, triangulated sexuality that the novel will go on to affirm in the scenes of Mrs Piggott's cautious public encounters with the Major, and in the episode also of Mrs Burkin-Jones's willed refusal to countenance her daughter's cooling affection for either of her schoolgirl friends, least of all the daughter of the valiant Mrs Piggott. Mrs Burkin-Jones's treatment of her husbandless compeer is so programmatically considerate that it can hardly fail to suggest a smothered apprehension of the threat Mrs Piggott poses to her own marriage. And yet the scandal of Major Burkin-Jones's overfamiliarity with the beautiful widow's 'cottagey house' – as Mrs Burkin-Jones tells her daughter, ostensibly à propos of Clare's reluctance to invite her friends to tea: 'It's not fair to be always round there at Feverel Cottage' (LG 114) – is shadowed and imaginatively reversed by the scandal of his possible innocence: for how then would we parse Mrs Piggott's lovely tea gowns and discreetly erotic paintings, the absence of a gong (a most suggestive indication of a household indifferent to the regularising function of mealtimes) and the superabundance of hothouse flowers? The hypothesis of the married lover may thus be understood to function not only as an opportunity for a substantial narrative revelation but also as a hefty bulwark against the otherwise altogether more troubling possibility of the voluptuous Mrs Piggott's sexual satisfaction in the absence of adult male company.

The possibility that Mother, who evidently wants a great deal, doesn't want a man, surfaces repeatedly in Bowen's writing. We may think, for example, of the long passage in *Pictures and Conversations* in which Bowen describes how she and Florence Bowen, living together on the south coast of England in the years following Henry Bowen's mental collapse, liked to entertain themselves by inspecting handsome suburban villas available to rent.

> Any empty premises that we liked the look of we entered, whether at that time requiring or contemplating a change of residence or not. Part of the fun of the game was to obtain the key from the house agent without the house agent; occasionally our entrances were unauthorised – I became as adept as a Fagin pupil at snaking in through some forgotten little back window, then finding a door to unbolt to admit her. The deserted rooms, downstairs in summer often embowered in shadows of

the syringa embowering the bewildered gardens, of which the lawns had grown high in hay, smelled intoxicatingly of wallpaper, sunshine, mustiness. With the first echo of our steps on the stripped floors, or of our voices excitedly hushed by these new acoustics, another dream-future sprang into being. We took over wherever we were, at the first glance. Yes, what a suppositious existence ours came to be, in these one-after-another fantasy buildings, pavilions of love. (PC 29)

In Chapter 1, we looked at the concept of the maternal No in its aspect as the paradigmatic instrument and embodiment of separation in the dyad. What I want to stress here is the importance of this psychical capability in structuring the sexuality of the mother herself. It seems to me that what Bowen is thinking about in her oneiric evocation of leisure-class house-breaking is not only the effect of the absence of a reliable maternal No on the child Elizabeth but also the consequences *for Florence* of the absence of such a function in herself. What is it like to be recognised, in the social world of Hythe, as an adult woman, and a wife, and a mother, without experiencing the internalised acceptance of separation that – properly confirmed by paternal law – would support the subject in the phantasmatic assumption of such a triangulated identity? The answer that Bowen experiments with here combines the intimation of a lyrical eroticism with a startling insistence on psychopathy, the tacit comparison of Elizabeth's mother to Fagin working at once to highlight the strangely maternal nature of Dickens's notorious thief and to characterise Florence's pedagogical relation to her daughter – Fagin, we will recall, tenders food and affection as part of his training-up of new recruits in the art of stealing – as a kind of criminal seduction or 'grooming'.

If the sojourn in Kent seems reminiscent of a lengthy period of courtship, complete with house-hunting expeditions around the local stock of 'pavilions of love', the achieved togetherness of the couple projected constantly forward into a 'suppositious' future, Bowen's account of her return with her mother to Bowen's Court in the summer of 1912 seems to bring into much closer prospect the consummation of their romance. Rich with honeymoon implications, the episode figures the utopian inauguration of an ideal domestic bliss:

> [T]he return to Bowen's Court seemed to promise everything [...] [I]t was to be a real, triumphant return. It was. June sun baked the steps and streamed in at the windows; the bare floors gave off their familiar smell. On my thirteenth birthday I woke up early and ran barefoot all over the house: already the windows were standing open, and the air was fresh with mosses and woods and lawns. Until my father joined us from Dublin my mother and I were alone: sleeping in her room with the blue Morris paper, at nights we heard herons utter their lost-soul cry. (BC 423–4)

Does Mother *really* want her child to be her lover? Is she, *really*, hoping for the consummation that seems in these passages to be hesitating at the perilous horizon of the possible, the extreme edge of what can be imagined or thought? The question comes to a head in 'Ivy Gripped the Steps', in the scene of Mrs Nicholson's tête-à-tête with Gavin by her drawing-room fire, upon their return from the dinner party at the Concannons' – the dinner party at which, as we saw in Chapter 1, Lilian Nicholson has worked hard to induce in her host and in the two male guests (or three, counting Gavin) an infantile state of consciousness akin to that of a baby at the breast. Back at home, Lilian seats herself on a low chair before the hearth, inviting Gavin to sit with her, encircled by her arm. 'In the fire a coal fell apart, releasing a seam of gas from which spurted a pale tense quivering flame. "Aren't you glad we are back"', Mrs Nicholson says to the eight- or nine-year-old child beside her, '"that we are only you and me? – Oh, why endure such people when all the time there is the whole world! [...] Why don't we go right away somewhere, Gavin; you and I? To Germany, or into the sun? Would that make you happy?"' Gavin's reply is obscurely non-compliant: '"That – that flame's so funny"', he says, 'not shifting his eyes from it'. It is certainly not what Lilian wants to hear. 'She dropped her arm and cried, in despair: "After all, what a child you are!"' '"I am not"', he responds stoutly, but she sends him up to bed (I 702).

In this passage, Bowen defines the nature of a psychotic maternal sexuality with formidable conceptual clarity as well as her characteristic poetic expertise. On the one hand, the episode decisively confirms that Mother does indeed fantasise that her child may be able to gratify her in her desire. At the same time, however, the passage establishes that such a hope rests on a categorical misrecognition of the putative potential lover as an adult, for when Gavin responds to his hostess's seductiveness with the authentic unformulated noncooperation of a nonplussed child, Mrs Nicholson's imagination of his potency is instantly disallowed, much to her displeasure. Thus the nightmarish spectre of a paedophilic threat to Gavin is swiftly replaced by the perils attendant on domestic intimacy with the common-or-garden shrew: Lilian's dismissal of the boy, upon the correction of her perception of him in the direction of his actual age and developmental state – 'After all, what a child you are!', is thoroughly reproachful, even punitive, and thus thoroughly unreasonable as well as intemperate. Indeed Lilian's pettish hostility, at this moment, may help us to recognise the immature nature of the desire that drives her here, a desire whose gratification we have seen her modelling in her phantasmatic evocation of breast-feeding at the Concannons' dinner party in the earlier part of the evening. We should recall at this point our exploration, in Chapter 1, of the symbolic association throughout Bowen's writing of Germany with the maternal, an association that we noted there to be observable in Lilian's emphatic defence of the country as against Admiral Concannon's imputation to it of bellicose designs: 'I have never been happier anywhere', she says of her year in Dresden. What the scene by the fire suggests, I think, is that what Mrs Nicholson really wants is neither the child Gavin, nor an adult masculine partner, but a powerful *maternal* lover, 'Germany', who would, like the mother of the dyad before separation, make herself infinitely available to her hungry, passionate child. Lilian's performance at the dinner party may thus be understood more precisely as a demonstration to the group of how to provide what she herself would want to be provided with, rather than as a scene from which she derives primary sexual satisfaction – except insofar as she identifies, in fantasy, with the men whom we see her treat as babies at the breast. When, then, in character as Gavin's object of desire, Lilian asks him if he would like 'to go right away' with her, to be 'only you and me', she may thus be observed to be speaking to him *as if to herself*, the prospect of an unbroken dyadic union with the all-encompassing figure of the mother before separation the desire as much of the ostensibly mature Mrs Nicholson as of her juvenile house-guest.

In fact, the fantasy may be rather less to Gavin's taste than to her own, for as we have seen his reaction to Lilian's offer of herself in the role of the pre-separation mother suggests at least some discomfort in the nine-year-old boy, as well, perhaps, as some inarticulate apprehension of the dangers inherent in her invitation. Although Mrs Nicholson's verbal construction may be easily rationalised as a metaphor, its socio-economic context the feasibility of foreign travel for leisured Edwardian Britons, the immediate oddity and force of her language are not to be gainsaid. 'To Germany, or into the sun', she proposes, as if the longed-for communion with the maternal object were identical with, or at least equivalent to, a kind of orgasmic celestial immolation, the ultimate gratification of a burning desire for Mother accomplished by unification with a fireball of cosmic proportions. Bowen's critics have not paid much attention to the thanatophilic quality of Lilian's sexual imagination, although there has been considerable discussion of what I think we may now recognise as a closely related scene – what I characterised, at the beginning of this section of the chapter, as the almost unappreciably strange conclusion to *The Last September*, the vision, that is, of the fiery immolation of Danielstown brought about by its torching by local republican forces. In fact,

> the death – execution, rather – of the three houses, Danielstown, Castle Trent, Mount Isabel, occurred in the same night. A fearful scarlet ate up the hard spring darkness; indeed, it seemed that an extra day, unreckoned, had come to abortive

birth that these things might happen. It seemed, looking from east to west at the sky tall with scarlet, that the country itself was burning [. . .] At Danielstown, half-way up the avenue under the beeches, the thin iron gate twanged (missed its latch, remained swinging aghast) as the last unlit car slid out with the executioners bland from accomplished duty [. . .] Above the steps, the door stood open hospitably upon a furnace. Sir Richard and Lady Naylor, not saying anything, did not look at each other, for in the light from the sky they saw too distinctly. (LS 206)

Critical discussion of the meaning of the text's conclusion is expressively polarised, split between, on the one hand, accounts that characterise the burning of the house as an 'atrocity' that confirms the novel's identity as a tragedy,[20] and, on the other, readings that identify in the episode, as in the narrative as a whole, the affirmation of a progressive politics. 'When the house does eventually burn', Mary Kelly writes, 'Bowen presents it as a welcomed prospect [. . .] As a 1929 commentary on the Irish war of independence and the broader history of colonialism in Ireland, Bowen's text retrospectively acknowledges and welcomes the end of Anglo-Ireland.'[21] Certainly the novel could not be accused of failing to prepare its reader to grapple with the significance of its concluding episode, for the text is replete with images of household fires – or rather with images, it would be more accurate to say, of the absence of household fires, since although Bowen's characters very frequently locate themselves in relation to the domestic hearth, the fireplaces of *The Last September* invariably show as empty. Near the start of the novel, for example, Lois notes in the guestroom prepared for Hugo and Francie '[t]wo arm-chairs fac[ing] round intently into the empty grate with its paper fan – in them Mr and Mrs Montmorency would sit, perhaps to discuss the experiences of the day' (LS 12). The association that is lightly established here of fireplaces with intimacy in couples is confirmed by virtually every subsequent reference to a domestic hearth in this novel. When Lois, for example, is questioned, encouragingly, by Francie, about her social life, she expressively seeks out the mantelpiece: to Francie's 'And I expect you are having a wonderful time now you've grown up?' Lois replies at first only 'Oh, well . . .', '[going] across to the fire-place and [rising] on her tiptoes, leaning her shoulders against the marble. [. . .] Having a wonderful time, she knew, meant being attractive to a number of young men' (LS 21). Later, Marda will adopt a similar stance on the day of her departure from Danielstown for marriage in England ('against the mantel-piece' she is 'bright and hard-looking in her coat and skirt' [LS 137]), and later still we will see Gerald pose assertively in Mrs Fogarty's parlour – he stands 'with an elbow planted among photo-frames on the mantelpiece' (LS 178) – while insisting, to Lady Naylor, on his intention to marry Lois. At the same time, the novel has left us in equally little doubt about the virtual or phantasmatic reality elsewhere of the fires that in Danielstown itself never get lit. The landscape around the estate is repeatedly characterised as flammable, incendiary, if not yet actually burning – 'Behind the trees, pressing in from the open and empty country like an invasion, the orange bright sky crept and smouldered' (LS 22) – while, as numerous critics have observed, both Lois and Laurence seem to look forward with some relish to the eventual conflagration of their family's hereditary home. 'I should like something else to happen, some crude intrusion of the actual', Laurence remarks, intentionally provocative but speaking nonetheless in good faith: 'I should like to be here when the house burns' (LS 44).

It is remarkably difficult, however, to specify the tone or effect of the novel's final image, although its scale is surely not in doubt: the scene has a physical and psychological grandeur that offers to dwarf most of what has come before in this novel of conversations, tennis-parties and country walks – notwithstanding the phantasmatic presence throughout of the violent sexual imagination that we have observed and discussed. For hitherto in every case the figurative expression of such a desire has acted in the direction of its minimisation. Marda's symbolic defloration by an armed fugitive is represented by a small flesh wound; the Naylors' fantasy of gang-rape dresses down as a scene of forcible hair-cutting; Laurence, surprised and overpowered by local republicans, by whom he expects to be fatally assaulted, is merely deprived of his shoes (and, temporarily, of his watch) and bitten by horse-flies. In contrast, the terminating vision of the Big House in flames, an image that partakes at once of the sublime and of the obscene, suggests rather the pushing towards its limits of the capacity of narrative representation by an experience or an idea that so nearly exceeds conceptualisation as to require for the attempt the full spectrum of the novel's resources, rhetorical and emotional. The result is a kind of total, perhaps even totalitarian, emblem, the formal correlative in the realm of representation of the psychical phenomenon of the mother-and-baby dyad before separation. Unstructured by the maternal No, such an emblem is at once absolute and absurd, figuring forth a thanatophilic *jouissance* impossible to reconcile with symbolic law. How, then, are we to parse the ultimate political logic of Bowen's novel? To account the destruction of Danielstown an affirmation, on Bowen's part, of the new dispensation in Ireland will struggle to persuade by exactly the extent to which such a reading fails to engage with the obscene quality of the novel's denouement, its characterisation of the 'fearful scarlet' scene as a kind of incestuous consummation, Danielstown's orgasmic potential at last ignited by republican 'executioners' in full view of Sir Richard and Lady Naylor, hapless representatives of the triangulated sexual order that could neither gratify the motherland's psychotic desire nor exclude it, finally, from the Big House. And yet to characterise the ultimate logic of Bowen's novel in terms of a clamorous conservative lament for symbolic law in the form of the Anglo-Irish Ascendancy and its imperial backers will fall short by exactly the extent to which it ignores the fierce amoral yearning that irradiates the image of Danielstown in flames.

## Notes

1. By 'Henry VI' Bowen means her father. She gives her Bowen forefathers regnal numbers throughout *Bowen's Court*.
2. Bowen, 'Preface to *The Last September*', p. 126.

3. My assertion that in Bowen's work the beloved invariably represents one or another version of the lover's mother will immediately beg the question of any and every variety of sexuality which appears to feature a masculine object of desire. As gender is a reality of the imagination we must allow the possibility that in any particular case either a male or a female partner may represent masculinity in the eyes of the lover. Thus it will not only be heterosexual women and homosexual men whose partners are to be acknowledged as masculine (although of course it is perfectly possible that some heterosexual women and some homosexual men will perceive in their male partners a representation of femininity), but also homosexual women, some of whom may look to their female partners for a representation of masculinity. So what, then, of my claim that in Bowen's work, all desire is for a maternal object? We will be able to see that the formulation is in no way problematised by the multitude of husbands, boyfriends and butch female partners in Bowen's writing if we recognise a distinction between *the sexual partner*, on the one hand, and on the other *the object of desire*. Plenty of Bowen's characters pursue or accept the attentions of a masculine partner: but in no such case is the sexual partner coincident with the object of desire. Rather, the masculine partner is valued on account of the relationship that he or she represents to the maternal beloved. He or she represents *Father*, which is to say a way of accessing Mother: he or she is not a representation of Mother herself.
4. Bowen, *Friends and Relations*, p. 12; hereafter cited as FR.
5. Bowen, *The Last September*, p. 85; hereafter cited as LS.
6. Kreilkamp, *The Anglo-Irish Novel and the Big House*, p. 157. In less celebratory spirit, Neil Corcoran characterises the episode at the mill as a scene of 'the return of the historically repressed', the IRA man's shooting of the Anglo-Irish woman pay-back for the English destruction of Irish industry (Corcoran, *Elizabeth Bowen: The Enforced Return*, p. 53): but in this, I think, Corcoran mistakes Marda for her fiancé, misrecognising as a gesture of political retribution what is in fact an unregenerate masculine jostling for power.
7. Hoogland, *Elizabeth Bowen: A Reputation in Writing*, p. 82.

8. Hoogland, *Elizabeth Bowen: A Reputation in Writing*, p. 47.
9. Bennett and Royle, *Elizabeth Bowen and the Dissolution of the Novel*, p. 17.
10. Corcoran, *Elizabeth Bowen: The Enforced Return*, p. 50.
11. Kreilkamp, *The Anglo-Irish Novel and the Big House*, p. 158.
12. Esty, 'Virgins of Empire', p. 263. Andrew Bennett makes a similar point on a larger scale: 'Marriage and the marriage plot', he writes with particular reference to *The Last September*, 'and *therefore even plot itself*, is largely interdicted [. . .] in early Bowen' (Bennett, 'Bowen and Modernism: The Early Novels', p. 32; my italics).
13. Gildersleeve, *Elizabeth Bowen and the Writing of Trauma*, p. 34.
14. Gildersleeve, *Elizabeth Bowen and the Writing of Trauma*, p. 43.
15. Gildersleeve, *Elizabeth Bowen and the Writing of Trauma*, p. 45.
16. In Chapter 1 we observed the symbolic association in Bowen's work of the mother of the dyad with carnations, in scenes, in particular, of figurative breast-feeding in *The Hotel* and 'Ivy Gripped the Steps'. Therefore, in light of the primitive maternal eroticism represented by Lois's Aunt Myra as against the claims put forth by Gerald on behalf of a mature triangulated sexuality, it is not surprising to notice that Lady Naylor's outfit, on the day of her meeting with Gerald, includes two carnations 'pinned in the lace' of her jabot – therefore, displayed prominently on her breast (LS 180).
17. Bowen, *The Little Girls*, p. 63; hereafter cited as LG.
18. Gildersleeve, *Elizabeth Bowen and the Writing of Trauma*, p. 148.
19. Ellmann, *Elizabeth Bowen: The Shadow Across the Page*, p. 199.
20. Ellmann, *Elizabeth Bowen: The Shadow Across the Page*, pp. 66–7.
21. Kelly, 'When Things Were "closing in" and "rolling up"', p. 292. Accounts that broadly concur with Kelly's assessment include Nicola Darwood's, which distinguishes between the political thrust of the novel as a whole and the conservative resistance figured by the house, so that, 'to the last, Danielstown,

personifying both the Naylors in particular and the Anglo-Irish more generally, opens its door "hospitably upon a furnace", still unwilling, or unable, to accept its fate' (Darwood, *A World of Lost Innocence*, p. 44), and Neil Corcoran's, which 'read[s] the burning of the house at the end of the novel as the register as much of authorial desire as of anxiety' (Corcoran, *Elizabeth Bowen: The Enforced Return*, p. 60). For a reading that chimes with Ellmann's, on the other hand, see Heather Bryant Jordan's view of the novel as an opportunity for Bowen 'to practice facing what she thought she could not bear in reality: the loss of her estate, an inheritance that was both her obligation and her joy' (Jordan, 'A Bequest of Her Own: The Reinvention of Elizabeth Bowen', p. 49).

# Chapter 3
# Reproduction; or, Legacy

In Elizabeth Bowen's view, the history of the Anglo-Irish demonstrates the perennial difficulty of securing, maintaining and reproducing political power when the men of a social class show themselves as intrinsically weak. In her essay 'The Big House' (1940), she traces a paternal deficit back to the earliest years of the Ascendancy, identifying an original financial inadequacy in her settler-colonial ancestors at the same time as she pays tribute to the quixotic Enlightenment ambitions of their construction projects. Hearty, unreflective landowners, the men who built the Big Houses were nonetheless guided by principal, moved to pay homage to an ideal: 'the European idea', 'humanistic, classic and disciplined'.[1] 'It is something to subscribe to an idea', Bowen remarks, 'even if one cannot live up to it':

> These country gentlemen liked sport, drink and card-playing very much better than they liked the arts – but they religiously stocked their libraries, set fine craftsmen to work on their ceilings and mantelpieces and interspersed their own family portraits with heroicized paintings of foreign scenes [. . .] All this cost money: many of these genial builders died badly in debt and left their families saddled with mansions that they could ill afford [. . .] [B]ig houses that had begun in glory were soon only maintained by struggle and sacrifice. (BH 27)

Emerging from Bowen's analysis as a familiar portrait of a well-intentioned but chronically disappointing man, the Anglo-Irish father in character as a patron of the arts is a figure rich in pretensions but embarrassed as to funds, his 'genial' claims to cultural leadership hopelessly under-resourced. We have seen that such figures feature prominently in Bowen's fictional writing about families; they occur with particular frequency in the generation of Bowen's protagonists' parents. In some particularly significant cases, the fictional father in question can be identified as a member specifically of the age-group of the historical Henry Bowen, Elizabeth's father. What makes these cases particularly significant is that they pertain directly to the question of the upkeep and the destiny of a fictional Big House, in novels which contemplate with some urgency the legacy of the Anglo-Irish. In Bowen's novel of 1929, *The Last September*, Sir Richard Naylor, direct fictional contemporary of Elizabeth's parents', has inexplicably failed to provide an heir for his estate. Perhaps his niece Lois is expected to inherit, but the question of Danielstown's destiny is never broached, and family discussions concerning Lois's future are strictly limited to the relative merits of art school or visits to Europe. In this light we might perhaps see something of a mercy killing in Danielstown's 'execution' by the IRA. In *The Heat of the Day* (1948), Cousin Francis, Anglo-Irish peer of the fictional Sir Richard and Lady Naylor and the historical Henry and Florence Bowen, gives every sign of intending to do his best for Mount Morris, equipping himself with a wife and showing a lively interest in the prospect of modernising the place. But although he 'had always looked kindly on new inventions' it was 'with a final reluctance to take advantage of them' (HD 77). Inviolate, Mount Morris retains throughout his tenure 'almost, its original state', and Francis dies in his mid-sixties without having fathered any children.[2] '[T]he master had a great time with ideas', as his Irish caretaker puts it, but '[t]here was nothing to show in the end of it all' (HD 314).

It is, however, in the generation to which the historical Elizabeth Bowen belongs that the enfeeblement of the tribal fathers attains its peak (unless we should rather say its nadir), for it is the generation born around the turn of the twentieth century that Bowen's writing consistently associates with the ultimate extinction of masculinity among the Anglo-Irish. In Chapter 2, we observed that Laurence assumes in fantasy a feminine identification: as he is the only young man among Lois's Anglo-Irish peers we might therefore wonder if to attain sexual maturity in his community were not invariably to occupy, at least in imagination, the place of the mother (*The Last September*). This demographic, or phantasmatic, peculiarity is highlighted by the plight of the Hartigan sisters, unmarried women – the bloom already somewhat off the rose – who despite their inveterate participation in the social round appear doomed to a perpetual virginity by the dearth of Anglo-Irish men. When Lady Naylor rejects the junior officers of the British Army as suitors for Lois and her female peers – 'these young men are not at all marriageable', she opines – her neighbour Mrs Trent replies, 'But I don't see what else the girls are to do. I mean, look at the Hartigans' (LS 174). Bowen's fictional Anglo-Irish contemporary in *The Heat of the Day* is Victor Rodney. Wounded in the First World War, Victor does manage, in 1921, to father a son, but he almost immediately thereafter defaults on his marriage, abandoning his paternal responsibilities in order to live with the woman who had nursed him in the war. He then, suddenly, dies. Thus by 1940, when Bowen sets out to define the position of the Big House in '[n]ew democratic Ireland', the absence of functional fathers among her own generation – now at middle age – seems to be a settled reality, with troubling consequences for the architectural totems of the tribe (BH 28). 'Big houses in Ireland', Bowen writes,

> are, I am told, very isolated. I say 'I am told' because the isolation, or loneliness, of my own house is only borne in on me, from time to time, by the exclamations of travellers when they arrive. 'Well,' they exclaim, with a hint of denunciation, '*you* are a long way from everywhere!' (BH 25)

The literal and figurative eccentricity of life in the Big House is as much a matter of pride as of deprecation here for Bowen; pejoratively, she characterises geographical and cultural centrality as the product of a vulgar modernity, as against the elegant simplicity of a former age. 'I suppose I see this [isolation] the other way round', she remarks, remotely:

> everywhere seems to have placed itself a long way from me – if 'everywhere' means shopping towns, railway stations or Ireland's principal through roads. But one's own point of departure always seems to one normal: I have grown up accustomed to seeing out of my windows nothing but grass, sky, tree, to being enclosed in a ring of almost complete silence and to making journeys for anything that I want. (BH 25)

But by thus explicitly invoking her experience of childhood, Bowen's defence of the 'isolation' or 'loneliness' of such houses indicates some loss of psychosocial sophistication in the architectural relics of the ascendancy. 'Each house seems to live under its own spell', she writes alluringly, alarmingly;

> and that is the spell that falls on the visitor from the moment he passes in at the gates. The ring of woods inside the demesne wall conceals, at first, the whole demesne from the eye: this looks, from the road, like a *bois dormant*, with a great glade inside. (BH 25)

Insofar as Bowen associates the characteristic condition of the Big House in the Ireland of 1940 with a regressive dyadic state, her account implies a definitive expiration of paternal function in the Anglo-Irish men and women of Bowen's own generation.

Of course, it is Elizabeth Bowen's historical peer group that would, in early adulthood, witness, contest, and participate in the end of British-backed Anglo-Irish rule in Ireland, and the foundation of the Irish Republic in the early 1920s. But to fully understand the complexity and the significance of the motif of masculine extinction we will need to attend as well to Bowen's account of how her personal identity was constructed in the family of her birth, for it is in these passages of *Bowen's Court* that we may discern in autobiographical form the archetype of a model that recurs throughout Bowen's explorations of reproductive failure in the generation born around 1900. Elizabeth's birth, nine years into the marriage of Florence and Henry, came as quite a surprise to the family at large, because although the arrival of the baby had been keenly anticipated everyone had expected a boy. 'Bowen's Court asked for an heir, who was to be called Robert': the heir was always named Robert or Henry, in alternation (BC 403).

> Henry's to-be son Robert came to be *the* Robert, superseding his grandfather in the right to that name. His arrival was late, so much so that, greeting each other, people would say: 'Any news of Robert yet?' And in the exact sense he never arrived at all, for the child who, at 15 Herbert Place, on the 7th June, 1899, came to a very difficult birth was, after all, a girl – whom they christened Elizabeth. (BC 404)

'The birth', Bowen assures us, 'was celebrated at Bowen's Court by immense rejoicings', and 'no one, from the moment the sex was announced, said a word against Elizabeth for not being Robert'. In the event, Florence would not go on to have any more children, but it is evident that the couple continued for some years to try. 'About four years after my birth', Elizabeth reports, 'the start of another set up a serious illness of which [Florence] nearly died.' After this near-disaster – evidently an early-term miscarriage – Bowen writes, 'Henry wasted no more wishes on Robert', a formulation which shows that, at least in Elizabeth's mind, the Bowens' abortive third child, like their unborn first, had been imagined as a 'Robert', which is to say, a son (BC 404).

Elizabeth wants it to be understood that she was a much-loved daughter. Her father, she writes, 'had [...] from his mother a high opinion of women', and Florence's reaction to the birth of her baby was 'above all sublimely triumphant' (BC 405). '[T]he Bowens were not bound by the Salic law', Bowen asserts, distinguishing the rules governing inheritance in her family from those of an antique European legal system best remembered for its prohibition of female heirs. Yet given Bowen's emphasis on her family's desire for a boy it is hard not to sense in her insistence on the value of her femininity some conviction of its categorical inadequacy, or lack. Furthermore, the imaginary figures of masculinity in relation to whom the girl Elizabeth is defined are no less troubled by failure, incapacity or loss. Elizabeth's virtual elder brother is an image at once of perfection and of impossibility, an ideal Robert who lived for nine months in the womb of his family's imagination before vanishing at the moment of birth. Less fantasy than nightmare, or fever-dream of defectiveness and death, the younger boy – Replacement Robert – had barely time to take shape in his parents' minds before dying in a miscarriage that would nearly kill his mother too. Thus to Bowen's Court's 'ask[ing] for an heir', Elizabeth and her imaginary brothers together present a sadly inadequate response, coming to the stewardship of the family legacy as a sibling trio in which each one of three gendered identities – two masculine, one feminine – is differently damaged or deficient.

My topic in Chapter 3 – which makes up the sixth and final section of the book – is the concern in Bowen's writing with the question of legacy and a very closely associated constellation of anxieties about reproductive capability. My analysis will build on my work in Chapter 2, specifically on my exploration in the first half of that chapter of Bowen's understanding of triangulated sexuality. We saw there that Bowen's work suggests considerable confidence in the symbolic efficaciousness of mature sexual roles; by assuming, at adolescence, either a masculine or a feminine identification, a subject may expect to achieve access to the maternal object of desire. In Chapter 3, my discussion will take as its context or field precisely this stage or formation of triangulated adult sexuality, but I am going to focus on a very particular nexus of worries about gender under the mandate of paternal law that is figured in the form of the sibling trio and that takes on increasing importance in the middle and later periods of Bowen's work. Both the terms of my investigation and the textual focus of its analysis thus differ significantly from important work on the topic of political 'infertility' by Elizabeth Cullingford and Jed Esty, each of whom concentrate on *The Last September*. Cullingford describes Bowen's second novel as 'anatomiz[ing] the centripetal life of the Anglo-Irish at the moment of its extinction [. . .] through a collection of characters who are all either childless or only children'.[3] 'Lois, and her equally virginal cousin, the world-weary Laurence', Esty writes, 'represent the historical dead end of a class that can neither reproduce nor transform itself.'[4] My investigation seeks to break new ground by addressing itself to novels from the 1940s, 1950s and 1960s, as well as by identifying in the virtual sibling trio a complex and crucial figure in Bowen's literary and conceptual exploration of reproductive dysfunction.

In the first part of the chapter I shall investigate in detail the three positions or roles that make up the trio as they are to be observed in Bowen's mid-period masterpiece *The Heat of the Day* (1948). Because the trio is a model for thinking about gender – specifically, gender under the mandate of paternal law – it is always defined in relation to the maternal object, in its triangulated form a totemic representation of patriarchal social value. After an initial discussion of trios in relation to such maternal figures as Stella Rodney and the Kelway family home, Holme Dene, I home in on Mount Morris and its inheritance by Roderick Rodney, in order to focus on the question of legacy in the specific context of Anglo-Irish history. In this novel of 1948, Bowen imagines a solution to the problem of Anglo-Irish political 'reproduction' in terms of Roderick's paternal fortification by conscription into the British Army. In the second half of the chapter I explore the figure of the sibling trio in Bowen's later novels *A World of Love* (1955) and *Eva Trout* (1969), again with the aim of investigating the cultural and political dimensions of these texts. The bulk of my discussion is devoted to *A World of Love*, a story in which the decline of a Big House and its people give evidence of the symbolic incapacity or illegitimacy of the Republic of Ireland. But whereas the prospect of Mount Morris's renovation would depend upon the good husbandry of the Anglo-Irish Roderick Rodney, the house and land of Montefort – and the cultural or class values that they represent – must look instead to the salvific symbolic action of a wealthy rancher from the United States, British imperial dominion having given way to the new American superpower in the decade after the Second World War. Child Number One is the Bowens' longed-for son, the heir who will ensure the family legacy. He is a perfect healthy child; he will grow into a magnificent young man. He accords in every way with his parents' hopes; he is Robert in ideal Platonic form. But because he vanishes at the moment that his mother is delivered of a baby, his existence, even as a fantasy, will always have something spurious about it. The problem is not mortality, but its absence: never having been born, this figure lacks a crucial ontological gravity, a quality related to the risk and the possibility of death. Ernestine Gibb née Kelway is a classic example of Child Number One, the exigencies of the Second World War scant pretext for her frantic vitality. 'Her being clad in the uniform of the W.V.S. added to her air of having been torn, or having on their account torn herself, from some vital war-time activity; but Stella guessed she would look like that at any time' (HD 107). Almost perpetually in motion, Ernestine's arrival upon any scene is abrupt to the point of absurdity, and shadowed by a kind of knockabout violence; as when, for example, she 'dashe[s]' up to the Kelway tea-table and immediately begins 'to saw at the loaf' (HD 111), or draws attention to her occupation of a car by means of an '[a]nimated thumping upon a window', before being discovered within, 'bundling round invisibly inside there like a ferret' (HD 182). Her greetings are shouts, cries, or inexplicable peals of laughter; she 'swoop[s]' on a visitor's hand, 'rapidly, as though securing a bargain, before [her brother] was under way with the introduction' (HD 106); her departures, characterised as boundings or shootings-off, are effected 'with unnecessary force' (HD 107). She is never wholly quiet or at rest: 'Though standing still for the moment, she vibrated with energy, seeming to be almost audibly ticking over' (HD 107). Tainted, or exemplified, by the intimation as of something mechanical, Ernestine is a thoroughly implausible being; as when she 'turn[s]' a 'look [. . .] from Stella to Robert [in which] the absence of human awareness was quite startling' (HD 107), the oldest child of the Kelways, for all her slapstick vibrancy, seems less a living creature than a robot, an untiring humanoid contraption designed to function in crudely life-like style. Like a robot, she appears to lack a sense of her own mortality, unless it is rather that she understands her incapacity to die; she has, however, been programmed to respond in a socially appropriate fashion when a human being alludes to the inevitability of death. In the novel's second scene at Holme Dene, for example, on the evening before Robert will fall or leap from the roof of Stella's flat, the topic of mortality is raised in the context of the Kelways' having received an offer from a would-be purchaser of their family home. Mrs Kelway pretends to urge her children to come to a decision without reference to her, as she '[has] had [her] life': 'you must not expect me to be with you long', she remarks. '"Muttikins," Ernestine shriek[s] out, "don't say such *dreadful* things!"' – to which Mrs Kelway, regarding Ernestine 'with contempt', responds: 'You talk [. . .] as though you expected not to die yourself. We shall all come to that, including the children' (HD 255).

This sadistic observation might appear at first sight gratuitous to the point of perversity: irrationally, Muttikins meets her daughter's obliging reaction to the poignant spectacle of the maternal deathbed with a sudden impulse of destruction, as if punishing her most loyal lieutenant for the sedulous obedience that Robert, for example, is less swift to display. We may observe a similar interaction later in the conversation, when, prompted by another of Muttikins's self-pitying self-stagings, Ernestine delivers a further well-trained performance of devotion. 'If you do not care for [the house], you had better say so', says Mrs Kelway. '"Oh but of course we care!" wail[s] Ernestine, hysterically thumping backward her green felt hat, with the W.V.S. lettering, from her forehead. "How can I ever forget this is my home?"' Again her mother responds with an assault: '"It would not be your home if your husband had not died," said Mrs Kelway, looking at Ernestine disparagingly' (HD 260). But at both of these moments we might guess that Muttikins fails satisfactorily to land her blow. Ernestine gives no sign of having been wounded or pained by her mother's capricious hostility, and her stolid occupation, throughout the evening in question, of 'a coffin stool collected by her father at an antique shop' suggests a virtually categorical alienation from the mortal vulnerability that the name of such an item might evoke (HD 260). When Robert surprises both women with an attempt to escape the collective psychological paralysis ('*I* say, sell!'), Ernestine's reaction models a mechanical processor's response to unprecedented input without suggesting the least existential tremor: emitting 'a quite new demoralized laugh', like the outraged whine of an engine kicked into top gear, she '[spins] round on the coffin stool to examine Robert as though for the first time' (HD 260). I find myself wondering, that is to say, if Muttikins's sadism does not perhaps include some experimental intention, as if what she is trying to do, when she attacks her oldest child, is locate some credible human emotion in her strangely synthetic daughter, to prove, by hurting her, that Ernestine has feelings that can be hurt.

Child Number Two is a real live baby – like the female child born to the Bowens on 7 June 1899 and christened Elizabeth. 'The name had Henry's mother and Florence's mother and the whole range of Bowen tradition behind it' (BC 404): thus at the very moment that the Bowens' daughter is distinguished from the son they had awaited by her incontrovertible achievement of aliveness, so too she is assigned to a maternal tradition and denied the identity of the heir. '[N]o one, from the moment the sex was announced, said a word against Elizabeth for not being Robert', Bowen insists, but the way in which the being of Elizabeth, to Elizabeth's infinite disadvantage, is predicated on the not being of Robert is suggested not only by the disobliging persistence of Robert in the wishes of Elizabeth's parents but also by the proneness, in Bowen's fiction, of Child Two to be persecuted by Child One, and to experience pain and stress in consequence, as well, perhaps, as some retaliatory rage. Figuring in starkly literal terms the categorical wrongness of Two, the middle child of the Kelway trio is bullied by her elder sibling, and by the family at large, on the grounds of her femininity tout court.

Amabelle, who early had heard the call of sex, to the accompaniment of suffusing blushes and a roundness as nonplussing to her wardrobe as to herself, had been martyred for it: no one could have been merrier on the subject than Ernestine, or more repudiatingly icy than the sisters' mother. (HD 257)

The unhappy predicament of Two is reiterated in the generation below by the figure of Anne Joliffe, the elder of Amabelle's two children, who occupies the middle position in the virtual sibling trio that is Muttikins's suite of grandchildren: Christopher Robin Gibb (Ernestine's son, an army cadet) and Anne and Peter Joliffe (aged nine and seven respectively). Anne 'love[s]' her uncle, Robert Kelway, 'with, in her respectable way, the first intensity of her life: so much so that the woman she would become stared askance [. . .] out of her child's features', which naturally provokes in her Number One aunt remorseless manifestations of hostility (HD 262). 'I'm afraid we are rather a case of hero-worship', Ernestine remarks of her niece to the tea-table at large, which causes 'Anne, with her eyes down, [to] angrily [suffer] a slow red blush' (HD 112) – a response that suggests some of the hatred inspired in Child Two by her sexual humiliation. Given that Amabelle never appears in the present of the novel's narration – 'having married into the I.C.S., [she] was now confined by the war to India' (HD 106) – it is more difficult to detect the exact nature of her feelings in relation to Ernestine. But the very effectiveness of her self-imposed exile suggests considerable determination, on Amabelle's part, to escape from the orbit of Child Number One, to efface herself from the family circle if she cannot efface from it the favoured elder sibling who had tormented her there.

Neither a phantom boy nor – unforgivably – a girl, the baby conceived by the Bowens a few years after Elizabeth's birth was both authentically human and believed to be the right kind of child. But the unfortunate death, in utero, of Elizabeth's presumptive younger brother makes of Child Number Three, in Bowen's imagination, a figure of complex vulnerability, an image at once of hyper-mortality and of development arrested at a frighteningly early stage. Replacement Robert's extreme juvenility at the time of his death, and the troubling puzzle of his death's relation to his mother's body, are registered in the combination of fear and aggression which characterises Child Number Three in his attitude towards representations of the mother. On the one hand, Three seems to sense that he has been cheated of his opportunity to develop; he must contrive to get back inside the womb in hopes of completing his foreclosed gestation. On the other hand, he remembers that the womb can be a place of death, his own death; he must ensure that he can escape from the maternal chamber that he is simultaneously plotting to re-enter.

The paradox is nowhere more neatly encapsulated than in the strategic choice of pastime adopted by the third child of the Kelway trio in teenage years: 'Robert in adolescence had taken to photography, which secured him an alibi, a dark room whose door he could respectably lock, and a more or less free pass out, for technical requirements, to the nearest town' (HD 257). The purpose of a dark room is to enable the development of photographs; light let in prematurely will arrest the process of development and spoil the images, which is why it is unexceptionable to lock the door. But the dark protective enclosure in the core of the family home might feel too much like a cell in a prison, the chamber, perhaps, of a condemned man, did the hobby not also entitle the novice photographer to 'a more or less free pass out' to the world beyond Holme Dene. The handy 'technical requirements' of photography thus give cover for breaking out and breaking in both, thereby suggesting a phantasmatic project of considerable urgency and internal tensions.[5] That Robert's life is ended by his falling from a roof – whether on purpose or by mistake – and that his position, as Child Number Three, is occupied in the trio of Kelway grandchildren by Peter Joliffe, Christopher Robin Gibb representing Number One, might put us in mind of a classic figuration of just such an ambivalent masculinity in children's literature, Peter Pan. The Pooh books end with Christopher Robin's maturation, and departure from the Hundred Acre Wood, but Peter Pan is a boy who never grows up, his ability to fly a correlative of his impenitent juvenility, although he nonetheless breaks back repeatedly into the nursery spaces that he is equally apt to evade.[6]

The self-contradictoriness of the sensibility is elaborated in the ostensibly adult realm of sexual adventuring by the character of Robert Harrison, Number Three in a virtual sibling trio in which the first and second positions are occupied by Francis Morris and Victor Rodney; the maternal object in relation to which this trio is constituted is played, in different relations, by Nettie Morris and Stella Rodney, both characters figuring the archetype of the insubordinate wife or beloved, a woman who threatens, in fantasy, to castrate her sexual partners. (We will look in more detail at the figures of Francis Morris and Victor Rodney below.) I want to highlight both the virtually foetal nature of Harrison's desire for Stella and the marked ambivalence of his sexual approach to her. 'I never have been loved' (HD 43), Harrison tells Stella near the start of the novel: 'Is it so odd', he has already asked her, 'I should want a place of my own?' (HD 34) At a later meeting, almost as if she has been turning over the implications of these remarks in her mind, Stella asks him: '*You* must have had a mother?' The question appears welcome at the same time as it poses some obscure difficulty: 'He seemed nonplussed but gratified. "More or less"', he replies; observes, inconsequentially, that his mother was a South African; and adds, 'She cleared out.' 'Were you sorry?' Stella asks: 'I was in Sydney', he replies, the non sequitur again suggesting the limitations of his emotional and cognitive capacities (HD 134). Such moments seem to confirm Stella's sense of Harrison as of someone unformed, a person defective as if in consequence of developmental failure in the womb. During the course of their acquaintance she has more than one opportunity to observe him undergo 'a crisis [. . .] of [. . .] emotional idiocy': 'it was as unnerving as might be a brain-storm in someone without a brain' (HD 42). Jessica Gildersleeve suggestively associates Harrison with a 'traumatic void':[7] he is 'unrecognizable', she writes, 'unidentifiable, and more than that, nullified'.[8] It is thus perhaps not wholly surprising that when on two separate occasions Stella appears ready to admit him to her bed, Harrison swiftly backs off and backs away, notwithstanding the persistent, provocative and probably illegal efforts that he has made to achieve exactly such an invitation. For nobody knows better than Harrison that the maternal body is the first place where human development may go wrong, 'the first place' – as he remarks to Stella of Holme Dene, *à propos* of her visit to meet Robert Kelway's family – 'where rot could start' (HD 131), as well as the first potential place of life and maturation. Thus if Harrison 'would not', as he tells Stella on another occasion, 'call it [a pity]' that he and Stella had ever met, 'there have been times', nonetheless, 'when [he has] called [their relationship] the very hell' (HD 137). That Stella is even more astonished than she is outraged by this statement demonstrates that she has no conception of the threat conjured up by the uterine character of her flat, even as it holds out the enticement of its potentially remedial capacity. Reacting against Stella's amazement and hostility, Harrison 'propel[s]' himself upright in the expressively endometrial armchair in which he is seated. 'No more, for him, those insidious pink springy depths – he repudiated the pretty dream of the room' (HD 137).[9]

The problem represented by the existence of the sibling trio pertains to the management of the maternal object under the mandate of symbolic law, the management, to be precise, of what we have defined in previous chapters as the mother of the triangle. As an individual subject may assume at adolescence an active paternal role and thereby at once access and bring into being the triangulated object of desire, so it is the heir's right, and his responsibility, to appropriate and furbish up the property that at once symbolises and instantiates the symbolic power of his family and of his community or class. It is a matter at once of inheritance and of good husbandry, the opportunity to enter into possession of the estate entailing a familial and class-related obligation to work and make fruitful the land, realising the phantasmatic and political value of what has been bequeathed and promoting its potential productivity in the future. But each of the three gendered positions making up the archetypal trio of Bowen's imagination is incapable – for different reasons – of exercising paternal function and thereby enabling the reproduction of the mother of the triangle, the object and totem of patriarchal power.

In the senior Kelway trio, the categorical disqualification of Child Number Two is confirmed by exclusion from ownership of the family home. Muttikins tells Ernestine, Child Number One, that Amabelle, Child Two, 'will be in no position to say' whether she wishes to inhabit Holme Dene upon her return from India. 'She has no claims of any kind', her mother insists.

> Your father dealt with her suitably when she married. If she and her husband expect more they are quite mistaken. I had always quite understood they understood at the time [. . .] This house is to be left to you, Ernestine, and Robert, jointly. (HD 260)

Of course Number One is granted a stake in the maternal totem: Ernestine's having been married is no bar, as if, figuring as a son in her parents' imagination, she had not – in contrast to Amabelle – taken receipt from them of a dowry upon her marriage. Child One professes to cherish the home of her youth, but in characteristically ineffectual style she can neither commit to keeping Holme Dene in the family nor embrace the opportunity to sell it. '"One way and another," [says Ernestine' – in fact her last recorded words in the novel – '"there seems to be quite a fatality against our deciding anything. How if I got a pencil and paper to jot down points?"' (HD 266). Robert Kelway, Child Three, in contrast to his elder siblings is both empowered to play the property market and fully willing to do so. And yet the decision that he voices – '*I* say, sell!' – gets no more traction with his mother than could at least three previous bids on his part to settle the question of the would-be buyers: 'We turn 'em down'; 'we jack 'em up'; 'jack 'em up still higher' (HD 254). Abortive attempts to compensate for Ernestine's inability to decide, each one of Robert's pronouncements is an exercise of paternal authority that expires before it can come to birth.

The question of who will undertake responsibility for the maternal totem in its specifically Anglo-Irish form is answered, in *The Heat of the Day*, by Francis Morris's naming as the heir to his estate in the Irish Republic Roderick Rodney, Victor and Stella Rodney's son. Although the text does not explicitly assure us that Roderick will survive the Second World War, the auguries are promising, in large part because the new master of Mount Morris is distinguished so carefully from a virtual sibling trio in the generation above: the three men – all, by the end of the novel, dead – whom Roderick himself thinks of as 'his three fathers – the defeated Victor, the determining Cousin Francis, the unadmitted stepfather Robert' (HD 312). '[T]he defeated Victor' is a classic Child Two, his identity defined by phallic lack, or symbolic castration: injured in the First World War, he is comprehensively unmanned, in the eyes of his family, by Stella's false representation of him as the victim of her adultery (see Chapter 1). Dead within three weeks of the finalisation of his divorce, Victor is no more a suitable master for the Big House than is Nettie Morris, who is Francis's widow, but a descendant, as well, of the family in her own right, her inadmissibility as an heir associated – as is Victor's – with the unsatisfactory status of the feminine. Robert Kelway, of course, is Number Three; his attitude towards Francis's bequest, to Stella's son, of the family property manifests a predictable ambivalence in relation to the desirability of the Big House thereby obtained. The estate is a burden: 'To unload the past on a boy like that – fantastic! [. . .] No, it's too silly, Stella!' And yet it is a boon: 'Anything's better than nothing', he 'admit[s]', 'with a touch of the impatience he often showed when one truth got in the way of another' (HD 160). Correspondingly, Robert refutes the value of the ambiguous maternal object in the form of Mount Morris at the same time as he affirms his desire for it in the form of Stella Rodney, his annoyance, during this same conversation, about Stella's visiting the estate on Roderick's behalf evincing considerable jealousy in relation to Roderick's benefactor, whose ineffable masculine predominance Robert seeks to discredit on the grounds of its sheer implausibility. 'The whole thing's a racket of that old lunatic's. To get you back', Robert says to Stella, petulantly. Stella tries to soothe him, as one might a fractious baby: 'After all, he's dead', she points out, 'if you mean Cousin Francis?' Robert's response sounds like a joke, but it nails the essentially bogus nature of Child Number

One. 'A little thing like that wouldn't bother him', Three quips, morosely, 'call[ing] up such a speaking picture that Stella laughed. "You might have known him," she said' (HD 160).

What are the political implications of Bowen's exploration of reproductive dysfunction among the Anglo-Irish, and its potential solution in the form of Roderick, in *The Heat of the Day*? For her part, Maud Ellmann doubts that the novel proposes seriously any restoration of Anglo-Irish prestige, but 'conveys [rather] a strong impression that the culture of the Big House is defunct'.[10] She suggests, moreover, that although Bowen's novel never wholly renounces a vision of 'the traditional sanctity and loveliness of Mount Morris', the text also hints strongly at the thoroughly ambiguous nature of the cultural tradition that it represents.[11] Referring to an Anglo-Irish relative of the Morrises who advises Stella, at Francis's funeral, that the house had better be demolished at once, Ellmann remarks that 'Colonel Pole may well be right to see Mount Morris as a poisoned gift, destined to ruin its possessor.'[12] In his substantial discussion of the political complexion of *The Heat of the Day*, Neil Corcoran too stresses the novel's ultimate ambivalence, the 'extremely lively but deeply uneasy' character of its conclusion in particular.[13] But he places considerable importance nonetheless on what he characterises as the novel's attempt to imagine an 'all[iance] and reconcil[iation] [of] divided traditions' in the form of Stella's apparent contemplation of a marriage between Roderick and one of the beautiful peasant daughters of Donovan, Mount Morris's Irish caretaker.[14] In Corcoran's view, Stella's fantasy constitutes both an 'apologia' for the depredations perpetrated by the Anglo-Irish Ascendancy and a creative effort to envisage in personal terms how Roderick may accept Cousin Francis's bequest in a politically progressive fashion.[15] Stella, Corcoran writes, 'recognizes that inheritance must now be more a matter of renovation and even rejection than the acceptance of any stable "tradition"'.[16]

It seems to me, in contrast, that while the novel does indeed communicate a deep imaginative commitment to the hope that Mount Morris may flourish under Roderick's good husbandry, the political character of this fictional project or prospect is emphatically conservative and, to some extent, authoritarian. Identified from his first appearance in the text as a 'soldier in battledress' (HD 49), Roderick appears to have been subject to a kind of virtual re-parenting, or re-fathering, by virtue of his conscription into the British Army. Bolstering up the phallic function so inadequately displayed, in their different ways, by Francis, Victor and Robert, the military remastering of Mount Morris's heir would seem to have supplemented Roderick's direct paternal heritage with a robust imperial masculinity, grafting the Anglo-Irish branch more closely to the parent tree. In contrast, Bowen's Big House novel of 1955, *A World of Love*, can envisage no such figure of masculine competence as emerging from the Anglo-Irish community, whether or not fortified by a virtual transfusion of British imperial blood, the historical originating power and erstwhile guarantor of the Ascendancy portrayed in this mid-century fiction as decadent and in decline. By the same token, however, the political logic of Bowen's contemporary cultural figuration of a crisis in reproductive function is if anything even more supportive of global formations of power in this later novel than in its predecessor. In the second half of this chapter I will look in detail at the figure of the sibling trio in two of Bowen's late novels – *A World of Love* (1955) and *Eva Trout* (1969) – in order both to investigate the political complexion of Bowen's treatment, in her novel of 1955, of the question of personal, familial and cultural legacy in the context of a new American world order, and to explore the psychological urgency that drives her last substantial meditation on the historical fate of the Anglo-Irish.

'In [*A World of Love*]', Bennett and Royle remark, 'perhaps more than in any of [Bowen's] preceding [novels], attention is concentrated not only on the intricate configurations of the past within the present, but also on the sense of what is dedicated, transferred, bequeathed to the future.'[17] Set in the early 1950s, *A World of Love* looks back to the end of the First World War to explain the context in which a plan to restore the prestige of an Anglo-Irish family was first conceived and set in train by Antonia, the owner of an estate in County Cork.

> Guy, one-time owner of Montefort, Antonia's first cousin and dear ally, had, when he fell in battle early in 1918, been engaged to Lilia – at seventeen a wonderful golden willow of a girl. That enchanting love-on-a-leave, that idealization undoomed – as he probably knew – ever to fade so far failed to connect in Guy with outside reality that he had forgotten to make a Will. When he was killed, therefore, any money he had went, together with Montefort, to Antonia, who apart from anything else was his next of kin. The fiancée was left unprovided for. Antonia had felt this unfair, as it more than was.[18]

We may recognise immediately in the figure of Antonia's predecessor Guy the meretricious dash and ontological *fainéantisme* characteristic of Child Number One, and identify in Antonia herself the put-upon figure of Two. We may note that the maternal totem in relation to which these virtual siblings act takes a human as well as an architectural form – Guy's fiancée Lilia, as much as his ancestral home, attesting to his patriarchal prowess and depending upon it for maintenance in the future. Furthermore, we may observe that Antonia's predicament in 1918 resembles that of the historical Elizabeth's upon the death of Henry Bowen in 1930: both women are charged with the care of a family asset – the family home, and the prestige of the family itself – which each woman, *as* a woman, appears manifestly unequipped to undertake. But whereas Bowen could look to her husband Alan Cameron to step into the place of her dead father, Antonia is a woman alone, her own brief marriage – which will end in divorce – still an event of the future. Thus Antonia's predicament more closely recalls that of Bowen's upon the death of Alan Cameron in 1952, because Guy's death leaves Antonia as well as Lilia a virtual widow. Unable to fulfil Guy's masculine responsibilities towards his house or his fiancée alike, yet obligated for the sake of family honour to ensure the productivity of both, Antonia seeks for nearly a decade to outsource paternal function to grazing tenants (in the case of Montefort) and the proprietors of various genteel businesses (in the case of Lilia), but neither makeshift works. The unnamed tenant farmers display 'fecklessness or ill-will' while 'decay get[s] a hold on the shut-up house' (WL 16), and Lilia, '[p]ushed off into a series of occupations, placed in vain in a series of gift shops, tea shops, brought in vain to the notice of likely friends', comes 'bobbing back again like a thing on water'. Like Montefort, Lilia too shows signs of decay in the absence of competent stewardship: 'Blight had cut short her early beauty, apathy mildewed what might have remained, and her dependence upon Antonia more and more went with a profound mistrust' (WL 15).

Bowen's final novel to be published, *Eva Trout* (1969), explores in detail a closely comparable situation. Guy's Number One counterpart in this novel is Willy Trout, a millionaire businessman and 'crack polo player' who puts in a hearty performance of paternal capability for long enough to marry and impregnate the Lilia-like figure of Cissie, before dramatically defaulting on his marital commitments by falling in love with Constantine: it is a 'total attachment', an 'obsession', that would last for the rest of Willy's life. Devastated, 'defrauded', by her husband's abandonment of her, Cissie pretends to have conceived an adulterous passion of her own, flees abroad, and 'was then almost at once killed in a plane crash'.[19] Baby Eva, two weeks old when Cissie runs away in despair, is left motherless for most of her childhood, until the role is at last undertaken by a teacher at her boarding school – Iseult Smith. 'Till Iseult came, no human being had ever turned upon Eva their full attention – an attention that could seem to be love' (ET 18); so that when, twenty-three years after deserting Cissie, Willy's figurative derogation is at last reiterated in literal terms by the event of his sudden death, the paternal responsibilities inherited by Willy's legatee include the management of Eva's surrogate mother, as well as of Eva herself and a large fortune.

The legatee in question is Constantine – Child Number Two – who thus finds himself occupying a guardian-type role in relation to Iseult, Eva and the Trout millions that closely resembles the role bequeathed by Guy to Antonia in relation to Lilia and the Montefort estate. Antonia cannot man up in relation to her almost-sister-in-law because she understands herself as a woman. In light of Constantine's relationship with the emphatically phallic Willy ('Willy'!), and of Willy's apparent preference for effeminate partners – his wife, after all, had always been a Cissie – I think we may discern in Constantine, too, a feminine identification.[20] Thus just as we have seen Lilia 'blight[ed]' by the combination of Guy's premature death and Antonia's inability to compensate for his absence so too we may observe that in the case of the central maternal figure in *Eva Trout*, represented first by Cissie and then by Iseult, the terrible falling-off of the first father (Child One) is compounded by the categorical unsuitability of the second (Child Two). In both novels, the sequence plays out as a kind of formal or generic declension, the hyperbolic failure of the butch or swashbuckling hero – Willy, Guy – represented as melodrama or even as tragedy, whereas the bathetic inaptitude of the lost lord's feminine replacement – Constantine, Antonia – leads to the mundane plot elaborations of women's popular fiction. Thus Lilia's exalted status as Guy's war-widow, or widow-maiden, declines under Antonia's mandate to the pot-boiling spectacle of the middle-class woman expected to take a job; while the devastating sexual rejection that in some way triggers the horror show that is Cissie's death ('an unspeakable end', as Constantine remarks, 'not a cinder left' [ET 39]) looks sadly banal when it is re-staged, in a restaurant, between Constantine, Willy's effeminate successor and Iseult, who at this point in the narrative stands in the position of a mother to Eva.[21] Iseult had been gratified, in the first place, to be invited to meet Constantine in London; 'the letter not only revivified, it was balm. Continuously being ignored by Constantine had mortified Iseult more than she admitted' (ET 33). But the encounter fails to deliver on its promise of sexual affirmation, despite what sounds like an unambiguous demonstration of appetite on Iseult's part:

> Iseult's enjoyment of her oysters was at once methodical and voluptuous [. . .] Greed softened and in a peculiar way spiritualized her abstruse beauty, with its touch of the schoolroom. Eating became her – more than once she had been fallen in love with over a meal. She gave herself up, untainted, to this truest sensuality that she knew. [. . .] How she ate, Eric had ceased to notice; and Constantine did not care. (ET 41)[22]

Who is Eric, whose gradual loss of focus on Iseult's desire is contrasted here with Constantine's vexatiously absolute lack of interest? Eric Arble is Child Number Three, the third and final 'father' in the sibling trio. Eric's counterpart in *A World of Love* is Fred Danby, who is drafted in to marry Lilia and move in to Montefort, ten years after Guy's death in the First World War. Eric's marrying of Iseult in the later novel thus corresponds to the first stage of the plan to rescue the legacy of Montefort from the combined effects of Guy's negligence and Antonia's incapacity. For like the 'County Cork man' to whom Bowen would sell her ancestral home in 1959, Eric and Fred are fertility gods, their action, it is fervently hoped, to bless and make fruitful the patrimonial lands that have lain barren under the mandate of their incompetent predecessors.

In both texts, the potency of Child Number Three is imagined to be guaranteed by humble social status. Whereas, in the novel of 1969, the millionaire Willy and his cosmopolite fancyman fail in their stewardship of the maternal totem, great feats of fecundation are looked for from the undistinguished provincial figure of Eric Arble, a '[t]remendous unsparing worker'. 'Always', we read of Eric, 'he had wanted to be a fruit farmer, or thought so. He had put his back, together with all he'd got from selling up a small business left him by his father, into the enterprise known as Larkins Orchards' (ET 22). The nature of the small business that makes possible the establishment of Larkins Orchards is left unspecified, as if to facilitate Eric's self-image as a horny-handed son of the soil, a fantasy – operative at least as powerfully in Iseult as in her husband – of the bridegroom as a kind of modern-day Green Man that might be more difficult to sustain if Arble *père* were brought into closer focus as a member of the petty bourgeoisie. Certainly Iseult's attraction to Eric – 'a cerebral young woman's first physical passion' (ET 18) – is inextricable from her wishful perception of his quasi-peasant identity and primitive rural sexuality. While onlookers ponder the 'one mystery' of this 'highly intelligent person, young still, of pleasing appearance and good character': 'why had she thrown herself away?' (ET 16–17), Iseult feeds greedily, in imagination, on the lush agricultural prospect of the 'obscure marriage' that has motivated her 'abandonment of a star career' (ET 18).

> She never foresaw their marriage, its days and nights, other than as embowered by dazzling acres, blossom a snowy blaze and with honeyed stamens, by sun then moonlight, till came later – fruited boughs bowed, voluptuous, to the ground, gumminess oozing from bloomy plums. She had been a D. H. Lawrence reader and was a townswoman. (ET 22)

Lilia too is alert to the social inferiority of the man whom it is proposed that she should accept in marriage: Fred, she 'incontrovertibly' asserts, is 'common' (ET 16), whereas she herself – so Bowen's narrative specifies – is a daughter of the English middle-middle or lower-middle classes, 'suburbia merging into the Thames Valley' (ET 15). Indeed, whereas a certain disingenuousness dogs Eric's neo-rural stylings from the start (and perhaps helps to explain the swift and definitive failure of Larkins Orchards not long into the Arbles' marriage), Fred's lowly social credentials and agricultural competence are not to be gainsaid, despite the tincture of some notional distinction contributed by his paternal ancestry:

> Fred was Guy's and Antonia's illegitimate cousin, byblow son of roving Montefort uncle. As to his mother, who vanished, little was known: it was generally held she'd had foreign blood, to which Fred's colouring gave support. He had been left in at Montefort, not reclaimed and allowed to grow up in the stable yards, attempts to school him having been dropped in view of his usefulness round the place. (ET 15)

How then does a wedding come to be arranged between Fred, Mellors-like denizen of the Montefort stables, and Lilia – in this respect very unlike Iseult – whose failure to imagine herself a second Constance Chatterley points up her unfamiliarity with the works of D. H. Lawrence? It is Antonia's idea, and her doing: after nearly a decade of failing to exercise productive paternal control over Montefort and Lilia alike, Antonia offers them as a package deal to Fred ('a woman [goes] with the land', she tells him: 'Take one, take both' [ET 16]). In return, he will halve the profits of the farm with Antonia, who will retain full ownership of the estate and visit it as she sees fit. Although Fred has never before laid eyes upon Lilia, it takes him just a few days – after Lilia is summoned to Montefort, unawares, for his inspection – to come to a decision: 'after thirty-six hours he was able to intimate that as far as *he* went, the thing was on. Would Antonia speak to the lady on his behalf?' (ET 16) Lilia is unimpressed by her rustic suitor; but after Antonia warns her that she, Antonia, will not 'prop [her] up any longer', and is 'sick of having Montefort run to ruin', Lilia too spends just three days 'stunned by the ultimatum, shocked by the outrage, mindless with indecision' before 'capitulat[ing]' to Antonia's plan.

> [A]s Antonia could not now wait to be off to London, the wedding went through almost at once. Having escorted the couple home from the church, Antonia leaped back into the beribboned hackney and made her habitual dash to the boat train. She looked behind her once – they still stood framed in the doorway, blankly watching her go. They put no face on the thing.
> It is not known what words Fred or Lilia then or in the following time exchanged. Left there to mate, they mated[.] (ET 18)

I think it no exaggeration to say that this plot event in what is an essentially realist novel is perhaps the single most extraordinary fictional proposition to be advanced anywhere in Bowen's oeuvre. For what the text insists on here is that a marriage between virtual strangers could be arranged and executed in the Republic of Ireland of the late nineteen-twenties, at practically the drop of a hat, on the say-so of a woman, the direct contemporary of the bride and groom, whose patent and more or less avowed concern, in the sexual and reproductive disposition of the human beings in question, is with ensuring the productivity of her family's ancestral assets. Impossible to credit as a proposition, in fictional terms, about the real world to which the fictional world of *A World of Love*, as a realist novel, for the most part plausibly refers itself, Antonia's preposterous 'marry[ing][-]off' of Lilia to Fred (WL 15) suggests by its overtly fantastical nature the difficulty of arranging for the maintenance of the maternal object under the mandate of paternal law.

By the same token, however, the episode is richly informational with regard to the ethno-social tropology of a certain Anglo-Irish *imaginaire*. Unable herself to make good on Guy's foreclosed commitments, Antonia is happy to press into service the working-class phallus, requisitioning Fred's masculine endowments as if he were a stallion and Lilia Antonia's mare. Indeed, having been 'allowed to grow up in the stable yards' and virtually without education (WL 15), Fred seems almost more horse than human, half-animal at least, a kind of plebeian centaur figure credited with exceptional potency from adolescence. 'At fifteen, mature for his age, he was said to be poaching salmon, going with women' (WL 15), the implicit comparison of Fred's sexual conquests of women (not 'girls') with the stealing of fish from landowners' streams contributing to the young man's portrait a very Mellors-like power to cuckold the enfeebled gentry. Not that there is anything of the natural aristocrat about Fred. When he puts in his first appearance as a middle-aged man in the present of the novel's narration his characterisation as virtually bestial is reinforced by the suggestion of an evolutionary primitivism and linked, in addition, to the 'foreign blood' inherited from his mixed-race Irish mother.

> [H]ere he was, standing in the kitchen, hastily drinking out of a thick Delft cup [. . .] Fred's shirt was open, showing the matted black hair, here and there glistening with tea drops, on his barrel chest. He now was a thickset man, about fifty-three, with a touch of the Latin about his pigmentation and cast of features. His skull was broad, with forehead receding somewhat; his muscle-webbed neck was short. His far-apart, dark and prominent eyes were inhabited by a look of curious patience, as though he had at one time been struck across them and might be so again. (WL 19)

The rhetoric of this description is redolent of scientific racism, notwithstanding an intermittent compassion for the simple sufferings of the creature under examination. At best, Number Three is envisaged here as a representative member of a slave race, his cognitive limitations enabling a brute resilience in the face of cruel treatment; at worst he is figured in literally subhuman terms, a lower primate that can, like a chimp at the zoo, be sketchily costumed and induced to participate in the unwitting burlesque of a tea party, guzzling from a specially tough cup and spilling tea down its black hairy chest. There is thus something grotesque to the point of obscenity in the vision of the congress of Lilia and Fred, whether it is evoked in prospect by '[the] air they wore on their wedding day, [the] air of having been thrown together' (WL 140), or projected back by the novel's portrayal of the couple in middle age: a white-skinned, blue-eyed, golden-haired Englishwoman ravished by a dusky *untermensch*; a lily despoiled by a gorilla.

As we have noted, the agricultural promise of Eric Arble's Lawrentian posturings speedily proves to have been false. Larkins Orchards has to be given up and sold off, the Arbles retaining only the house, 'which the purchaser did not want, a lopsided barn, [and] a half-acre of land' (ET 22), while Eric goes to work as the foreman of a garage in the local town. That he acquits himself creditably in this modest but by no means primitive or bucolic role, that he shows himself 'a first-rate mechanic', 'a born one', only exacerbates the damage to his relationship with Iseult; ultimately the marriage, cut down, as it were, to an unassuming detached house, an only faintly picturesque outbuilding, and what is in effect – by the standards of lower-middle-class suburbia – a rather generous lawn, will not survive the destruction of its founding myth, the loss of its phantasmagorical orchards, its oneiric groves of 'bloomy plums'.

In contrast, the popular supposition of Fred Danby's fecundity is swiftly confirmed by what seems to have been his immediate impregnation of Lilia upon their marriage, Antonia's vision of a future for Montefort thus appearing to have been inspired by a sound apprehension of Fred's potentialities. And yet as early as evidence of Lilia's pregnancy is to be discerned there are manifest also uneasy intimations of something amiss, unpleasing, in the very figure of the expectant mother that Child Two has contrived, by executive action, to engineer. Returning to Montefort – for the first time, it is implied, since the Danbys' wedding – Antonia is 'aghast' at what she finds. For a start, the couple show signs of authentic mutual desire, an unlooked-for development from Antonia's essentially agricultural perspective: 'something monstrous seemed to her to be under her own roof. These two engendered a climate; the air around them felt to her sultry, overintensified, strange; one could barely breathe it' (WL 18). Gone, we are to understand, is the bovine surrender of the couple on their wedding-day, their air – as of livestock set to breed – 'not so much of misgiving as of subservience' (WL 140). Worse, however, for the childless Anglo-Irish landowner, is the transformation of the 'flaccid' (WL 16) middle-class virgin into an idol of social and reproductive transcendence.

> For Lilia that was an epoch, not to occur again, of ascendancy over her former patron. She was again in beauty, of a lofty late lightless inert kind; her pregnancy added to and became her, and this great never quite smiling snow-woman, come into being almost overnight, was formidable. She neutrally and abstractedly eyed Antonia, heard her speak or spoke to her from a distance – she was queening it, and, which was still worse, queening it naturally, unawares. Smug, thought Antonia, cutting that visit short. (WL 18)

The passage forms a striking contrast to the image of the newly pregnant Florence Bowen at the Bowens' winter residence in Dublin – a vignette in *Bowen's Court* (1942) that we looked at briefly in Chapter 1. In both cases the figure of the mother-to-be is counterpointed by that of another woman, not an inhabitant of the house, but closely apprised of its intimate business. 'Mrs Gates' – we thus read – 'a Bowen's Court neighbour much in Florence's confidence, called at Herbert Place to find Florence, elated and serious, on the drawing-room sofa, with her Persian cat Tory (after Queen Victoria) curled up in her skirts'

(BC 404). But whereas Mrs Gates's point of view allows us to appreciate the charismatic self-sufficiency of the pregnant Florence Bowen, casting Elizabeth's mother as a late-Victorian Madonna del Parto, an image at once humorous and sacred, chthonic and light-hearted, Antonia's perspective on the 'great never quite smiling snow-woman', 'queening it' over the Big House, is full of resentment. Like a nymph or a maiden impregnated by a god, Lilia appears to have assumed – 'naturally, unawares' – the 'lofty' status of her lover, a presumptuousness that the true-born daughter of the king would punish if she could. Unable to challenge the equivocal Madonna of Montefort, Antonia takes what comfort she can from a curt private dismissal of the woman's uppitiness and from what she imagines as an aggressive departure ('Smug, thought Antonia, cutting that visit short'). Better days are to come, however, after the birth of the baby: 'When next Antonia came to Montefort Jane was an infant, and Fred's kind, unfailing patience with Lilia confirmed the rumours that he was off again, back to his loves in the lanes' (WL 18–19).

Neil Corcoran reads the novel as a complicated but emphatic denunciation of the Ascendancy class represented by Montefort's historical proprietors. '[I]f Anglo-Irish regret, melancholy, and envy are part of the emotional structure of *A World of Love*', he writes, 'so too is a strong sense of accusation': in Corcoran's view, the novel delivers 'a terminal judgement' on 'Anglo-Irish arrogance'.[23] I will come in due course to the meaning of the novel's conclusion, but I would like to observe at this point that any characterisation of the novel's political complexion as liberal, let alone progressive, would seem to be seriously compromised by virtually every aspect of the novel that we have considered so far, not least the episode of Antonia's reaction to Fred's impregnation of Lilia. Antonia's ambivalence in relation to Lilia's pregnancy – she organises for it to be brought about, yet responds to its achievement as if to an assault upon social hierarchy – demonstrates that Child Two's marrying-off of One's widowed fiancée, and handing over of the operation of the estate, to Three, a 'byblow son of roving Montefort uncle', cannot represent a definitive response to the imperative to reproduce tribal prestige. For I think what is demonstrated by Antonia's perception of the pregnant Lilia as an inadmissibly parvenu mother is that Child Three's phallic capability is both literally and symbolically illegitimate.

Fred's relation to his Anglo-Irish father is informally accepted by everyone, but at the same time it is not registered in law. There could have been no question of Fred's inheriting Montefort on Guy's death, for example. Fred has no legal relationship to his cousins Guy and Antonia, and his social identity as a bastard must mean that the name 'Danby' comes from his mother. Most critical work on Bowen assumes that Fred, Antonia and Guy share a surname, but in fact Bowen never refers to the legitimate descendants of the Montefort dynasty as Guy Danby or Antonia Danby, and the phrase 'the Danbys' is used exclusively to denote the married couple of Fred and Lilia or the nuclear family comprised of them and their two daughters, Jane and Maud. Thus while Fred's mixed-race, working-class maternal inheritance endows him with a robust fecundity, his symbolic capacity to create of his wife a figure of sociosexual exaltation or 'ascendancy' (WL 18) is intrinsically limited. The virtual staging of Lilia as a queen consort or maternal idol is 'formidable' while it lasts, but it is 'lightless' and 'inert', and it does not endure very long. And when the paternal prohibition has ceased entirely to glorify the figure of the mother she shows as a strangely degraded object, as Lilia is simultaneously rejected by her husband and humiliated in the eyes of onlookers such Antonia, who understands Fred's 'kind, unfailing patience' towards his wife as a sign that he desires her no longer.

As the novel opens, twenty years later, on the scene of Montefort and its grounds one fine summer's morning in the early 1950s, the results of Fred's illegitimate mastery are evident in the slovenly look of the Big House, 'the small mansion [wearing] an air of having gone down' (WL 9).

> The door no longer knew hospitality; moss obliterated the sweep for the turning carriage; the avenue lived on as a rutted track, and a poor fence, close up to the house, served to

keep back wandering grazing cattle. Had the façade not carried a ghost of style, Montefort would have looked, as it almost did, like nothing more than the annexe of its farm buildings – whose slipshod gables and leaning sheds, flaking whitewash and sagging rusty doors made a patchwork for some way out behind. (WL 9)

I want to focus here on determining the specifically political bearings of Bowen's critique of the symbolic function of the third member of the sibling trio in distinction to his incompetent paternal predecessor Child One. A stock figure of romantic, virtually aristocratic Anglo-Irish masculinity, Guy – Child One – is no less ineffectual than he is impetuous in his attentions to women and land alike. He can recognise a pretty girl and sweep her off her feet, but he fails to establish definitively his mastery over her. There is a suggestion in the novel's description of Guy's whirlwind courtship of Lilia 'by the ballroom blue moonlight of Maidenhead' that he stopped short of taking her virginity, the maidenhead, as it were, of her Home Counties girlhood (WL 15); this might put us in mind of Francis Morris, whose wife, Nettie, refused sexual relations with him, a situation that is paralleled by the failure of Francis's projects to modernise his Big House. And if Guy had in fact succeeded in deflowering his fiancée he nonetheless neglected to achieve any registration of that event in law, the 'enchanting love-on-a-leave [. . .] so far fail[ing] to connect in Guy with outside reality that he had forgotten to make a Will' (WL 14). Guy's lordly incompetence in relation to Lilia thus assorts suggestively with his patronage of his land: at once ostentatious and unaccountable, Number One's 'overweening sentiment' for Montefort 'went [. . .] with neither wish nor ability to stay [there] always' (WL 14).

Fred, in contrast, is no absentee landlord: he is a peasant, and a bastard, installed in the master's place. As the previous passage makes clear, the Big House under the control of Child Three is unmistakably subject to symbolic prohibition – guarded by a 'poor fence', Montefort is approached, if no longer ceremonially, then with plenty of inconvenience, by way of a 'rutted track'. There is no question here of regression to a dyadic state; the paternal mandate that should secure the mother of the triangle is certainly operative, to some extent or in some manner. But it is inefficacious, illegitimate; hard at work, maybe, but not working stylishly or well. All the social graces of the place have withered or flaked away, the front door fallen out of use, the 'sweep for the turning carriage' obliterated by the unchecked growth of moss; prestigious no longer, Montefort shows as horribly debased, its essentially agricultural identity barely at all ennobled by the architectural 'ghost of style' that lingers about the façade. The court as of a lovely Madonna has given way to an unlovely farm, its 'slipshod' and 'sagging' aspect fully congruent with a workaday productivity. Where Guy typifies the Anglo-Irish father as a purebred gentleman patron of the land, a stylish lover if ultimately an ineffectual one, Fred figures the modern Republic as the byblow son of the *ancien régime*, a rough-and-ready mongrel demonstrably up to the task of fertilising Mother Ireland but incapable of spiritualising her femininity, securing her glamour, her aura as of something sacred, holy.

In the final episode of the novel, the twenty-one-year-old Jane Danby, daughter of Lilia and Fred, is driven to Shannon airport, with her younger sister Maud, by Harris, an English chauffeur. Harris is employed by the Danbys' English neighbour, Lady Latterly, who inhabits an 'unusually banal' castle in the vicinity of Montefort (WL 75); the purpose of the expedition in Lady Latterly's vehicle is to collect from the airport a visiting American, a house-guest – and former lover – of Lady Latterly's. Presumably wealthy, the American in question, one Richard Priam, lives in Colorado and is thought to be connected with ranching. Richard descends from the plane to Jane awaiting him on the tarmac: they are strangers to one another, and yet as their eyes meet – in the final line of the novel – 'They no sooner looked but they loved' (WL 149). Any reading of this scene today will be indebted to articles by Edwina Keown (2010) and Jeannie Im (2015) which explore the symbolic significance of Shannon airport. At mid-century, Keown writes, the airport was

> not only a window on the modish world but also a strategic centre, an economic and political crossroads of post-war capitalist modernity. Shannon marked the new shift in world economics and power from Europe to New York, and Ireland's shifting policy from a focus on Britain [. . .] and its own internal affairs, to direct foreign investment with America.[24]

Building on this recognition of the airport's role in the political reorientation and economic revitalisation of Ireland, Im stresses the significance of the passage to the allegorical work of the novel as a whole. Thus the Richard-and-Jane episode at the novel's conclusion emerges from Im's bracing analysis as the prime example of the text's romanticisation of international realpolitik in the years after the Second World War, its 'romantic emplotment of Ireland's entry into global capitalist networks'.[25] The scene of their love at first sight is the sign of a kind of political 'dreamworld' afloat in Bowen's novel – 'a fantasy where postcolonial nationalism is absorbed into late capital modernity'.[26]

Disembarrassed of its cod-Shakespearean mystifications, the novel's conclusion becomes legible in terms of a startlingly hard-headed analysis of the possibility of political redemption for the Anglo-Irish in the wake of British imperial decline. Or, to put it another way, the conclusion addresses the final part of the action plan to salvage the prestige of Antonia's family. As in *The Heat of the Day*, the reproductively incompetent trio – in the earlier novel, Roderick's 'three fathers' (HD 312); in the latter, Guy, Antonia and Fred – must be superseded by a salvific patriarch who can assure the glamour of the maternal totem. But whereas Mount Morris represented the mother as a virtually virginal figure, Montefort, as we have seen, is an all-too-prosaic wife, as slovenly as she is productive. Who would want her now? This is where Jane comes in as the representative daughter of the Anglo-Irish. For as if in defiance of Jane's debased parental inheritance, the Danbys' first child – bred, we will remember, at the behest of Antonia – has been virtually adopted by the female proprietor of Montefort. 'The cost of Jane's education – first at expensive boarding school, lately at a select London secretarial college – had been met by Antonia' (WL 14), to such satisfactory effect that by the time Jane reaches her majority 'this golden changeling was, in so far as she belonged to anybody, Antonia's' (WL 52).

Early on in the novel, 'Jane could now be held to be qualified for her first post', Bowen's narrator remarks disingenuously: 'what it should be or when she should take it up was not yet decided' (WL 14). I say 'disingenuously' because nobody at Montefort seriously imagines that Jane will undertake paid employment. At a moment of annoyance with her protégée, Antonia threatens her with talk of work, but Jane's response clearly demonstrates that she understands the remark as an expression of anxiety and ill humour rather than of an authentic expectation on Antonia's part that her protégée will take a job. Hearing that Antonia has offered Lilia a little holiday in London, and that Fred will be left behind in Ireland, Jane 'declare[s], in a tone which defied the world to detect in it any loss of her golden confidence: "Then *I* ought to stay and look after him!"' (WL 128) 'Just when had you thought of beginning to earn your living?' Antonia responds, pettishly. Jane at first parries, as if meeting a joke – 'Not, I do hope, while it's so hot' – before answering soberly, if provocatively, 'But in a way I'd have thought I already did. – Does this mean we're stony again, Antonia? In that case, who's going to pay for mother?' Antonia is duly provoked: 'What d'you mean, "you thought you already did"?' – but this is a disingenuous gesture too. For as Jane recognises perfectly well, she has been designed to gratify and attract. 'I've been a pleasure', 'she at last replie[s] to Antonia' (WL 128). Perhaps then it is not so much disingenuous as euphemistic on the part of Bowen's narrator to describe as a 'post' the occupation for which Jane has been 'qualified' by her upper-middle-class education – if we understand marriage, for a woman of the class to which Antonia has promoted her surrogate daughter, as exactly such a formal undertaking to function as the object of patriarchal desire.[27] The very model of a 1950s debutante, Jane's job is to attract and secure on behalf of her people – her adopted people, Antonia's people: the Anglo-Irish people – the patronage of a powerful man. Several recent readers of the novel have remarked on Fred Danby's feelings for his daughter: feelings that, as Corcoran puts it, '[border] on the incestuous'.[28] Ellmann connects this directly with the malaise afflicting Montefort, a psychical sickness that Ellmann identifies with a failure of adequate mourning in relation to the long-ago death of Guy. In this melancholic environment 'the taboo against incest is at risk: a danger made explicit in Fred's festering passion for his daughter Jane'.[29] If, however, we understand Jane as a kind of bait or lure designed to attract a high-status husband, we may perceive her desirability to her own father as evidence of the success of Antonia's plan. Fred's passion for his daughter – which contrasts strikingly with his sexual disaffection with his wife – is less a sign of trouble at Montefort than it is an intimation of the possibility of rescue by a patriarch from another tribe. The descent from the skies of the rich American rancher to the waiting Jane thus represents the ultimate triumph of Antonia's struggle to redeem herself as the heir of Montefort, her securing of the prestige of her family at once the production of a legacy of her own.

The solution that Bowen proposes in 1948 to the problem of the reproduction of Anglo-Irish power figures the class in question as a young man whose phallic capacity could be fortified by means of his conscription into the British imperial project. Published in 1955, *A World of Love*, in contrast, imagines the former proprietors of Ireland in the shape of a beautiful girl, classed up by the elite finishing schools of London whose cultural revalorisation of Anglo-Irish femininity thus parallels the British Army's re-invigoration of Roderick. Jane is consistently associated with, and pictured in terms of, gold: her 'easy golden hair' (WL 10) – smartly cut, of course – is repeatedly remarked on; her behaviour in childhood is said to be 'as good as gold' (WL 92); she imagines her own attention as a 'golden apple' (WL 58); her profile is suggestively described as 'coinlike' (WL 81). These images do not merely emphasise Jane's function as a resacralised figure of the Anglo-Irish mother, a Lilia re-gilded and glamourised anew. The golden tropes suggest also a certain imaginary material transformation in the representation of the maternal totem, a re-embodiment, at mid-century, of the symbol of tribal honour in distinctively fiscal form. Conceived more as a hoard of gold than as a Big House, Jane figures a new portability in the cultural capital of the Anglo-Irish, an aptness for transfer within and across national territories illustrated by the ease with which Lady Latterly arranges for Jane's delivery to Shannon airport to await the incoming Richard like a gleaming idol deposited on the runway. Thus the scene confirms also the dramatic transformation, in *The World of Love*, in the figuration of the erstwhile guarantors of Anglo-Irish rule. The warlike British father of *The Heat of the Day* is transmogrified into Lady Latterly, who puts Jane in the way of her American ex-boyfriend as if repentantly or unrepentantly compelled to assist in securing a new global patron for the daughter of the Anglo-Irish. Loveless, rotten, a caricature of post-menopausal decadence, Lady Latterly's sexual machinations in relation to Jane show as the actions, in effect, of a very high-class madam. If the British can no longer act the bridegroom, they can certainly play the pimp.

## Notes

1. Bowen, 'The Big House', p. 27; hereafter cited as BH.
2. Francis Morris is sixty-five at the time of his death in 1942, which indicates that he was born in 1877. Henry Bowen was born in 1862 (and Florence in 1866); I think it appropriate to describe Francis and Henry as generational peers because Henry, as the oldest of eight children, will have had at least one or two siblings of very close to Francis's age.
3. Cullingford, '"Something else"', p. 291.
4. Esty, 'Virgins of Empire', p. 259. See also Vera Kreilkamp's analysis of how political deterioration in the Anglo-Irish Ascendancy is figured in terms of reproductive exhaustion in families (Kreilkamp, *The Anglo-Irish Novel and the Big House*, pp. 22–3).
5. See p. 183 of *Elizabeth Bowen: The Enforced Return* for Neil Corcoran's somewhat different discussion of the function of

Robert Kelway as 'an autobiographical inscription' in *The Heat of the Day*.
6. The contrast between Christopher Robin and Robert Kelway is further articulated in relation to the question of being photographed, as Robert – Child Three – was not only an adolescent practitioner in the medium but acted as a photographic subject on numerous occasions in his childhood and youth. This enables his bedroom in Holme Dene to be rendered remarkable by the 'sixty or seventy photographs, upward from snapshots to crowded groups [. . .] hung in close formations on two walls. All the photographs featured Robert. By himself or with friends, acquaintances or relations he was depicted at every age' (HD 116). 'Yes, quite a galaxy, aren't they?' Ernestine remarks to Stella. 'Robert has always photographed well; whereas my own boy Christopher Robin, unlike his uncle, flees from a camera at sight' (HD 124). Robert's lover, and some significant recent readers of the novel, have concurred in their estimation of the rumness of this bedroom decor, which, Robert specifies, is the handiwork of his mother and Ernestine. Wallowing enjoyably in the ghastliness of the Kelways, Stella, '[c]omfortably slipping her arm through [Robert's]', comments that 'they've only made this room as though you were dead' (HD 118). In her trauma-oriented reading of *The Heat of the Day* Gildersleeve endorses Stella's characterisation of the deadly and deathly implications of the room, arguing that the photographs '"empty" the room of its occupant's existence, in the past and in the present' (Gildersleeve, *Elizabeth Bowen and the Writing of Trauma*, p. 127), while Corcoran, writing more broadly on the significance of photography across Bowen's work as a whole, observes that 'Bowen knows as keenly as Roland Barthes in *Camera Lucida* that photographs are spectres [. . .], as keenly as Susan Sontag in *On Photography* that "all photographs are *memento mori*"' (Corcoran, *Elizabeth Bowen: The Enforced Return*, p. 68). While I agree that the photographs of Robert contribute to his characterisation as a figure too emphatically marked by mortality, I would want also to underline the differently troubling evasiveness of a man such as Christopher Robin Kelway who 'flees from a camera at sight'. As we have seen, Number One is rendered less plausible, rather than more, by his strange alienation from death.

7. Gildersleeve, *Elizabeth Bowen and the Writing of Trauma*, p. 120.
8. Gildersleeve, *Elizabeth Bowen and the Writing of Trauma*, p. 121.
9. In her discussion of Harrison's intrusion into Stella's home, Maud Ellmann characterises the flat as 'a space that grows and shrinks with disconcerting elasticity' (Ellmann, *Elizabeth Bowen: The Shadow Across the Page*, p. 154).
10. Ellmann, *Elizabeth Bowen: The Shadow Across the Page*, p. 161.
11. Ellmann, *Elizabeth Bowen: The Shadow Across the Page*, p. 160.
12. Ellmann, *Elizabeth Bowen: The Shadow Across the Page*, p. 162.
13. Corcoran, *Elizabeth Bowen: The Enforced Return*, p. 201.
14. Corcoran, *Elizabeth Bowen: The Enforced Return*, p. 190.
15. Corcoran, *Elizabeth Bowen: The Enforced Return*, p. 191.
16. Corcoran, *Elizabeth Bowen: The Enforced Return*, p. 193.
17. Bennett and Royle, *Elizabeth Bowen and the Dissolution of the Novel*, p. 104.
18. Bowen, *A World of Love*, p. 14; hereafter cited as WL.
19. Bowen, *Eva Trout or Changing Scenes*, pp. 17–18; hereafter cited as ET.
20. Such a hypothesis is supported by Constantine's barely disguised hostility in relation to feminine women, whom he recognises as his direct rivals for the attention of manly men. Thus his initial characterisation of Cissie, when questioned by Iseult about Eva's mother, as 'delightful' – '"Such enchantingly girlish ways, so charming so often. So deliciously" – his eye skated lifelessly over his guest – "dressed, always. One was devoted to her"' (ET 39) – gives way very rapidly to the assertion that she was '*not* normal' (ET 41). 'Delightful she could be, could have been. One so wished that she should be', he goes on, his hypnotic transitions through grammatical moods a kind of formal manoeuvring in preparation for sticking in the knife: 'But possessive, vindictive? – frankly, she was maniacal. Willy she wore to a shadow. Such scenes . . .' [sic] (ET 41).
21. That Eva's birth mother pretended to flee into the arms of a lover – when in fact she seems to have expected to be

alone – and met her end in the conflagration ensuing from a plane crash may remind us of the trope of the Big House in flames, and of our exploration, in Chapter 2, of the figure of the dyad mother who resists separation in favour of a shockingly destructive psychotic jouissance. Cissie's holocaustic dissolution thus associates her with the women of Danielstown – Laura Naylor, Lois and her Aunt Myra – and with Mrs Piggott and Mrs Nicholson, whose putative affairs with married men may provide cover for exactly such a primitive maternal eroticism (*The Last September*; *The Little Girls*; 'Ivy Gripped the Steps'). As she is a wealthy citizen of Edwardian England, when Mrs Nicholson desires to 'go right away somewhere' she imagines a journey '[t]o Germany, or into the sun' (Bowen, 'Ivy Gripped the Steps', p. 702); half a fictional century later, and enabled by the faithless Willy's millions, Mrs Trout's heliotropic flight gets as far as the skies above South America before crashing and burning in the Andes (ET 40). Disjointed reminders of Cissie's 'unspeakable end' recur at unpredictable intervals throughout the novel, by turns lurid, enigmatic, or numb: in, for example, Eva's identification with Joan of Arc ('*Elle fut carbonisée*', remarks a fellow pupil [ET 51]); in the figure of the female sculptor to whom Eva briefly entrusts her adoptive son, and on whose watch the child is even more briefly abducted (she moves 'as though taking part in an *auto-da-fé* procession of one', speaks 'with the melted smile of a martyr out of the flame', and presides over a house whose 'scant furnishings were memorial pieces [. . .] In the fireplace were (which recalled something?) the white, deadened ashes of a wood fire' [ET 199, 197, 202]); or in the report of an encounter with Iseult on a bus ('I thought', another character remarks, 'they had a car of sorts': 'It is being decarbonized, I believe she told me', comes the reply [ET 74]).

22. How are we to assess the political bearings of Bowen's representation of male homosexuality in *Eva Trout*? On the one hand, the novel's portrayal of a community of homosexual men is strikingly rancid. Willy identifies a rival for Constantine's affections in the figure of an experimental educationalist: '[i]nspirational Kenneth of the unclouded brow and Parthenon torso' (ET 48). To keep Kenneth out

of Constantine's way, Willy sets him up as the head of a school 'two hundred miles out of town', entirely undeterred by his belief that Kenneth has predatory sexual designs on the male pupils. Moreover Willy's self-knowledge is so defective and his narcissism so robust that he can misrecognise his own ruthlessness as its opposite: 'Though in the throes of a jealousy aggravated by chronic mistrust of Constantine, Willy was not unscrupulous – boys, he would not have signed over like this for a single instant; but in a mixed school could Kenneth get up to much?' (ET 48) On the other hand, *Eva Trout* is populated in large part by grotesques. It is beyond the scope of a note to itemise the social, emotional, psychological and developmental abnormalities manifest in the novel's characters; suffice it to say that while it is true that Willy, Constantine and Kenneth make up a picturesque exhibit in the freak show, there are plenty of other acts on the bill. Furthermore – and to change tack somewhat – a comparison such as I have offered of Guy and Willy, Antonia and Constantine, works more to typicalise the homosexual men in the two pairings than to pathologise the heterosexuals. Willy's desertion of his wife in favour of a male beloved is simply another example, or figure, of the paternal defaulting of which Guy is equally guilty, and Constantine's disinclination to play the man in relation to Iseult is no more acutely discreditable than is Antonia's in relation to Lilia. Indeed I think the structural parallel that associates Constantine with Antonia offers us some fascinating insight into how Bowen may have been reflecting, around the time of her composition of *Eva Trout*, on her own inheritance of Bowen's Court and her inability, as a woman, to maintain it. Constantine, that is to say, might plausibly be understood as the author's self-portrait as an effeminate male homosexual.
23. Corcoran, *Elizabeth Bowen: The Enforced Return*, p. 64.
24. Keown, 'New Horizons', p. 230.
25. Im, 'Elizabeth Bowen's Negative Epics', p. 462.
26. Im, 'Elizabeth Bowen's Negative Epics', p. 475.
27. Im's demystificatory reading of the novel wavers only in its sympathetic characterisation of Jane Danby as a woman

who will have to earn a wage. 'Jane's fate is uncertain before she meets Richard: with the recession and unemployment exacerbated by the war, she, like so many generations before her, contemplates emigrating to London' (Im, 'Elizabeth Bowen's Negative Epics', p. 474).
28. Corcoran, *Elizabeth Bowen: The Enforced Return*, p. 65.
29. Ellmann, *Elizabeth Bowen: The Shadow Across the Page*, p. 180.

# Bibliography

Bennett, Andrew, 'Bowen and Modernism: The Early Novels', in Eibhear Walshe (ed.), *Elizabeth Bowen*, foreword by Neil Corcoran, Dublin: Irish Academic Press, 2009.

Bennett, Andrew and Nicholas Royle, *Elizabeth Bowen and the Dissolution of the Novel*, Basingstoke: Palgrave Macmillan, 1995.

Blodgett, Harriet, *Patterns of Reality: Elizabeth Bowen's Novels*, The Hague: Mouton, 1975.

Bowen, Elizabeth, 'The Apple Tree' (1934), in *The Collected Stories of Elizabeth Bowen*, introduction by Angus Wilson, London: Vintage, 1999.

Bowen, Elizabeth, 'The Big House' (1940), in *The Mulberry Tree*, selected and introduced by Hermione Lee, San Diego: Harcourt Brace Jovanovich, 1987.

Bowen, Elizabeth, *Bowen's Court* [1942; reissued 1964] & *Seven Winters: Memories of a Dublin Childhood* [1943], introduction by Hermione Lee, London: Vintage, 1999.

Bowen, Elizabeth, 'The Cat Jumps' (1934), in *The Collected Stories of Elizabeth Bowen*, introduction by Angus Wilson, London: Vintage, 1999.

Bowen, Elizabeth, *The Collected Stories of Elizabeth Bowen*, introduction by Angus Wilson, London: Vintage, 1999.

Bowen, Elizabeth, 'Coming Home' (1923), in *The Collected Stories of Elizabeth Bowen*, introduction by Angus Wilson, London: Vintage, 1999.

Bowen, Elizabeth, 'Confessions' (1949), in *Listening In: Broadcasts, Speeches, and Interviews by Elizabeth Bowen*, ed. and introduced by Allan Hepburn, Edinburgh: Edinburgh University Press, 2010.

Bowen, Elizabeth, 'A Conversation between Elizabeth Bowen and Jocelyn Brooke' (1950), in *Listening In: Broadcasts, Speeches, and Interviews* by *Elizabeth Bowen*, ed. and introduced by Allan Hepburn, Edinburgh: Edinburgh University Press, 2010.

Bowen, Elizabeth, 'The Cost of Letters' (1946), in *Listening In: Broadcasts, Speeches, and Interviews by Elizabeth Bowen*, ed. and introduced by Allan Hepburn, Edinburgh: Edinburgh University Press, 2010.

Bowen, Elizabeth, 'The Cult of Nostalgia' (1951), in *Listening In: Broadcasts, Speeches, and Interviews by Elizabeth Bowen*, ed. and introduced by Allan Hepburn, Edinburgh: Edinburgh University Press, 2010.

Bowen, Elizabeth, *The Death of the Heart* (1938), introduction by Patricia Craig, London: Vintage, 1998.

Bowen, Elizabeth, 'Do Conventions Matter?' (1941), in *Listening In: Broadcasts, Speeches, and Interviews by Elizabeth Bowen*, ed. and introduced by Allan Hepburn, Edinburgh: Edinburgh University Press, 2010.

Bowen, Elizabeth, *Eva Trout or Changing Scenes* (1969), introduction by Eibhear Walshe, London: Vintage, 1999.

Bowen, Elizabeth, 'The Fear of Pleasure' (1951), in *Listening In: Broadcasts, Speeches, and Interviews by Elizabeth Bowen*, ed. and introduced by Allan Hepburn, Edinburgh: Edinburgh University Press, 2010.

Bowen, Elizabeth, *Friends and Relations* (1931), London: Penguin, 1943.

Bowen, Elizabeth, *The Heat of the Day* (1948), introduction by Roy Foster, London: Vintage, 1998.

Bowen, Elizabeth, *The Hotel* (1927), London: Vintage, 2003.

Bowen, Elizabeth, *The House in Paris* (1935), introduction by A. S. Byatt, London: Vintage, 1998.

Bowen, Elizabeth, 'The Idea of the Home' (1953), in *Listening In: Broadcasts, Speeches, and Interviews by Elizabeth Bowen*, ed. and introduced by Allan Hepburn, Edinburgh: Edinburgh University Press, 2010.

Bowen, Elizabeth, 'Ivy Gripped the Steps' (1945), in *The Collected Stories of Elizabeth Bowen*, introduction by Angus Wilson, London: Vintage, 1999.

Bowen, Elizabeth, *The Last September* (1929), introduction by Victoria Glendinning, London: Vintage, 1998.

Bowen, Elizabeth, *Listening In: Broadcasts, Speeches and Interviews by Elizabeth Bowen*, ed. and introduced by Allan Hepburn, Edinburgh: Edinburgh University Press, 2010.

Bowen, Elizabeth, *The Little Girls* (1964), introduction by Penelope Lively, London: Vintage, 1999.
Bowen, Elizabeth, 'The Living Image – 1' (1941), in *Listening In: Broadcasts, Speeches, and Interviews by Elizabeth Bowen*, ed. and introduced by Allan Hepburn, Edinburgh: Edinburgh University Press, 2010.
Bowen, Elizabeth, 'The Living Image – 2' (1942), in *Listening In: Broadcasts, Speeches, and Interviews by Elizabeth Bowen*, ed. and introduced by Allan Hepburn, Edinburgh: Edinburgh University Press, 2010.
Bowen, Elizabeth, *The Mulberry Tree*, selected and introduced by Hermione Lee, San Diego: Harcourt Brace Jovanovich, 1987.
Bowen, Elizabeth, *Pictures and Conversations*, foreword by Spencer Curtis Brown, London: Allen Lane, 1975.
Bowen, Elizabeth, 'Preface to *The Last September*' (1952), in *The Mulberry Tree*, selected and introduced by Hermione Lee, San Diego: Harcourt Brace Jovanovich, 1987.
Bowen, Elizabeth, 'Tears, Idle Tears' (1941), in *The Collected Stories of Elizabeth Bowen*, introduction by Angus Wilson, London: Vintage, 1999.
Bowen, Elizabeth, *To the North* (1932), introduction by Hugh Haughton, London: Vintage, 1999.
Bowen, Elizabeth, 'The Visitor' (1926), in *The Collected Stories of Elizabeth Bowen*, introduction by Angus Wilson, London: Vintage, 1999.
Bowen, Elizabeth, *A World of Love* (1955), introduction by Selina Hastings, London: Vintage, 1999.
Bowen, Elizabeth and Charles Ritchie, *Love's Civil War: Elizabeth Bowen and Charles Ritchie, Letters and Diaries 1941–1973*, ed. Victoria Glendinning with Judith Robertson, London: Simon and Schuster, 2009.
Corcoran, Neil, *Elizabeth Bowen: The Enforced Return*, Oxford: Oxford University Press, 2004.
Cullingford, Elizabeth, '"Something else": Gendering Onliness in Elizabeth Bowen's Early Fiction', *Modern Fiction Studies*, Special Issue: Elizabeth Bowen, 53:2, Summer 2007, pp. 276–305.
Darwood, Nicola, *A World of Lost Innocence: The Fiction of Elizabeth Bowen*, Cambridge: Cambridge Scholars, 2012.
Deer, Jemma, '"Addressed to You": Nonhuman Missives from Elizabeth Bowen's *A World of Love*', *Mosaic*, 50:3, September 2017, pp. 175–89.

DiBattista, Maria, 'Elizabeth Bowen's Troubled Modernism', in Richard Begam and Michael Valdez Moses (eds), *Modernism and Colonialism: British and Irish Literature, 1899–1939*, Durham, NC: Duke University Press, 2007.

Ellmann, Maud, *Elizabeth Bowen: The Shadow Across the Page*, Edinburgh: Edinburgh University Press, 2003.

Esty, Joshua, 'Virgins of Empire: *The Last September* and the Antidevelopment Plot', *Modern Fiction Studies*, Special Issue: Elizabeth Bowen, 53:2, Summer 2007, pp. 257–75.

Gildersleeve, Jessica, *Elizabeth Bowen and the Writing of Trauma: The Ethics of Survival*, Amsterdam: Rodopi, 2014.

Hoogland, Renée C., *Elizabeth Bowen: A Reputation in Writing*, New York: New York University Press, 1994.

Hu, Jane, 'Interception as Mediation in *A World of Love*', *Textual Practice*, 27:7, 2013, pp. 1197–215.

Im, Jeannie, 'Elizabeth Bowen's Negative Epics: Landscape and Realism in *The Last September* and *A World of Love*', *Twentieth-Century Literature*, 61:4, December 2015, pp. 460–83.

Jordan, Heather Bryant, 'A Bequest of Her Own: The Reinvention of Elizabeth Bowen', *New Hibernia Review*, 12:2, Summer 2008, pp. 46–62.

Jordan, Heather Bryant, *How Will the Heart Endure?* Ann Arbor: University of Michigan Press, 1992.

Kelly, Mary, 'When Things Were "closing in" and "rolling up": The Imaginative Geography of Elizabeth Bowen's Anglo-Irish War Novel *The Last September*', *Journal of Historical Geography*, 38, 2012, pp. 282–93.

Keown, Edwina, 'New Horizons', in Edwina Keown and Carol Taaffe (eds), *Irish Modernisms*, Oxford: Peter Lang, 2010.

Kershner, Jr., R. B., 'Bowen's Oneiric *House in Paris*', *Texas Studies in Literature and Language*, 28:4, Winter 1986, pp. 407–23.

Kreilkamp, Vera, *The Anglo-Irish Novel and the Big House*, Syracuse, NY: Syracuse University Press, 1998.

Kreilkamp, Vera, 'Bowen: Ascendancy Modernist', in Eibhear Walshe (ed.), *Elizabeth Bowen*, foreword by Neil Corcoran, Dublin: Irish Academic Press, 2009.

Laird, Heather, 'The "Placing" and Politics of Bowen in Contemporary Irish Literary and Cultural Criticism', in Eibhear Walshe (ed.), *Elizabeth Bowen*, foreword by Neil Corcoran, Dublin: Irish Academic Press, 2009.

Mooney, Sinéad, 'Unstable Compounds: Bowen's Beckettian Affinities', *Modern Fiction Studies*, Special Issue: Elizabeth Bowen, 53:2, Summer 2007, pp. 238–56.

O'Brien, Valerie, '"A genius for unreality": Neurodiversity in Elizabeth Bowen's *Eva Trout*', *Journal of Modern Literature*, 42:2, Winter 2019, pp. 75–93.

Osborn, Susan (ed.), *Elizabeth Bowen: New Critical Perspectives*, Cork: Cork University Press, 2009.

Osborn, Susan, '"How to measure this unaccountable darkness between the trees": The Strange Relation of Style and Meaning in *The Last September*', in Susan Osborn (ed.), *Elizabeth Bowen: New Critical Perspectives*, Cork: Cork University Press, 2009.

Osborn, Susan (ed.), *Modern Fiction Studies*, Elizabeth Bowen Special Issue, 52:2, Summer 2007.

Oxindine, Annette, 'Resisting Dissolution: The Salvific Turn in Elizabeth Bowen's *The Heat of the Day*', *Renascence*, 69:4, Fall 2017, pp. 200–20.

Parkes, Adam, 'Elizabeth Bowen's Mélisande', *Texas Studies in Literature and Language*, 59:4, Winter 2017, pp. 457–76.

Pearson, Nels C., 'Elizabeth Bowen and the New Cosmopolitanism', *Twentieth Century Literature*, 56:3, August 2010, pp. 318–40.

Rau, Petra, 'Telling It Straight: The Rhetorics of Conversion in Elizabeth Bowen's *The Hotel* and Freud's *Psychogenesis*', in Laura Doan and Jane Garrity (eds), *Sapphic Modernities: Sexuality, Women and National Culture*, Basingstoke: Palgrave Macmillan, 2006.

Rose, Jacqueline, 'Bizarre Objects: Hallucination and Modernism – Mary Butts and Elizabeth Bowen', in *On Not Being Able to Sleep: Psychoanalysis and the Modern World*, London: Vintage, 2004.

Seiler, Claire, 'At Midcentury: Elizabeth Bowen's *The Heat of the Day*', *Modernism/Modernity*, 21:1, 2014, pp. 125–45.

Stevens, Julie Anne, 'Bowen: The Critical Response', in Eibhear Walshe (ed.), *Elizabeth Bowen*, foreword by Neil Corcoran, Dublin: Irish Academic Press, 2009.

Towheed, Shafquat, 'Territory, Space, Modernity: Elizabeth Bowen's *The Demon Lover and Other Stories* and Wartime London', in Susan Osborn (ed.), *Elizabeth Bowen: New Critical Perspectives*, Cork: Cork University Press, 2009.

Underland, Nathaniel, 'Disaffection and *Realpolitik* in Elizabeth Bowen's *The Heat of the Day*', *Textual Practice*, 33:9, 2019, pp. 1507–33.

Walsh, Keri, 'Elizabeth Bowen and the Futurist Imagination', *Journal of Modern Literature*, 41:1, Fall 2017, pp. 19–39.

Walshe, Eibhear (ed.), *Elizabeth Bowen*, foreword by Neil Corcoran, Dublin: Irish Academic Press, 2009.

Watson, Barbara Bellow, 'Variations on an Enigma: Elizabeth Bowen's War Novel' (1981), in Harold Bloom (ed.), *Elizabeth Bowen*, New York: Chelsea House, 1987.

# Index

Page numbers followed by n refer to notes

adolescence
  'Bowen's Court', County Cork, 112–13
  *The Heat of the Day*, 184, 186
  'Ivy Gripped the Steps', 118–20
  *The Last September*, 129, 137
  *A World of Love*, 197
architecture, 1–2

barristers, 1–3
Bennett, Andrew, 46–7
  *Elizabeth Bowen and the Dissolution of the Novel*, 5–6, 135
Big House, 109–13, 115, 122–69, 173–6, 179–80, 189–207
Blodgett, Harriet, 10
Bowen, Elizabeth
  'The Apple Tree', 15
  'The Big House', 173–6
  *Bowen's Court*, 2–3, 55–6, 94–5, 105–8, 145, 176–8, 199–200
  'The Cat Jumps', 12–13
  Christian novels, 9–10
  'Coming Home', 67–8
  'The Cost of Letters', 2
  'The Cult of Nostalgia', 14
  *The Death of the Heart*, 8
  'Do Conventions Matter?' (radio talk), 1–2
  *Eva Trout*, 190–207, 209–12n
  expected to be a boy, 21, 94, 100n, 177–8, 182
  *Friends and Relations*, 119–22
  'The Idea of the Home', 13–14
  *The Little Girls*, 156–62
  'The Living Image – 1', 14
  *To the North*, 15
  'Notes on Writing a Novel', 14

Bowen, Elizabeth (*cont.*)
nursery pictures, 21–3, 25–6, 93–4
'Out of a Book', 11
*Pictures and Conversations*, 58, 77–8, 153–6, 162–3
*Seven Winters*, 21–3, 52–3, 56–7
stammer, 14, 72, 102n
'Tears, Idle Tears', 15
'The Visitor', 66–7
*A World of Love*, 190–207
see also 'Ivy Gripped the Steps'; *The Heat of the Day*; *The Hotel*; *The House in Paris*; *The Last September*
Bowen, Florence (mother)
birth of Elizabeth, 177–8
death, 58, 67, 78
looked at villas to rent, 162–3
maternal No, 52–3
pregnancy, 94–5, 199–200
return to 'Bowen's Court,' 163–4
and signature story, 27
Bowen, Henry (father)
breakdown, 57–8
compromised prestige, 55–7
and fictional characters, 174, 207n
Irish War of Independence, 108–9
as lawyer, 2–3, 56–7
Republicans at 'Bowen's Court,' 112–13, 115–17
and signature story, 27
Bowen, Robert Cole (grandfather), 55–6
'Bowen's Court', County Cork, 3, 55–6, 105–17
breastfeeding, 29–33, 50, 60–1

cake, 32, 62–4, 82–4, 88
Cameron, Alan (husband), 107, 110, 191
carnations, 29–31, 60, 65, 171n
Caruth, Cathy, 24
Casabianca, 21–3, 25, 55
'castration', 90–1, 97–8, 185, 188
clocks, 66–7
complex developmental failure, 21–99
conventions, 1–2, 5, 55, 119
Corcoran, Neil
Anglo-Irish and *A World of Love*, 200
Bowen as conservative novelist, 43
burning of the house in *A World of Love*, 172n
*Elizabeth Bowen: The Enforced Return*, 5–8
incestuousness in *A World of Love*, 206
laurel as icon of war, 135

on 'Out of a Book', 11
photography in Bowen's
  novels, 208n
politics of *The Heat of the
  Day*, 189
ruined mill scene, 170n
on Stella (character),
  103n
war, 102n
'County Cork man', 107,
  110–11, 194
Cromwell, Oliver, 3
Cullingford, Elizabeth,
  11–13, 34, 102n, 178–9

Dáil Éireann, 105
Darwood, Nicola, *A World
  of Lost Innocence: The
  Fiction of Elizabeth
  Bowen*, 8, 171–2n
death
  'death drive', 44–5
  deathlessness, 69–70
  of Mother in stories,
    26–7, 65–8
desire, 118–44
  of Mother, 53–4, 160–9,
    170n
  objects of, 116, 170n
Dublin, 21–3, 56–7

Ellman, Maud
  Big House, 189
  on burial, 158
  *Elizabeth Bowen: The
    Shadow Across the
    Page*, 5–8
  Oedipal triangle, 31

on 'Out of a Book', 11
sickness in *A World of
  Love*, 206
symbolism of wound in
  *The Hotel*, 47
violets in *The House in
  Paris*, 100n
eroticism, 29–30, 92, 94,
  150, 163, 171n, 210
Esty, Joshua, 141, 179
ethics, 8–9, 109–72
external voice of law, 22–3,
  40, 49–51, 64, 66–7

fascism, 85–7, 99
Father
  breakdown of authority,
    57–8
  gender and paternal law,
    178–9
  intervention of, 40–1,
    50–1, 64–5
  outlawing of intimacy,
    49–50
  paternal failure, 60–1,
    101n
  symbolic violence against
    paternal authority,
    89–92, 95
First World War, 71–7,
  102n
flowers, 100n, 171n
  carnations, 29–31, 60,
    65, 171n
food, 32–3, 61, 80–2,
  88, 163
Freudian analysis, 11–14,
  44

gender roles, 1–4, 113–69
Germany and motherhood, 74–5, 79–80, 103n
Gildersleeve, Jessica
  on burial, 158
  'death drive' in *The Hotel*, 44
  *Elizabeth Bowen and the Writing of Trauma:The Ethics of Survival*, 5, 24
  ruined mill scene, 145
  suicide in *The House in Paris*, 41–2
  trauma and Bowen's novels, 8–9, 11
  trauma in *The Heat of the Day*, 185, 208n
grotesque
  arboreal corpse, 155
  dyad and separation, 116, 156
  *Eva Trout*, 211
  fascism, 85
  Madame Fisher (character), 36–8
  ruined mill scene, 146
  *A World of Love*, 198
  'guardian cat', 93–5, 199–200

happy endings, 25, 28–47, 49
*The Heat of the Day*
  Anglo-Irish, 174, 175
  High Modernism, 7
  re-birth, 9–10
  sibling trio, 180–90, 208n
  signature story, 70–99
  Stella Rodney (character), 103–4n
Hemans, Felicia, 23
homosexuality, 170, 210–11
Hoogland, Renée C., 133, 135
*Horizon*, 'The Cost of Letters', 2
*The Hotel*
  Germany and motherhood, 75–7, 79
  happy endings, 28–47
  local clarity and intertextual clarity, 10
  Mrs Kerr (character), 60, 92–3
  puppies and monkeys, 63–4
  war, 102n
*The House in Paris*
  Big House, 150–2
  Germany and motherhood, 74–7
  happy endings, 28–47
  paternal failure, 101n
  transgressiveness, 86–7
  triptych-style texts, 157–8
  violets, 100n

Im, Jeannie, 203–4, 211–12n
incestuousness, 59–60, 95, 169, 206
inhibition, 12, 48–9
Ireland
  Anglo-Irish, 2–5, 173–207
  Anglo-Irish Treaty, 105–6

## Index

Big House, 109–13, 115, 122–69, 173–6, 179–80, 189–207
  Civil War, 105–9, 114–17, 122–44
  Irish Free State, 105
  as Mother and her children, 116–17
  Northern Ireland, 105
  Republic of Ireland, 2–5, 105, 179–80
  Republicans, 105–9, 112–13
'Ivy Gripped the Steps'
  Casabianca, 101n
  eroticism, 210n
  'guardian cat', 94
  Mother's desire, 160–1, 164–6
  trauma and psychosis, 48–70
  triangulated sexuality, 118–19
  war, 27, 72–4, 77

Jordan, Heather Bryant, 'A Bequest of Her Own: The Reinvention of Elizabeth Bowen', 172n

Kelly, Mary, 'When Things Were "closing in" and "rolling up"', 167, 171–2n
Keown, Edwina, 203–4
Kershner, R. B., Jr., 100n
Kreilkamp, Vera, 102n, 133–4, 141

*The Last September*
  Anglo-Irish, 171–2n, 175
  carnations, 171n
  High Modernism, 7
  reproductive dysfunction, 174
  sexuality, 109–69
  signature story, 70
  legacy, 108, 173–211

maternal dyad
  Anglo-Irish, 116–17
  Big House, 176
  carnations, 171n
  death, 66, 68–70
  definition, 24–6
  desire, 53–4
  happy endings, 28–47
  *The Heat of the Day*, 99
  *The House in Paris*, 100n
  'Ivy Gripped the Steps', 62
  metaphors, 93–4
  and sexuality, 144–69
  trauma, 109–10
  violence, 74
  war as, 76–9, 85
monkeys, 63–4, 86–7, 94
monstrousness, 36–8, 78–9
Mooney, Sinéad, 7, 47
Mother
  death of in stories, 26–7, 65–8
  desire, 53–4, 160–9, 170n

Mother (*cont.*)
Germany and
motherhood, 74–5,
79–80, 103n
Ireland and her children,
116–17
and masculine desire,
170n
maternal beauty and
seductive deathliness,
39
maternal No, 25, 34,
51–4, 58, 117, 169
maternal No (Florence
Bowen), 163–4
maternal 'place',
122–44
psychotic maternal
sexuality, 164–5

Oedipal triangle, 31, 102n,
124
Osborn, Susan, *Elizabeth
Bowen: New Critical
Perspectives*, 7
Oxindine, Annette, 9–10

prohibition
and sibling trio, 202–3
First World War, 77
Henry Bowen, 57–8
inheritance laws, 177–8
'Ivy Gripped the Steps',
65
paternal, 27, 67, 111,
149, 201
'transmutation', 49

psychoanalyst figures,
14–15
psychosis, and trauma,
48–70
puppies, 63–4

rape fantasies, *The Last
September*, 134–9,
168–9
Rau, Petra, 34
re-birth, 9, 46, 87
reproductive dysfunction,
political implications of,
173–207
Ritchie, Charles (lover)
diary, 14, 102n
letters to, 13
Rose, Jacqueline, 103n
Royle, Nicholas, *Elizabeth
Bowen and the
Dissolution of the
Novel*, 5–6, 135
ruined mill, *The Last
September*, 117, 130–1,
144–6, 155–6

*The Saturday Book*, 1
Second World War, 77–8,
93, 102n
Seiler, Claire, 7
separation, 21–99
Big House, 112
death, 156, 160
Germany and
motherhood, 165–6
ruined mill scene,
144–7

Index 225

sexuality and the dyad, 152–3
war, 102n
sexuality
  *affair of roles*, 112–13, 118–44
  and the dyad, 144–69
  *The Heat of the Day*, 95–7
  homosexuality, 170, 210–11
  psychotic maternal, 164–5
  role-based sexuality, 114–15
  rule-based sexuality, 114–15
sibling trio, 180–207, 208n
signature story, 21–99
social inequality, 3–4
socio-sexual order, 3–4
Stevens, Julie Anne, 7
suicide, 37–8, 41–2
symbolic law
  Bowen's belief in, 10
  and desire, 153
  *The Heat of the Day*, 81–2, 85, 88, 98–9
  *The Hotel*, 47
  *The House in Paris*, 43
  inequality of access to, 3–4
  *The Last September*, 139, 169
  *The Little Girls*, 157
  sibling trio, 186

Towheed, Shafquat, 11
transmogrification, 31, 36, 79–80, 207
transmutation, 48–9
trauma
  in Bowen's novels, 8–9, 11
  definition, 24–6
  happy endings, 28–47
  *The Heat of the Day*, 78–9, 93, 95, 98–9, 185, 208n
  'Ivy Gripped the Steps', 77
  and psychosis, 48–70
  ruined mill scene, 144–5
triangulated sexuality, 112–44
  Big House and, 109–10
  and the garden, 147
  *The Last September*, 146, 169, 171n
  *The Little Girls*, 161

uncanny garden, 153–60

Walshe, Eibhear, *Elizabeth Bowen* (essay collection), 7
war
  as dyadic, 76–7
  First World War, 71–7, 102n
  *The Hotel*, 75–7, 102n
  *The House in Paris*, 76–7

war (*cont.*)
  'Ivy Gripped the Steps',
    72–4, 77
  Second World War, 77–8,
    93, 102n
  war wound, 71–3, 78
Watson, Barbara Bellow,
  'Variations on an
  Enigma: Elizabeth
  Bowen's War Novel',
  103–4n
weaning
  *The Heat of the Day*,
    81–3, 90
  *The Hotel*, 31–3, 38,
    60–2
separation, 16, 24–6, 51
witnessing, 9, 11